ADVANCE PRAISE FOR

Making It on Broadway

"If you think working in theater is glitzy and ritzy, you've gotta read *Making It on Broadway.* It's a heartbreaking, humbling, and hilarious look at today's Great White Way, told by pros who know every stage of showbiz."

—**Wayman Wong,** *New York Daily News* **and Playbill.com**

"The Broadway performers reporting in this devastating multiple-memoir on the real life of actors are hilarious, grim, rueful, resigned, even forgiving, but somehow, in every mood, their recollections are inspiring and transparently honest. Loving intensely what they're looking for, and even looking for it in what should be the right place—Broadway—they're pretty much shocked by the reality. But like saints and lunatics, they never lose the vision, see it as real, and sometimes, even for a moment, find it.

When you start out in New York with little money, and with rats in the walls of a closet you're supposed to think of as a whole apartment, it is not, God knows, any part of the dream that got you there. And then, when you find out later that life after 'making it' is not all that different, and certainly not different enough—there's reason to be discouraged. But like a torturous love affair, there is, after all, at the bottom of it, love. So, if this book is a warning, it is also PR for a hard, still proud, way of life."

—**Leon Katz, Emeritus Professor, Yale School of Drama**

"How is a life in the theater possible when 'making it' is a false concept and 'Broadway' is no one's permanent address? This book is a wise, uncompromising, and invaluable document, featuring the passionate voices of those wrestling with the question and living the answer. Long live their history!"

—**Mel Shapiro, Head of Acting and Musical Theater, UCLA**

"Usually, when you climb to the top of the beanstalk, you discover a giant monster. This book describes that trip up, and what's there when you arrive. Some of the contributors to this book were once told what life would be like once they finally 'made it' on Broadway . . . but they didn't believe it. Now, the actors in this book tell it like it is—they destroy the myths and inject the truth. Yet, will it discourage any young artist? Not likely."

—**Arthur Bartow, Artistic Director, Undergraduate Department of Drama, NYU Tisch School of the Arts**

"Irving Berlin lied, but David Wienir and Jodie Langel have told the truth: When it comes to show business, everything about it is NOT appealing. Wienir and Langel conducted interviews with scores of people who have trod the boards—and have been trod upon by management, audiences, and their coworkers. Many a book has been called 'an eye-opener,' but *Making It on Broadway* is an 'EYES-opener' in showing that life upon the wicked stage is more wicked than we might have imagined. Anyone who's considering a theatrical career must read this book—twice. They may still wind up wanting to go into the business, and that's fine—but at least they will now be well-prepared for this life after all that they've learned from Wienir and Langel's book."

—Peter Filichia—*The New Jersey Star-Ledger* and Theatermania.com

"*Making It on Broadway* strips away the thin veneer of glitz on Broadway and exposes the true iron and steel needed to 'make it' on the Great White Way. It's the truth, spoken by the soldiers in the trenches. This book doesn't sugarcoat the experience of being a Broadway actor. It shows the real blood, sweat, and tears that make up our profession. It shows through the B.S. and tells it like it is."

—Rick Sordelet, Broadway Fight Director

"This book is important reading for anyone who cares about Broadway. There is no other book like it."

—Gil Cates, Producing-Director of the Geffen Playhouse
and Producer of The 75th Academy Awards

"*Making It on Broadway* is a must-read for anyone who has dreamed of one day performing on the Great White Way. It is honest, thorough, and inspiring, and lends important insight into the world of show business."

—Jamibeth Margolis, Director/Casting Director

"The names in this book range from the familiar . . . to the unknown, and every story is equally fascinating and engrossing. A must-read for anyone who has ever dreamt of life on the wicked stage—or just loves going to see live theater."

—Jeffrey Epstein, Senior Editor, *Out* magazine

MAKING IT ON BROADWAY

Actors' Tales
of Climbing
to the Top

DAVID WIENIR
AND
JODIE LANGEL

ALLWORTH PRESS
NEW YORK

To all those who have ever dreamed of a life on Broadway

© 2004 David Wienir and Jodie Langel

09 08 07 06 05   8 7 6 5 4

Published by Allworth Press
An imprint of Allworth Communications, Inc.
10 East 23rd Street, New York, NY 10010

Cover design by Derek Bacchus
Page composition/typography by Sharp Des!gns, Inc.

ISBN: 1-58115-346-5

LIBRARY OF CONGRESS CATALOGING-IN-PUBLICATION DATA
Wienir, David.
Making it on Broadway: actors' tales of climbing to the top / by David Wienir
and Jodie Langel; foreword by Jason Alexander.
p. cm.
Includes index.
ISBN 1-58115-346-5 (pbk.)
1. Theater—New York (State)—New York. 2. Actors—New York (State)—
New York—Interviews. I. Langel, Jodie. II. Title.
PN2277.N5W48 2004
792.02'8'097471—dc22
2003024694

Printed in Canada

Contents

Part 1: The Early Years

 • *Not by Choice* • *Church and Tractor* • *A Young Passion for Music*
 • *Cheerios, Indians, and Show Tunes* • *A Special Talent*

 • *Tickets, Please* • *Field Trip* • *Broadway Dreaming*

 • *Play Ball* • *What's Wrong with the Family Business?* • *Proving
 Parents Wrong* • *Plan for the Future*

Part 2: Getting Settled

 • *A Special City* • *Driving into Town* • *Taxi!* • *Sharing the Wealth*
 • *Adjusting to City Life*

 • *Roll Out the Red Carpet* • *Where's My Carpet?* • *The N.Y.C. Wildlife*
 • *Loving the Landlords* • *Dealing with the Devil* • *Leaks, Freaks,
 and Gregory Hines*

 • *The Toilet Scrubber* • *The Fitness Instructor* • *Welcome to Macy's*
 • *The Ice Sculpture* • *The Telemarketer* • *The Waiters* • *Pebbles, Winnie,
 and The Count*

 • *Bar Hopping* • *Hava Nagila* • *All Aboard* • *On Guard*
 • *Carrots and Hamburgers* • *Life before the Union*

Part 6: A New Era

Part 7: When Dreams Come True

The Voices

Jason Alexander
Joan Almedilla
Ana Maria Andricain
John Antony
Michael Arnold
Frank Baiocchi
Antonio Banderas
Roger Bart
Anastasia Barzee
Bryan Batt
Gary Beach
Craig Bennet
Michael Berresse
Michael Berry
Sarah Uriarte Berry
Geoffrey Blaisdell
Jeff Blumenkrantz
Matt Bogart
Ron Bohmer
Kelly Briggs
Steven Buntrock
Kerry Butler
Liz Callaway
Ann Hampton Callaway
Joseph Cassidy
Patrick Cassidy
Dave Clemmons
Daniel C. Cooney
Nick Corley
Ann Crumb
Charlotte d'Amboise
Lea DeLaria
Erin Dilly
Jonathan Dokuchitz
Kip Driver
Robert DuSold
Daisy Eagan
Jeff Edgerton
Susan Egan

Jarrod Emick
Cory English
Robert Evan
William Thomas Evans
Harvey Evans
Gina Ferrall
Allen Fitzpatrick
Hunter Foster
Alison Fraser
Boyd Gaines
Jeff Gardner
Deborah Gibson
Anita Gillette
Randy Graff
Debbie Gravitte
Brian Lane Green
Jeff Gurner
Danny Gurwin
James Hadley
Marsh Hanson
Sam Harris
Paul Harman
Heather Headley
Ruthie Henshall
Wilson Heredia
Philip Hernández
Tom Hewitt
James Hindman
Brian d'Arcy James
David Josefsberg
Betsy Joslyn
Kevin Kern
Davis Kirby
Marc Kudisch
Jodie Langel
Jane Lanier
Michael Lanning
Sondra Lee
Daniel C. Levine

DeLee Lively
Jose Llana
Angela Lockett
Kevin Loreque
Rebecca Luker
Heather MacRae
Terrence Mann
Marin Mazzie
Sal Mistretta
Andrea McArdle
Christie McCall
Sean McDermott
Gerry McIntyre
Donna McKechnie
J. Mark McVey
Idina Menzel
Ann Miller
Jessica Molaskey
Mark Moreau
Donna Murphy
Christiane Noll
Nancy Opel
Brad Oscar
Ken Page
Sean Jeremy Palmer
Hugh Panaro
Joe Paparella
Erin Leigh Peck
Lonny Price
Paige Price
Faith Prince
Steve Pudenz
Kelli Rabke
Anthony Rapp
Lee Roy Reams
Alice Ripley
Chita Rivera
Darcie Roberts
Ray Roderick

Craig Rubano
John Rubinstein
Daphne Rubin-Vega
Sophia Salguero
Lea Salonga
Alex Santoriello
James Sassar
Craig Schulman
Jane Sell
Roger Seyer
Brooke Shields
Emily Skinner
Doug Storm
Rena Strober
Jerry Tellier
Lea Thompson
Clarke Thorell
Robert Torti
Lucy Vance
Andrew Varela
Donna Vivino
Ray Walker
Barbara Walsh
Jim Walton
Amanda Watkins
Laurie Wells
Colm Wilkinson
Jessica Snow Wilson
Patrick Wilson
Marissa Jaret Winokur
Pamela Winslow
Scott Wise
John Leslie Wolfe
Deborah Yates
Lee Zarrett
Karen Ziemba
Adrian Zmed

Foreword

A very wise man once uttered a sentence that made little sense to my adolescent mind but has become a great truth in my maturity. The man was Lt. Spock, first officer of the starship Enterprise and a Vulcan. It was on the occasion of having to fight for the right to marry his betrothed. After victory, he inquired why she chose to have him battle for her hand. She explained she wanted another man more, and that she believed the outcome of the fight would guarantee her wishes. It was at that moment that Spock uttered his memorable line: "After a time, you may find that having is not so pleasing a thing, after all, as wanting. It is not logical, but it is often true."

This statement embodies what so many of us have come to know in regard to our greatest love, Broadway. The small stretch of streets on New York's west side has been a beacon seen round the world by all whose hopes and fantasies center upon the theater. It is Mecca, the holiest of holies. It is the stuff of dreams—shimmering, elusive, seductive, and mysterious. To be held in its embrace is to know paradise. To be accepted to its ranks is to walk with the gods.

Or so we believe.

I have sat in the audience of Broadway's theaters since I was a little boy. I have worked on its stages on five glorious occasions. And I have been honored with its highest award. Broadway excites me like no other place in the world—for it is like no other place in the world.

But like all living things, Broadway is constantly undergoing change. Its patrons and artists come and go. And their unique abilities and agendas come and go with them. Audiences grow and diminish. Their sophistication and appetites constantly vary. Business and budgets inflate. Unions and managers clash. Critics and pundits herald its demise and then, paradoxically, reverse themselves to pronounce its rebirth.

The truth is that Broadway is neither dying nor thriving. It is, however, constantly changing. Look at a photo of Times Square from fifteen years ago and compare it to what stands today. What do you see? Massive change. And what is the most glaring element of that change? Industry. Broadway has become an industry. That is why so many corporations have bought their way in. And they are affecting how that industry is run. I always thought of each individual theater as a "mom-and-pop shop" that got along with each other as a great neighbor.

The "mom-and-pop shops" are gone. Broadway is now a great big mall and each theater competes as if it were a Gap or a Sam Goody. There are no more friendly salespeople. Everything is automated and computerized. You can still buy a great product, but your shopping experience has changed.

That is what this book is about—change. If you are going to enter this mall either as a merchant or buyer, you need to truly know the marketplace. Actors who come to the Great White Way with only their dreams are in for harsh awakenings. So too, composers and directors.

And so too, the audience. Perhaps no other single element of Broadway is as responsible for this metamorphosis. The Broadway audience is the buyer, the connoisseur, and in some ways, the director. The audience's tastes dictate what material will be tried, as well as what will succeed or fail. It is the audience's behavior that determines the relationship between the stage and the seats. It is the audience's attendance that ultimately determines if Broadway is relevant and thriving, or frivolous.

So then, this book is one of insight and delight to anyone who has reason to walk through the doors of a Broadway theater. In these pages you will share the experiences of a variety of performers whose paths you may have crossed or hoped to follow. It is hoped that those experiences will help temper and enhance the dreams of what Broadway is and what it has become. Fear not; no dream is diminished by reality. And no illusion is diminished by truth.

If you dream of working on Broadway, this book will help to prepare you for what it takes to "make it," maintain it, and go on loving it. If you live to see a Broadway show, this book will give you insight into the joys and struggles that go into serving you, the audience. It will also empower you. It will empower you to face the theater as a partner. It will make you responsible for maintaining its beauty and majesty. It will make you demand more from it and from those who work in it. It will connect you. It will make Broadway less of a dream and more of what it should be— a soul mate.

Having had a long life on Broadway, I can in fact understand the words of Mr. Spock—the having is not always as pleasing a thing as the wanting. But, oh, what a sumptuous, satisfying delight it is. I wouldn't trade it for the world. So, also in the words of Mr. Spock, may it "live long and prosper."

Jason Alexander

Jason Alexander began his Broadway career while enrolled as an undergraduate at Boston University, having been cast in Stephen Sondheim's Broadway musical *Merrily We Roll Along.* He subsequently went on to win a Tony Award for his participation in *Jerome Robbins' Broadway.* In total, Jason has performed in five Broadway shows and starred in the Los Angeles production of *The Producers.* In 1990, he was cast as George Costanza in *Seinfeld,* one of the most popular television shows of all time. His extensive film credits include *Pretty Woman, Shallow Hal, The Mosquito Coast, Jacob's Ladder, The Hunchback of Notre Dame, North, Blankman,* and *Love! Valour! Compassion!*

Opening Thoughts

Tony Award Winner Scott Wise

I used to give seminars at colleges. Some of the teachers started complaining. They said I wasn't being positive enough. I wasn't playing it up and saying, "Broadway is great. Broadway is neat. Being on that stage is the most amazing thing in the world."

Those things are true, but I try to give the reality. The teachers simply didn't want me to do that. They wanted their students to go mindlessly into the profession. They wanted one of their students to make it big so they could say, "See, I taught them."

Tony Award Winner John Rubinstein

If someone tells me, "I love the theater. I have always acted, sung, and danced throughout high school and college. While it's my favorite thing, I also love marine biology. I am torn. What should I do with my life?" Then to that person, the absolute rock-solid advice is, "Stay away from show business and go into marine biology."

I am not even being cynical. A dedication to a life on Broadway requires you to overlook so many impediments, obstacles, and discouragements. There is always a statistical avalanche rolling against you as you try to walk up the hill.

If there is anything else that lights your fire, go that way. Avoid this mess. The only way to walk up that hill, with the avalanche pouring down on you, is if it's the only direction you can possibly go.

Tony Award Nominee Sam Harris

When I was younger, I always thought that if I did A, B, and C, then D, E, and F would happen. I was told that's the way it works. I was always told, "You are so talented. If you work really hard and you study, if you take your classes and go to auditions, you are going to be a big fat star." That is simply not true in musical theater anymore, but you can't tell that to an eighteen-year-old. The reality is that if you do A, B, and C over and over again, maybe, once in a while, D, E, and perhaps F will happen.

Tony Award Nominee Daphne Rubin-Vega

A successful career in musical theater is like skiing. Getting to the top of the slope and making it down. And going back up and coming down, successfully—and enjoying that trip. That's success. It's not a constant. Nobody tells you that.

Introduction

Over the past two decades, mega-musicals such as *Les Misérables, The Phantom of the Opera, Beauty and the Beast,* and *The Lion King* have toured the world, exposing millions to Broadway and fueling the dreams of countless young hopefuls. However, the grandeur of these multimillion-dollar spectacles has not only re-landscaped the musical theater industry, but has left ticket holders with profound misconceptions about the lives of the performers who have moved them.

Through the candid words of more than 150 of today's Broadway performers, including 55 Tony Award winners and nominees, *Making It on Broadway* unravels these misconceptions and provides unprecedented insight into the struggle to stardom and beyond. The stories in this book will not only entertain and astonish anyone who has ever attended a Broadway musical, but will serve as a sobering reality check for future generations of students who are considering a career in theater.

The timeliness of this book is underscored by the arrival of Disney and the Cameron Mackintosh mega-musicals to the Broadway scene, a topic that has already generated significant media attention. As these producers have broken from past tradition and reshaped the musical theater profession, the shows themselves, rather than the actors who perform in them, have become the stars. Furthermore, as these mega-musicals squat in Broadway theaters, there are fewer opportunities for Broadway performers to star in new productions and to originate new roles. *Making It on Broadway* explores these changes and the effect they have had on the performer, the audience, and Broadway itself.

The book is divided into seven sections that guide the reader on a journey through the performer's never-ending struggle to reach the Broadway stage.

Part One begins with Broadway performers recounting the moment they first fell in love with the theater and their childhood dreams of Broadway. They share stories about their education and the advice they received from parents and friends. Part Two explores actors' challenging first months in New York City, their first apartments, their financial struggles, and the jobs that were necessary to make ends meet. Next, Part Three recounts stories of the audition process and the innovative and dramatic ways in which performers have broken through into the Broadway community.

Once cast, in Part Four, actors make it clear that the life of a performer is not all routine, recounting comical and terrifying moments on stage when things did not go exactly as scripted. Also, actors tell stories of interactions with audience members and relationships with adoring fans. In contrast, Part Five explores the daily routines, drudgeries, and sacrifices of a Broadway performer, showing that the life of a performer is not as glamorous as it might seem. Performers speak candidly about personal relationships, life on the road, and sex.

Ultimately, however, in Part Six, performers reflect on how megamusicals and the "Disneyfication" of Broadway have impacted their lives and their dreams, and have even compromised the integrity of Broadway itself. In Part Seven, actors revisit the closing of a show, the sorrowful return to the unemployment line, and the realization that, more than ever, a career on Broadway is fleeting, and for most, unsustainable.

Once a performer "makes it" on Broadway, there is usually only one direction to go—back to square one. Not even Tony Award winners and nominees are immune from this new reality. In a heartfelt and forthright manner, they reflect on how being nominated or even winning the coveted Award can still be followed by years of unemployment and self-doubt. After all, the base of the Tony Award is not gold, nor stone, but plastic.

Many books have been written about the history of Broadway, celebrating its past and reminiscing about the glory to be found on the Great White Way. Needless to say, this book is not one of them. Over drinks in a Montreal café, this book began as an insider's look into the lifestyles of Broadway performers in the new millennium. The authors recognized that the book would require an unprecedented degree of candor and honesty from those who are generally hesitant to share their most personal stories and expose their offstage struggles and fears. Furthermore, it would require performers to surrender hours of their lives and reflect on some very sensitive topics.

Not only were performers willing to talk, but they did so with a sense of urgency and passion that neither of the authors could have ever anticipated. Without a doubt, there is a growing sense of unrest within the theater community. Many explained that there is nothing short of a crisis underway on Broadway. And while just about every contributor expressed his or her love for Broadway, many also shared feelings of sadness. The Broadway which they had imagined, or had even once known, is now nowhere to be found.

The interviews in this book took place over a period of three years. Most of the interviews were conducted in the homes of the authors and the contributors, lasting several hours apiece. A few were conducted elsewhere. While beginning with laughter, many interviews ended in tears. With each new interview, the message of the book gradually changed. No longer was the book simply a behind-the-scenes look into the lives of Broadway performers, despite how valuable such a book might have been. Rather, what evolved was something of far greater significance—a powerful look at how corporate theater has interfered with the dreams and careers of Broadway performers, and how Broadway has changed as a result.

Making It on Broadway neither criticizes nor questions the brilliance of Claude-Michel Schönberg, the composer of *Les Misérables, Miss Saigon,* and the ill-fated *Martin Guerre.* Nor does this book attempt to disparage the contributions of Sir Andrew Lloyd Webber, or the music of Disney. Their music has touched millions, and many of their melodies approach the divine. The musicals, and the composers who wrote them, shoulder no blame. Rather, this book looks to how these mega-musicals have been produced, promoted, and managed, and the effect they have had on professional theater and the lives of those who have "made it" on Broadway.

To be sure, each Broadway performer is unique. Each has his or her own tale of climbing to the top. Furthermore, there are thousands of Broadway musical theater performers in New York, and this book features only 154 of them. However, while this book does not profess to speak for everyone in the Broadway community, it would be hard to disagree that many of the experiences and sentiments in the following pages are shared.

Broadway has changed. Through the stories and confessions in this book, performers have opened up their personal lives with the hope of restoring a certain intimacy to Broadway which many feel has been lost. It is the authors' hope that, through fostering such a renewed intimacy and understanding in the pages that follow, Broadway will change yet again.

Key to Broadway Credits

[O]	=	Original Broadway Company
Normal type	=	Broadway Company
*	=	Broadway National Tour
[T]	=	Tony Award® Winner
[t]	=	Tony Award® Nominee
u/s	=	Understudy
s/b	=	Standby

The Broadway credits attributed to each contributor were last updated on January 1, 2004. While diligent efforts have been made to ensure the accuracy of the biographical information, the authors and publisher offer no warranty of its accuracy. While most if not all Broadway appearances are listed for each contributor, the authors do not warrant or represent that each biography mentions every appearance or role in a Broadway company or Broadway national tour. Where possible, credits are listed according to opening night production credits. In many circumstances, performers have gone on to assume other roles in the same production. Such credits are usually not listed. Furthermore, Broadway national tour appearances are not listed when the performer appeared in the same production on Broadway. Where contributors appeared in the ensemble, usually no role is listed. Original company members and original company members of a revival of that same production are collectively referred to as members of an "Original Broadway Company." Where included, Canadian companies and pre-Broadway national tours are referred to as Broadway national tours for the purposes of this book.

PART ONE

THE EARLY YEARS

CHAPTER 1

Singing on the Coffee Table

A love for performing can start at an early age, and often does. Fueled by either destiny or desire, or both, the path to Broadway often begins long before ever seeing a Broadway show, and for many, long before hitting puberty. The desire to perform does not always begin in drama class. Some begin the journey in response to a playground dare. Others develop their young passion for music while singing in church or singing over the sounds of a South Dakota tractor. Either way, the love can be pure and all-encompassing.

For those taken in at such an early age, life without theater is simply unimaginable. Performing isn't something they want to do, but something they have to do. It provides a sense of self, and a source of pride. A life in theater no longer becomes a choice, but a calling. Many begin the long journey to Broadway thousands of miles from New York. Some begin the journey without even knowing the journey has begun. Once underway, there is usually no turning back.

Not by Choice

It is funny how we get into things. When I was about nine or ten, there was a girl who used to practice ballet in the playground. I used to see her practice all the time. At the time I was a tomboy, but inside I really wanted to be a girl.

One day, I remember telling the girl that I thought doing ballet in the playground was a bit sissy. I was trying to be the tough guy. She said, "Well, if you think it's sissy, why don't you try it? I bet you couldn't do it." The gauntlet was down. I said, "Yes, I can. Of course I can do that!"

I fell in love with the first ballet class I had. I was a child who had a lot of passion, and I didn't know where to put it. I was very hyperactive. I just needed an outlet. My mother called me "banana fingers" because my hands looked like they were a bunch of bananas. I had never danced before that moment. I started very late. Yet from the moment I went to ballet, I felt special. I never had great technique. What I had was great passion.

> **Ruthie Henshall.** *Putting It Together* (The Younger Woman) [O], *Miss Saigon* (Ellen), *Chicago* (Velma)

For certain people, Broadway is a dream. I did it because I had to. It was my calling. When I was fifteen years old, I auditioned for a high school musical as a gag. It was a big joke. I was a jock. My friends and I laughed at theater stuff. So, in full football attire, with the football team watching through a window, I went up on stage. With my football helmet in one hand and a microphone in the other, I sang "Yesterday" by the Beatles. The entire football team started jeering, "Look at him, that big jerk! Look at him, he can sing!"

Until that moment, I didn't know I had a voice. I always thought that someday I'd play on a professional baseball or football team. From that point forward, I just had to take a different route.

> **Robert Torti.** *Starlight Express* (Greaseball) [O][t], *Joseph and the Amazing Technicolor® Dreamcoat* (Pharaoh) [O]

One afternoon when I was in tenth grade, I missed the bus to go home.

Some girl said, "If you wait for about half an hour while I help paint the set for the school play, my mom will drive you home." I said, "Fine."

While I was waiting, my English teacher said, "Well, here is a paintbrush. Do you want to help?" I said, "Okay."

Then my teacher started complaining because one of the students didn't show up to help with the set. She asked if I wanted to sit behind the cardboard tombstone during the play that weekend.

I said, "Sure," and that was how it all started.

> **James Hindman.** *A Grand Night for Singing* [O], *City of Angels* (Stine) [O], *1776* [O], *The Scarlet Pimpernel* (Ben), *Once Upon a Mattress* (Princess), *Dancing at Lughnasa** (Michael), *Falsettos** (Marvin), *Joseph and the Amazing Technicolor® Dreamcoat** (Simeon), *Cats** (Gus)

Because I was so young, it wasn't a decision I made on my own. It was a decision made around me. My whole family knew that I could sing. I would sing on the coffee table. But I never really thought of it as a career.

One of my cousins was very active in a local repertory company. She suggested to my mom that I audition for *The King and I.* My mom brought me to the audition, and I got in. I never said, "Momma, please send me to the audition. I would like to be a performer." No, the decision was made for me. I was just tossed into the deep end of the pool, without saying I wanted to go in. I knew no fear.

I was going to be a doctor. I was in pre-med when I auditioned for *Miss Saigon.* I didn't think of it as a career. I enjoyed performing, but back home, I was more geared into thinking against theater as a career. It seemed more prudent to go into medicine, or another profession. Financially, I knew that it was difficult to be a performer.

But I went to Mass one day, and the priest said, "All of us have been given our gifts. God has given us all talents. Use your talents to the best of your ability." I knew it was going to be this.

Lea Salonga. *Miss Saigon* (Kim) [O][T], *Flower Drum Song* (Mei-Li) [O], *Les Misérables* (Eponine)

Church and Tractor

I lived in Trinidad until I was fifteen. My father was a pastor, and I grew up above a church. I knew I could sing and follow a tune, but I didn't know how well. I enjoyed performing, singing, and playing piano.

Every afternoon after school I would go to church by myself and stay there for three to four hours. In my little head, I would literally see thousands of people in the pews. I would pretend I was someone I saw perform on television, or somebody I saw sing in church, and I would one-up it and make it an even better performance.

I remember practicing. If I would mess up or do something I didn't like, I would start all over again. That's what I did every day after school. I didn't go outside and play with the other kids. The irony of it is that I do the same thing today. I go into my apartment, turn out all the lights, and see whatever I see. That's how I practice.

Heather Headley. *Aida* (Aida) [O][T], *The Lion King* (Nala) [O], *Ragtime** (Sarah u/s)

I'd spend hours on a tractor. It sounds crazy, but that's where I used to sing a lot. I had to level, cultivate, rake, cut, or whatever. Many hours were spent on a tractor. We had a Case 890 and a couple of Case 200s. The Case 890 was incredibly loud. I would sit right behind the engine for six or seven hours, unless I wanted to take a whiz or eat. That was basically my day.

I sang a lot when I sat on the tractor. It gave me time to think. When I was done driving, I would fix an old fence, get water, feed the lambs, or whatever. There was always something to do, which is probably another reason why I got the hell out of there. It was really hard work.

Jarrod Emick. *Damn Yankees* (Joe Hardy) [O][T], *The Boy from Oz* (Greg Connell) [O], *The Rocky Horror Show* (Brad) [O], *Miss Saigon* (Chris), *Les Misérables** (Enjolras u/s)

I used to plow the fields and drive the tractor a lot. I was exposed to a lot of different things growing up on a farm. I was in 4-H, and in a kids' program for raising animals. We raised the animals and brought them to the county fair. I showed sheep and cattle. My brother showed hogs, rabbits, and chickens.

Theater was a departure from the people who graduated high school, skipped college, and got a job working in a factory. I yearned for a lot more.

Matt Bogart. *The Civil War* (Sam Taylor) [O], *Aida* (Radames), *Miss Saigon* (Chris), *Smokey Joe's Cafe* (White Guy)

A Young Passion for Music

I remember when I was about fifteen months old—it's weird, but I remember things from when I was a baby. My mother sang to me constantly. Lullabies, children's songs, Disney songs. Starting at about eighteen months, I could sing all the songs. That's all I did. Sing.

When I was almost three, I got a blue dump truck and a record player for Christmas—one of those little white plastic record players. I thought it was a suitcase. From that point forward, everybody would give me albums for gifts. I had all the Disney albums. *Mary Poppins* was one of my favorites. When I was four, I decided I wanted to be in movie musicals like Judy Garland. I just knew.

In eighth grade, we were desperately poor. When I was three, my parents divorced and my mom entered the church as a missionary. I went to live separately from her on a farm for about three and a half years. It was like a commune, and it really nurtured my imagination.

Things got harder in junior high school. That's when I first started becoming aware of fashion and the value of things. I had really short pants because I was always growing. I had high-waters. In the fifth grade, people would ask, "Where's the flood?"

In the seventh grade, it really started to kick in. Many girls in my school had barrettes with weaved ribbons. They were a "luxury," so my mom said I couldn't get them. I wanted them because all the cool kids had them. When the barrettes finally went on sale, I got them. But by then, no one was wearing them anymore.

One girl would tease me and say, "Your dad is a garbage man." He wasn't a garbage man. Kids were awful—they knew I was poor. I always knew I was going to be on Broadway someday. I remember thinking, "You are going to wish you were kinder to me." I couldn't wait for the day.

Sarah Uriarte Berry. *Taboo* (Nicola) [O], *Les Misérables* (Eponine), *Beauty and the Beast* (Belle), *Sunset Boulevard** (Betty Schaeffer), *Carousel** (Julie Jordan)

When I was in kindergarten, we did a production of *Goldilocks and the Three Bears*. I was a brunette, but for some reason they cast me as the blonde. One night, when the curtain came down, I was standing too far downstage. The curtain fell behind me, instead of in front of me, and suddenly I was all alone onstage.

At first, I was very embarrassed. But then I started doing something silly, clowning, and the embarrassment evolved into delight.

Donna Murphy. *Passion* (Fosca) [O][**T**], *The King and I* (Anna) [O][**T**], *Wonderful Town* (Ruth) [O], *The Mystery of Edwin Drood* [O], *The Human Comedy* (Bess Macauley u/s) [O], *Privates on Parade* [O], *They're Playing Our Song* (Swing)

I was ten years old when we moved into a townhouse community in Canada. I got some friends together, none of whom were even remotely interested in theater, and said, "We are going to do a show. We are going to do *Annie*."

I rented the movie and wrote down all the lyrics. I gave everyone parts. I went to the thrift store and bought everyone costumes. We rehearsed for two days. We put up little chairs in the garage. My mom made popcorn. We charged fifty cents. We did four shows in one day, and then we all went to the candy store and spent the money.

Jessica Snow Wilson. *Little Shop of Horrors* (Audrey u/s) [O], *Les Misérables* (Eponine), *A Funny Thing Happened on the Way to the Forum* (Philia)

My family moved from Brooklyn to Long Island when I was two years old. My parents came from no money. We had been living in my grandmother's basement. My parents decided to get a piano in the house before they even bought a couch. We had a kitchen table and a piano.

I hogged the piano. When I would hear something on my sister's stereo, I would run to the piano and play it by ear. I was four years old. I remember doing shows in the living room. It brought the whole family together.

Deborah Gibson. *Cabaret* (Sally Bowles), *Les Misérables* (Eponine), *Beauty and the Beast* (Belle), *Grease!* (Rizzo), *Joseph and the Amazing Technicolor® Dreamcoat** (Narrator)

Cheerios, Indians, and Show Tunes

In fourth grade I started listening to my parent's records. I was always running around the house, singing, and putting on little plays. I would use empty cereal boxes to play the other characters. I would move the cereal boxes and talk to them. The Cheerios box was usually the other main character.

Jeff Edgerton. *Parade* (Fiddlin' John) [O], *Grease!* (Eugene u/s)

When I was a little girl I listened to music. I didn't know my father yet. He was fighting in the Second World War. I used to dance in the living room with my arms up over my head. My mother thought I was trying to emulate a ballerina. When I was three years old, in my mind, I imagined that my father was an Indian chief. I don't know why I chose that. I always connected to the music, and to the yearning. It was less about movement and more about expressing myself, connecting to my father, and the need to be loved.

Donna McKechnie. *A Chorus Line* (Cassie) [O][**T**], *Company* (Kathy) [O], *State Fair* (Emily Arden) [O], *On the Town* (Ivy Smith) [O], *Promises, Promises* (Vivien Della Hoya) [O], *The Education of Hyman Kaplan* (Kathy McKenna) [O], *How to Succeed in Business without Really Trying!* (Dancer) [O], *A Funny Thing Happened on the Way to the Forum** (Philia), *Call Me Madam** (The Princess), *Sweet Charity**, *Annie Get Your Gun**

I was an odd kid. I would go to the library and rent show albums. For a little kid, for a black kid, for a St. Louis kid, and whatever else you want to throw in there, Broadway was a strange thing. When I would try to take ten albums out at a time, the lady would say, "You can only take four." Then I would have a dilemma. Which four would I want? She'd always laugh.

Ken Page. *Cats* (Old Deuteronomy) [O], *Guys and Dolls* (Nicely-Nicely Johnson) [O], *Ain't Misbehavin'* [O], *The Wiz* (Lion), *Purlie**

A Special Talent

Being a kid who was teased a lot, acting was a way of showing off. I found a way of stepping beyond those teasing kids and found something that I could really be good at. I never thought about a life on Broadway. I never thought about anything. It was just about showing off.

When I was a child, I was diagnosed with dyslexia and with attention deficit disorder. I spent many weekends with psychiatrists. I was always being tested. I was put on too much Ritalin, taken off Ritalin, and then put on it again. And for a long time, I had a very difficult time with the whole psychiatric world. I thought it was a bunch of crock. I was a kid with a lot of energy. But when someone captured that energy, watch out. That's what theater did for me.

The first show I ever did was called *Treasure Island*. I was a pirate. My only line in the entire show was "treasure." I felt like I was the king of the world.

Steven Buntrock. *Jane Eyre* (Mr. Eshton) [O], *Oklahoma!* (Joe/Curley) [O], *Titanic* (Frederick Barrett), *Les Misérables* (Enjolras), *Martin Guerre** (Arnaud), *Joseph and the Amazing Technicolor® Dreamcoat** (Reuben)

CHAPTER 2

First Impressions

There are few things in the world more powerful than the imagination of a child, and perhaps nothing can unleash its full potential more than seeing a Broadway show. The experience can be magical and intensely personal. It can provide a form of intimacy and comfort otherwise unknown. Its spell is more powerful than any drug, for the love of theater does not fade, but only intensifies with time.

Every once in a while, a special musical comes along which shapes a whole generation of performers and inspires thousands to pursue careers on Broadway. Perhaps no show in history has done so more than *Les Misérables*. Before *Les Misérables*, shows like *Annie, West Side Story*, and *Pippin* accomplished such a task. As the actors in this chapter explain, the magic of these shows can be intoxicating to a young mind, and the intensity of their dreams can blind them from the reality that awaits.

Tickets, Please

For my tenth birthday, my parents took me to see the first national tour of *Annie*. Nothing has impacted my life more. There was something inside of me—I don't know if I can ever explain it. It was complete awe. In a sense, I wanted to be Annie. Don't get me wrong!

We got the record, and for almost a month and a half I would listen to *Annie* all day long. I kid you not. I almost went into a kiddie depression. I wanted to do that show. I made up scenarios of me being the only male orphan. It was almost like when I first found out what sex was like. It was emotional content that was hitting me so hard. And as a ten-year-old child, I had no idea where to place it.

Steven Buntrock. *Jane Eyre* (Mr. Eshton) [O], *Oklahoma!* (Joe/Curley) [O], *Titanic* (Frederick Barrett), *Les Misérables* (Enjolras), *Martin Guerre** (Arnaud), *Joseph and the Amazing Technicolor® Dreamcoat** (Reuben)

I used to watch *West Side Story* on television. I loved the songs, the performance, and the dancing. The funny thing is, I didn't know I was watching musical theater. I'm a boy of Dominican descent who was born in Brooklyn. I wasn't exposed to musical theater. I would watch *West Side Story* and *The Music Man* on television. I just thought they were great movies with music. I didn't put it all together. I didn't know it was a genre. I can't really explain it to you. It was almost like I had a piece of metal in my diaphragm and the theater was a huge magnet. I always had a gut feeling pulling me towards the stage.

Wilson Heredia. *Rent* (Angel) [O][**T**]

I was born in Grenada, and my parents moved to New Jersey when I was young. I started going to Catholic school in East Orange, New Jersey. I was overweight and had braces. I hated my life so much that I would just sit at home and watch television. It was my fantasyland. My mother would say, "Stop watching the television or you will go blind!"

One day, I saw a commercial for *Pippin*. The commercial said, "This is thirty seconds of *Pippin*, the Broadway musical. If you want to see the next hundred-plus minutes, come to the theater and check it out."

I thought, "Oh, my God." I didn't know what it was, but I knew that it was going to save me and make my life completely different. It was

Pippin. © Martha Swope

going to be my joy and passion for the rest of my life. The clouds opened. I felt a reason to be here.

Gerry McIntyre. *Once on This Island* (Armand) [O], *Joseph and the Amazing Technicolor® Dreamcoat* (Judah) [O], *Anything Goes* (Purser) [O], *Uptown . . . It's Hot!* (Little Richard) [O], *Chicago** (Billy Flynn), *Annie 2** (Punjab)

When I was young, I wanted to be a magician. However, my whole life changed when I was twelve years old and saw *Pippin*. Even though I was serious about magic, I wasn't very good. I have very small hands and could barely palm a card. At the age of twelve, I was really distraught, and thought, "I don't know what I'm going to do with my life."

Pippin was everything that I loved all in one place. It was rock music, theater, and magic, all rolled into one. Not only rolled into one, but rolled into Ben Vereen. He seemed to have complete metaphysical control of everything that happened on stage. I was blown over by the performance. At that very moment, I thought, "This is what I want to do."

So, I went on this ridiculous quest to become Ben Vereen. He radiated at such a high energy level. I was under the illusion that his whole life was always glittering and exciting. He was incredibly powerful, joyful, surprising, and mysterious. I thought his whole life had to be just like that.

Jason Alexander. *Jerome Robbins' Broadway* (Emcee) [O][T], *Merrily We Roll Along* (Joe) [O], *The Rink* (Lino/Lenny/Punk/Uncle Fausto) [O], *Broadway Bound* (Stanley) [O], *Accomplice* [O], *The Producers** (Max Bialystock)

Up until the time I was twelve years old, I was very sure that I was going to be a veterinarian. My uncle was our family doctor, and I thought he was great. Because I was an animal nut, I was going to be a vet.

One day, my parents saw a number from a new Broadway musical called *Annie* on *The Today Show*. It was a big deal because Andrea McArdle was a local girl from Philadelphia. My parents thought, "Oh, that might be fun. It sounds cute. It sounds like it's for kids."

They got tickets, and we drove to New York City. I had never seen a Broadway show before. I didn't even know what Broadway was. I didn't know anything about it. Yet from the time the curtain went up, I was perched on the edge of my seat. I didn't blink once.

In the car ride home, my parents kept talking about Andrea McArdle. "That kid from Philadelphia is amazing. I've never heard a kid sing like that." They were going on and on. Finally, I said, "Well, I can do that."

They said, "What do you mean? You've never even opened your mouth."

"Just because I haven't sung before doesn't mean I don't know I can."

It was late when we got back home that night. At two in the morning, I sat down at our piano and played "Tomorrow" and "Maybe." I just sat down and started playing. I started singing too.

"We never knew you could sing. Where did that come from?"

"Well, you never asked me."

All of a sudden I was singing for everybody. I would sing everything Andrea sang, in her key. I sounded like a high belting little girl. My brother used to torment me. He would say, "Better be careful. We're going to put you in a red dress and a red wig and send you out!" I discovered something that I could do that would get praise. I was a fat little kid who couldn't play sports. I was pigeon-toed. I basically ate and played the piano.

Hugh Panaro. *Side Show* (Buddy Foster) [O], *The Red Shoes* (Julian Craster) [O], *The Phantom of the Opera* (Phantom/Raoul), *Les Misérables* (Marius), *Showboat* (Ravenal), *Martin Guerre** (Martin)

I was raised in a really small town in Montana. I had no idea how one became an actor. I had no idea of the process. When I was a kid, I thought you were chosen, that somebody picked you. I didn't know that there were schools and things.

The first play I ever saw was *Titus Andronicus*. I was eleven years old. I had no interest in seeing it whatsoever. *Star Trek* was on that night. My parents dragged me kicking and screaming. That play literally changed my life.

The show began with archaic language. While I had no idea what was going on, it was beautiful. The production was breathtaking. Then really strange things started to happen. Lavinia got her arms and tongue cut out. When they cut her tongue out, she was lying backwards on the stage and they pulled a ribbon out of her mouth—a big long red ribbon which draped across the stage. Then they cut off her arms and pulled red ribbons out of her costume. I'm getting chills just thinking about it, those simple red ribbons. It was so poetic, terrifying, violent, and beautiful. It was like a horror cartoon coming to life. I had no idea Shakespeare could do that, that plays could do that. It was a big thing for me.

Tom Hewitt. *The Rocky Horror Show* (Dr. Frank N. Furter) [O][t], *The Boys from Syracuse* (Antipholus of Ephesus) [O], *Art* (Serge u/s) [O], *The Lion King* (Scar), *School for Scandal* (Charles Surface), *Sisters Rosensweig* (Geoffrey), *Urinetown** (Officer Lockstock)

The most earth-shattering experience was seeing the landmark production *Of Mice and Men* with James Earl Jones as Lenny. I was eleven years old. At intermission, I asked my mother, "How did they get a mentally retarded man to memorize so many lines?" I had been seduced by the performance. She said, "Read his bio." I read that he had been in Shakespeare and some other amazing shows. I was a bit overwhelmed that it was possible to be so completely taken in.

Jeff Gardner. *The Wild Party* (Burrs u/s) [O], *The Scarlet Pimpernel* (Mercier) [O], *Cyrano—The Musical* (Sylvian) [O], *The Queen and the Rebels* (Traveler) [O], *Jerome Robbins' Broadway* (The Setter u/s), *Les Misérables** (Foreman)

When I was eight years old, I went to see the touring company of *Carousel.* I sat up in the mezzanine. In the second act, there was a blackout. People came running down the aisles with flashlights, and shined the lights upon the stage. The actors kept performing and finished the show.

At the end of the show, John Raitt came out and said, "I don't want anyone to go anywhere. There's been a blackout in the city. They don't want people to move right now, so I'm going to sing for you." He sang for about forty-five minutes.

I will never forget that moment. To me, that was the magic of theater. Every night is different. Every audience is different. I just love the magic.

Marin Mazzie. *Kiss Me, Kate* (Lilli Vanessi) [O][t], *Ragtime* (Mother) [O][t], *Passion* (Clara) [O][t], *Man of La Mancha* (Aldonza), *Big River* (Mary Jane Wilkes), *Into the Woods* (Rapunzel)

Field Trip

I grew up in Alabama, and I had to get out. During my senior year in high school, my drama group was making a trip to New York City. I begged my parents to let me go. They did. I was so excited. I had never seen a Broadway show before. My first night in town, we saw *Cats.*

During high school, I worked at a place called Chess King. That's how I saved the money to go on the trip. I bought a really cool Chess King double-breasted tuxedo and I had a skinny red sparkly tie. I also had pants that I could tuck into my boots. I was feeling pretty darn cool. I went to the Salvation Army and bought a pair of tap shoes. So, when I went to see *Cats,* I was prepared. I put on my tap shoes, the skinny red tie, and the Chess King tuxedo, and tapped all the way down Broadway to the Winter Garden Theater.

Kip Driver. *Martin Guerre** (Swing), *Cats** (Munkustrap), *Les Misérables**

When I was sixteen and living in Chicago, I would visit New York City by myself on the weekends. I'd go to the TKTS booth in Times Square and buy tickets. I'd see as many shows as I could. I had pizza for lunch and pizza for dinner. I stayed in little cheap hotels. My parents let me do this. They trusted me. I remember going to The Drama Bookshop and buying the book *Audition.* It was so exciting.

Liz Callaway. *Baby* (Lizzie) [O][t], *Miss Saigon* (Ellen) [O], *Merrily We Roll Along* (Nightclub Waitress) [O], *The Three Musketeers* (Lady Constance Bonacieux) [O], *The Look of Love* [O], *Cats* (Grizabella)

I grew up in Houston. All I ever wanted to do my whole life was be in *A Chorus Line.* I took dance classes from the time I could walk. I started singing when I was nine. A group of us took a trip to New York to see *A*

Chorus Line. I sat in the next-to-last row. I almost needed a Dramamine because I was so high up. When I saw Valerie Clark come on stage with her pigtails and white outfit, I thought, "That's who I want to be." She sang the song "Tits and Ass," which had the "F-word" in it. Growing up in Houston, I wasn't even allowed to think about the "F-word." I thought, "How am I going to be able to do this show and not upset my parents?"

DeLee Lively. *Smokey Joe's Cafe* [O][t], *A Chorus Line** (Val)

Broadway Dreaming

I didn't even know what Broadway was. I didn't know it was a street. I just knew that Broadway was what I wanted to do. I remember thinking that I didn't care if I was poor. I didn't care if I was living in a little apartment with cockroaches, or working as a waitress, as long as I was pursuing what I really wanted to do.

Jessica Snow Wilson. *Little Shop of Horrors* (Audrey u/s) [O], *Les Misérables* (Eponine), *A Funny Thing Happened on the Way to the Forum* (Philia)

When I was growing up in a small Vermont town, I thought Broadway had an element of glamour. I watched the Tony Awards. I thought the life of a Broadway actor was comparable to the life of a Hollywood star. I thought everyone in a Broadway show had a limousine and went to fancy parties.

Ray Walker. *Jesus Christ Superstar* (Annas) [O], *Grease!* (Doody), *Les Misérables* (Marius), *Whistle Down the Wind** (Preacher), *Music of the Night** (Principal Soloist), *Joseph and the Amazing Technicolor° Dreamcoat** (Joseph u/s), *Falsettos** (Whizzer)

In 1982, we drove into New York City on a bus. We saw *A Chorus Line* and I forgot my glasses, so I could barely see the show. Yet I had worn out the album, so I knew every word. When I saw the actors coming out of the stage door, I thought they were all famous and lived in penthouse apartments. I thought all they did was go to interviews and sign contracts. I had no idea that they were probably making $450 a week and were struggling to survive. To me, they were the same as movie stars.

Marsh Hanson. *Les Misérables* (Marius), *Joseph and the Amazing Technicolor° Dreamcoat** (Brother)

CHAPTER 3

Don't You Dare Call My Child a Thespian!

For some parents, there is nothing more disturbing than having their child dream of becoming a Broadway actor. Overcoming a parent's urgings to become a doctor, lawyer, UPS worker, or car salesman is often the first obstacle a young performer must hurdle just to get his or her journey to Broadway underway. Often, the pilgrimage to Broadway begins alone, without the support and enthusiasm of family and friends.

Play Ball

When I was ten years old, I was a terrible athlete. Every summer, my dad would introduce me to a new sport. However, it seemed like every time there would be a game, there would also be a movie-musical on television. I would con my dad into letting me stay home from the game. I would fake illness. Finally, he caught on, so I would have to be honest. I would say, "Dad, *Jesus Christ Superstar* is on television. I can't miss it." He finally just gave up.

Joe Paparella. *Jesus Christ Superstar* (Swing), *Les Misérables* (Thénardier u/s), *Martin Guerre** (Martin u/s), *Mamma Mia!** (Eddie), *Joseph and the Amazing Technicolor® Dreamcoat** (Swing), *Ragtime**, *Big**

Growing up in Tennessee, it wasn't the coolest thing to pursue the arts. It was all about football and sports. Guys who were interested in the arts were immediately labeled sissies. I didn't get any support from my school.

Not only was my stepfather a jock football player, but he was really religious. He was firmly convinced that if I went down to the theater to hang out with "those fags," I would become one. He did everything he could to stand in my way. My mother had to sneak me out of the house for auditions. We could only tell him after I was cast. In a weird way, it made my resolve even stronger.

Dave Clemmons. *The Scarlet Pimpernel* (Ben) [O], *The Civil War* (Sergeant Virgil Frank/Auctioneer's Assistant) [O], *Les Misérables* (Jean Valjean), *Whistle Down the Wind**, *Jekyll & Hyde** (Bishop)

What's Wrong with the Family Business?

When I took acting class in high school, I was told, "Ninety-nine percent of all Equity members are unemployed at any given time." It was supposed to scare me. It didn't. My dad would try to talk me out of doing summer stock theater. He was very logical.

He would say, "Honey, why don't you come home and get a job at UPS? Hmm, let's think. You can do summer stock in Indiana at the Red Barn Theater for very little money each week, or you can get paid eight dollars an hour at UPS and live at home."

"Dad," I said, "I have to do this." I just knew. I couldn't take my eyes off the road.

Alice Ripley. *Side Show* (Violet Hilton) [O][t], *The Rocky Horror Show* (Janet Weiss) [O], *Sunset Boulevard* (Betty Schaefer) [O], *King David* (Bathsheba) [O], *James Joyce's The Dead* (Mrs. Molly Ivors) [O], *The Who's Tommy* [O], *Les Misérables* (Fantine), *Little Shop of Horrors** (Audrey)

My dad's first reaction when I told him I wanted to go to college and study theater was, "Well, I'm not going to pay for school if it's for theater." He was always very practical. He would say, "Well, you can go for a couple of years and then come back and work with me in the car industry."

My argument was always, "Dad, we will be doing the same thing. You sell cars. I will be selling myself. I will be doing the same thing you are doing, except I will be my own product. You are very good at what you do, and, so far, I think I am pretty good at what I do." It was an argument that he couldn't really refute.

Jeff Edgerton. *Parade* (Fiddlin' John) [O], *Grease!* (Eugene u/s)

Proving Parents Wrong

Nobody in my family had ever pursued art as a career. Everyone was a doctor, a lawyer, or some sort of businessperson. My mother was extremely worried and very against my going to a conservatory. Once, I overheard a conversation between my mother and stepfather just before

I was going to the city to audition for the drama program at Carnegie Mellon University.

I was coming downstairs to say good night and I heard my stepfather say, "It's really good of you to let her try to do this."

She said, "Yeah, yeah."

He said, "You realize that if she gets in, you are going to have to let her go."

My mom replied, "Oh, she's not going to get in. Don't worry about it. They don't accept just anybody."

I was sitting there quietly on the steps, thinking, "Just because of that, I'm going to go."

Sophia Salguero. *The Green Bird* (Singing Apple) [O], *The Capeman* (Bernadette) [O], *Juan Darien* (Green Dwarf) [O], *Martin Guerre**, Carousel*

Plan for the Future

When I was fifteen years old, I told my mother that I was going to buy a motorcycle and move to "the Village." I didn't know what "the Village" was. I thought it was a little village in New York City—a little artist's village. I told her that I was going to be a backup dancer for Janet Jackson or Madonna. I had no idea what the business was about.

She cried. It scared the hell out of her. She wanted me to go to college and have something to fall back on. I could minor in dance, but she didn't want me to be a dancer. I grew up in a farm town. In my graduating class, I was the only male dancer. It always set me apart.

Mark Moreau. *Cats* (Swing), *The Music Man* (Traveling Salesman), *The Will Rogers Follies, Grease!*

I decided to pursue acting much to my parents' chagrin. They wanted me to be happy and stable and not hit them up for cash too often. They were concerned about the instability of the business. They are very practical, conservative people. Although loving, they managed to be supportive but not encouraging.

The reason I went into theater was because it was what I loved, and it came easy to me. I went to Rutgers University with the understanding that if it didn't click I would minor in business, get another degree, and try to figure out something else to do.

Roger Bart. *You're a Good Man, Charlie Brown* (Snoopy) [O][**T**], *The Producers* (Carmen Ghia) [O][**t**], *Triumph of Love* (Harlequin) [O], *King David* (Jonathan) [O], *Big River* (Tom Sawyer), *The Who's Tommy* (Cousin Kevin), *The Secret Garden* (Dickon), *How to Succeed in Business without Really Trying!* (Bud Frump)

When I told my parents I wanted to be a dancer, there was just a lot of silence.

It was unexpected.

They didn't see it coming. I think they were disappointed. They expected me to be a star scholar, and they thought I was throwing it all away. I was just dashing my future on the rocks of stupidity.

Deborah Yates. *Contact* (Girl in the Yellow Dress) [O][t], *Dream* (Swing) [O]

PART TWO

GETTING
SETTLED

CHAPTER 4

Welcome to Gotham City

To be sure, New York City is one of the most special places on Earth. Nevertheless, it is not country living, and those moving into town have some adjusting to do. Just as Ellis Island once served as the gateway for millions of immigrants, Penn Station and John F. Kennedy Airport now serve as the modern portals through which many actors are steered. Hoping to be "discovered" upon arriving in the city, some are shocked to find themselves only discovered by lustful cabdrivers. That being said, while an actor's first few months in New York City can be overwhelming, they can also be inspiring.

A Special City

New York City is one of the most spiritual places I have ever come across. If you are looking for something, whatever it might be, you will find it in New York. The energy is really special. I can't tell you how many times I have been to Central Park. I know God is everywhere, but as far as I am concerned, God lives in Central Park. So far, the greatest gift of my life has been the time that I have spent in New York City.

> **Ruthie Henshall.** *Putting It Together* (The Younger Woman) [O], *Miss Saigon* (Ellen), *Chicago* (Velma)

I used to live on 74th Street between Amsterdam and Columbus. Steve's Ice Cream was right around the corner. In the ice cream parlor was a piano. Over the piano was a chalkboard. The chalkboard read, "*Play and sing the song of the day for a free scoop of ice cream.*" Every day, a different song was written in chalk.

In the mornings, I would walk by and glance at the song of the day. I would then go back to my apartment, go through my music, find the song, and learn it. Almost every day, I would play and sing the song for the ice cream. New York was pretty cool.

Hugh Panaro. *Side Show* (Buddy Foster) [O], *The Red Shoes* (Julian Craster) [O], *The Phantom of the Opera* (Phantom/Raoul), *Les Misérables* (Marius), *Showboat* (Ravenal), *Martin Guerre** (Martin)

Driving into Town

When I was nineteen years old, I drove into Manhattan in a little four-hundred-dollar car that my brother gave me. I had just finished doing a summer stock production of *West Side Story.* I thought, "I'm coming to New York, and I'm going to be a star!" As I came into the city, I had a little jam box which was wrapped in duct tape to hold in the batteries. It was playing the music to *Les Misérables.*

By pure coincidence, while the music was still playing, I drove by the *Les Misérables* theater. Mind you, this was 1989. I thought, "Oh, my God, there's *Les Misérables.* I have to see it." I got out of my car and ran into the theater. I only had about $200 to my name.

At the ticket booth, I asked, "Can I get a ticket for tonight?" They started laughing.

"No, really," I said. "I would like a ticket."

They said, "We are sold out for a year."

Some guy then said, "Go stand on that line." After standing in line for a while, he called me over. "There are two tickets that just became available. You'll have to buy them both. So, do you want to see the show or what?"

I said, "I don't have the money, and I only want one."

Just as I said that, a lady came over and said, "I'll take one."

So I paid my fifty-eight bucks for the ticket. Since I only had $200 to my name, I was kind of screwed after that. Also, I parked my car in an illegal spot, so now I was actually down to about $70.

I sat in the eighth row, dressed in jeans and a T-shirt. I watched the guys in the show run around and sing their high notes. I thought, "I can do that!"

That was the first Broadway show I ever saw. I was in heaven. Afterwards, when I was walking around the city, it was like I was on a drug. I was just blown away.

Daniel C. Cooney. *Les Misérables* (Marius u/s), *The Civil War** (Swing), *Evita** (Che), *Fiddler on the Roof** (Perchik)

I graduated from Carnegie Mellon University and came to New York City with five buddies. We packed up all of our stuff in a U-Haul. Moments before we arrived at the last exit before the Lincoln Tunnel, I realized I had no cash. I asked my friends if I should stop for money. One of my friends said, "No, don't worry about it. I have enough to get us through."

We waited in rush-hour traffic for over an hour before we got to the tunnel. Before we pulled up to the tollbooth, I said, "Wouldn't it be funny if we didn't have enough money to even get into New York City?"

I asked my friend, "How much money do you have?"

"Four bucks," he said. It just so happened that it was exactly four dollars for a truck to go through the tunnel.

When we got up to the tollbooth window, the lady said, "That will be six dollars."

"Sorry?"

"Six dollars."

"I thought it was four," I said.

"You have an extra axle. You are a truck with two axles. It is two dollars for each extra axle."

I just started laughing. I said, "We don't have an extra two dollars!" There we were, moving to New York City for the first time, and we couldn't even get into the damn city. She got on the phone. Meanwhile, I realized that my license had expired. We were in a code red.

We pulled the truck off to the side of the tunnel. My friend leaped to the back of the truck and started frantically scooping up whatever change he could find. And then the police arrived.

I told the cop, "We just came from Pittsburgh. We are moving here, and we have no money." Then he looked at my license.

I said, "I am going back to Florida next week to get a new license. I just graduated from college and I am an actor. Please. I just got here."

He just looked at me, and asked, "Are you really going to Florida next week?"

"I promise."

"All right," he said. We scrounged up the extra two dollars and he let us go. It was a rough move to New York.

Patrick Wilson. *The Full Monty* (Jerry Lukowski) [O][t], *Oklahoma!* (Curley) [O][t], *The Gershwin's Fascinating Rhythm* [O], *Carousel** (Billy Bigelow), *Miss Saigon**

Taxi!

I loved New York the minute I got here. It started with the cab ride from the airport. The cabdriver was Caribbean, and he threw earphones in the back seat for me to listen along to some jazz. I thought, "What a great city." It was just a magical entrance.

Everything seemed to go well, even though I didn't have a lot of money and I was alone. It was a big move from Birmingham, Alabama. I don't know what gave me the courage—maybe my naïveté. I just remember feeling that I belonged and that I would be happy here.

Rebecca Luker. *The Music Man* (Marian) [O][t], *Showboat* (Magnolia) [O][t], *The Sound of Music* (Maria) [O], *The Secret Garden* (Lily) [O], *The Phantom of the Opera* (Princess/Christine) [O], *Nine* (Claudia)

I arrived at JFK Airport with only a big suitcase. I told the cabdriver that I was moving to New York. He said, "I can't hear you in the back seat. Why don't you come up here in the front with me?" I said okay.

Stuck in traffic, he started putting his hands on me. He said he wouldn't charge me for the ride if I went to a hotel with him. It was horrible. I had my suitcase in the back and there was simply no way for me to get out of the cab. I never feared for my life, I didn't think I was going to be raped, but this guy was definitely manhandling me. That was my first day in New York City.

Liz Callaway. *Baby* (Lizzie) [O][t], *Miss Saigon* (Ellen) [O], *Merrily We Roll Along* (Nightclub Waitress) [O], *The Three Musketeers* (Lady Constance Bonacieux) [O], *The Look of Love* [O], *Cats* (Grizabella)

When I got off the train at Penn Station, I had to wait in a horrible line in order to get a cab. While I was waiting, some guy came over to me and asked, "Hey, do you need a cab?"

I said, "Yeah."

"Follow me," he said.

I followed him to 8th Avenue, and he hailed a cab. He then said, "That will be five dollars." When I opened my wallet to get the money out, he said, "Give me that," and he grabbed my wallet. He took all the money out, handed back my wallet, and ran away. The cabdriver started screaming. "What are you? An idiot? Is this your first time in New York or something?" I was petrified.

Mark Moreau. *Cats* (Swing), *The Music Man* (Traveling Salesman), *The Will Rogers Follies, Grease!*

Sharing the Wealth

I was taking some classes at HB Studio and I wanted to save my money. That meant saving my subway tokens. It was a nice evening, so I decided to walk from the Village to the Upper West Side. It was dusk when I was coming through midtown. When I was somewhere between Macy's and Times Square, this dude started walking along beside me, asking for money.

I said, "No, I'm sorry. I don't have any."

He said, "Well that's too bad, because I'd really hate to have to stab somebody." And he pulled a knife on me.

I stopped, shook my head, and said, "Look, dude," turning my pockets inside-out, "this is all I have." I pulled out a handful of change. "Look, I'm even saving that subway token. I'm walking home so I can save that subway token for later!"

He said, "Really? This is all you have?"

"Yeah."

He asked, rather puzzled, "So what's in the bag?"

"Theater books and scripts. Nothing of any value."

He started poking through the bag. "Nah, nothing in there I want. Let me see your change again." I reached deep into my pocket and grabbed everything I could find. He reached into my hand and picked out all the coins, leaving the pennies. Politely, he said, "Okay, thanks man," and just walked off.

And there I was, standing with a handful of pocket lint and pennies, thinking, "You've got to be kidding me."

Doug Storm. *Dance of the Vampires* [O], *The Scarlet Pimpernel* (Leggett), *Les Misérables* (Feuilly)

On my first Halloween in New York, I had a callback for a show. I was supposed to look like I was twelve. When I went down into the subway, I took off all my jewelry and put it in my purse. Sure enough, when I got off the train, I was mugged. They grabbed my purse and I lost everything.

I chased after them and soon found myself at a school for delinquent minors. Being at the school was even more horrifying than being mugged. When I walked away from the school, all I wanted was a frozen yogurt. As soon as I couldn't get one—because I had no purse and hence no money—I started to cry.

I went to my manager's office and said, "I can't go to my callback. I was mugged."

They said, "You can still make it."

I looked like shit, and thought, "Are you crazy?"

Paige Price. *Saturday Night Fever* (Stephanie) [O], *Beauty and the Beast* (Silly Girl) [O], *Smokey Joe's Cafe*

I lived in an apartment on West Street on the West Side Highway. It had a two-door entrance. One night, someone followed me to the second door. He pinned me up against the wall, took my keys, and told me he was going to make a copy. Then he said he was going to take the copy and bury it in a "special place." Only he knew where. It was awful.

Suddenly, there was a noise outside, and he looked the other way. I grabbed my keys and ran up the stairs. He followed me. I slammed the door in his face and called the cops. I put all the windows down. It was like a *Cagney & Lacey* episode—quite traumatic.

Ray Walker. *Jesus Christ Superstar* (Annas) [O], *Grease!* (Doody), *Les Misérables* (Marius), *Whistle Down the Wind** (Preacher), *Music of the Night** (Principal Soloist), *Joseph and the Amazing Technicolor® Dreamcoat** (Joseph u/s), *Falsettos** (Whizzer)

Adjusting to City Life

New York is so expensive. People pay for the privilege to live in this town, and yet so much of this town is nasty. It is dirty. There are homeless people everywhere. There are drug addicts and there is dog shit all over the sidewalks. The subway stations smell like urinals.

You can't even feel free to walk around in your own apartment because you might disturb the people below you. There are cockroaches that come from the apartment above when they spray. The cockroaches have to escape somewhere, so they come to your apartment, even though you keep your apartment really clean. Being from the West Coast, I was miserable.

Even when you order a coffee, people treat you like crap. They say, "What do you want? Coffee? Coffee regular? Light? What?" They are so mean.

Sarah Uriarte Berry. *Taboo* (Nicola) [O], *Les Misérables* (Eponine), *Beauty and the Beast* (Belle), *Sunset Boulevard** (Betty Schaeffer), *Carousel** (Julie Jordan)

It was so overwhelming—all the people, all the buildings, and the energy. I couldn't take everything in fast enough. It took me six months to figure out the difference between north and south. I could never figure out which was uptown and which was downtown.

One day, I was on 78th Street and Broadway, and I saw a guy sitting on the street. He was a homeless guy, or a "bum," as we used to call them. He was sitting there playing with some bullets—taking the bullets out of the cartridge and pouring out the gunpowder. "Shit, man, that's scary," I thought. He didn't have a gun, and I don't know what he was going to do except blow himself up. That image is etched in my mind.

Terrence Mann. *Les Misérables* (Javert) [O][t], *Beauty and the Beast* (Beast) [O][t], *Cats* (Rum Tum Tugger), *The Scarlet Pimpernel* (Chauvelin) [O], *Barnum* (Chester Lyman) [O], *Rags* (Saul) [O], *Getting Away with Murder* (Gregory Reed) [O], *Jerome Robbins' Broadway* (Emcee), *The Rocky Horror Show* (Dr. Frank N. Furter)

During school break from Juilliard, I went back home to California. One day, when I was talking to my father in a shopping mall, a little boy walked up behind me with two cap pistols. I didn't see him. He shot me and I jumped about ten feet in the air. It scared me so bad. My father said, "So, you live in New York City, do you?"

Boyd Gaines. *Contact* (Michael Wiley) [O][T], *She Loves Me* (Georg Nowak) [O][T], *The Heidi Chronicles* (Peter Patrone) [O][T], *Anything Goes* (Lord Evelyn Oakleigh) [O], *Company* (Robert) [O], *The Show Off* (Aubrey Piper) [O], *Cabaret* (Clifford Bradshaw)

CHAPTER 5

New Home and New Friends

New York is one of the most expensive cities in the world, and only a select few are lucky enough to arrive on a red carpet. The reality is that most can barely even afford their own carpet, and struggle from day one to make ends meet. From sharing apartments with over a thousand cockroaches to giving late-night massages to skinny eighty-year-old landlords who parade around in the nude, many of today's brightest stars have had humble beginnings. When living in a three-hundred-square-foot apartment in the middle of town is considered a luxury, you know you've arrived in the Big Apple.

Yet for most young performers, sharing a closet with a roommate and a family of rats for almost a thousand dollars a month is a price they are willing to pay. That is, unless the place is possessed by the devil. The experience of being a young performer and living in Manhattan is second to none. There are friends to be made, and there is a life to begin.

Roll Out the Red Carpet

When I first came to New York, I walked into an apartment on 67th Street that Disney had provided. Somebody picked me up at the airport. When I walked in, there were flowers on the piano.

I am not a New York girl. I am from the Caribbean and from Indiana. It was a little much for me. I don't understand how people can come to New York without everything being set. I would have sat in the middle of Times Square and thought, "Slit my wrists, kill me now."

Heather Headley. *Aida* (Aida) [O][T], *The Lion King* (Nala) [O], *Ragtime** (Sarah u/s)

Where's My Carpet?

I got off the train and took my huge boxes out of the taxicab. I was so excited to be in New York. But my hotel lost my reservation. There I was. I didn't know a soul in New York. I didn't have a place to go, and I had no money.

I was on the street crying. I asked someone passing by, "Do you know if there is a place I can stay?" I got the address of a hotel. What I didn't know was that it was a hotel for welfare people, alcoholics, and prostitutes. It was really seedy. There was no phone in my room, so I had to go to the corner to make calls. Guys would drive up and ask, "Hey, baby, how much do you charge?"

Ann Hampton Callaway. *Swing!* [O][t]

I came from the West Coast, where I paid five hundred bucks a month for a large one-bedroom apartment, with a yard and a covered garage. In New York, the least expensive thing I could find was a studio for eight hundred bucks a month. It was fifteen by fifteen. It was like living in a closet.

I probably pissed some people off because I'd tell them, "I can't live like this!"

They would say, "This is a really nice place. I don't know what your problem is."

I soon learned that if you come to New York and want to be an actor, this might be the way you will live for the rest of your life. It's about having a place to lay your head, take a shower, and go to your show.

Michael Berry. *Les Misérables* (Enjolras u/s), *Sunset Boulevard** (Artie)

The N.Y.C. Wildlife

There was a horrible smell in our apartment. We couldn't figure out what it was. It was a combination of curry and urine. Sometimes it would disappear for a day or two. And then it would come back. We had no idea what the hell it was.

Finally, a month and a half into living there, when I was doing work in the kitchen, I pulled the oven away from the wall, and there it was— a roach motel. It was one of those old Black Flag Roach Motels. It had been baking back there with the heat of the oven for years perhaps, with all those crispy critters—just the nastiest combination of smells.

Clarke Thorell. *Hairspray* (Corny Collins) [O], *Titanic* (Jim Farrell) [O], *The Who's Tommy*

In my first apartment, I slept on an old gray vinyl sofa. It was all I could afford. I even shared it with other people. There was no air conditioning.

During the summer I would stick to the vinyl. It was horrible. Once, I was asleep and I felt a scurrying across my face. It woke me up and I screamed like a girl. It was a cockroach. That was the glamour of just getting my $100,000 degree in acting.

Jeff Gurner. *The Lion King* (Ed the Hyena)

I lived with four other guys in a two-bedroom apartment on 47th Street. Sometimes I'd go home at night and find big old rats—the kind of rats that would come up and start hassling you for change.

One night, when I was sitting in my room reading a book, I saw one of my roommates go chasing after something that was scurrying down the hallway. I thought it was a rat. When he cornered it, it turned out to be an enormous cockroach. I thought, "Oh, my God, this is Spartan living."

The back of our apartment faced the piano bar, Don't Tell Mama's. Down on Restaurant Row, it can get kind of stinky from all the restaurant garbage. In the summertime, we had to leave our windows open. Otherwise, we couldn't sleep. We were too poor to run the air conditioner.

Early in the morning, you could hear the boys over at Don't Tell Mama's going into their Judy Garland routines. They would sing songs from *La Cage Aux Folles* at full voice, never missing a note.

I remember lying there, listening to show tunes, saying, "Oh, dear God. Oh, stop. Oh, c'mon, Merman!" At the same time, it was pretty wonderful. Those boys love what they do. They love getting up in those piano bars and singing. Even though I couldn't sleep, I thought, "Yeah, it's New York."

Doug Storm. *Dance of the Vampires* [O], *The Scarlet Pimpernel* (Leggett), *Les Misérables* (Feuilly)

I found an apartment on West 47th Street. I came into the apartment and it was a mess—dirty and yucky. The first day I moved in I had no furniture, so I slept on the floor. I woke up and felt this thing in my ear. When I sat up, a roach fell out. I opened up the cupboards and there were roaches all over the cabinets. I had never seen a roach before. I didn't know what they were. There were no roaches in Rockford, Illinois. There were mosquitoes, but no roaches. I had to "bomb" the apartment. I put the aerosol cans in the apartment and left for about ten hours. When I came home, there were a thousand dead roaches all over the apartment. Welcome to New York City.

Marin Mazzie. *Kiss Me, Kate* (Lilli Vanessi) [O][t], *Ragtime* (Mother) [O][t], *Passion* (Clara) [O][t], *Man of La Mancha* (Aldonza), *Big River* (Mary Jane Wilkes), *Into the Woods* (Rapunzel)

Loving the Landlords

The blessing about my apartment in New York was that my landlord skipped town. There was no one to pay rent to, so I lived rent-free for about three years. It was a real blessing.

Anthony Rapp. *Rent* (Mark Cohen) [O], *You're a Good Man, Charlie Brown* (Charlie Brown) [O], *Precious Sons* (Freddy) [O], *Six Degrees of Separation* (Ben) [O], *The King and I** (Louis)

There was a little old lady with an eight-room apartment. Her name was Ruth. She was eighty years old, or more. She charged us forty-five bucks a week. We each had our own bedroom.

Some nights she would wake us up, screaming. She was just out of her mind. A skinny, little, old, osteoporosis-ridden Jewish woman. She would walk down the hall with her walker, practically naked. She would have a nightshirt on, but nothing underneath.

One night I woke up out of a dead sleep.

"Sean! Sean! Sean!"

I ran in. I thought she was dying or something. She was hanging off the end of her bed. She couldn't get her sock off.

"Sean! I can't get my sock off!" Butt naked, eighty years old.

I ran in, got the sock off, and went back to bed. For three or four months, we dealt with Ruth. It was forty-five bucks a week.

Sean McDermott. *Starlight Express* (Prince of Wales) [O], *Miss Saigon* (Chris u/s) [O], *Falsettos* (Whizzer), *Grease!* (Danny Zuko)

Dealing with the Devil

We went to a rental agency. In those days, all you had to do was say hello, look fairly decent, hand them a check, and you had an apartment. It was easy. Nevertheless, my friend Carol said, "Let them think this is my place." I am black, she is white, and we weren't sure if they would rent to me. This was 1974.

When we got into the apartment, it was small. All the furniture was painted red, which we didn't get. There was a lamp which was covered in tinfoil. All the books in the bookcases were also covered in tinfoil. We thought it was odd, but mind you, we are from St. Louis.

After a while, we would run into people in the elevator. People would ask, "Are you the new people in 7D?" We wondered, "How do these people know? Why so much interest?"

One day, a lady told us that her friend had just moved into the penthouse apartment. We asked her if she would take some of the extra furniture in our apartment and give it to her friend.

We told the doorman, "The guy who just moved into the penthouse is going to take some of our furniture."

The doorman said, "He's been living in the penthouse for years. What is she talking about?"

Several days later, we saw a guy taking our picture at a street fair. Later, we saw that same guy in the building. We asked the doorman, "Who's that guy?"

"That's the guy who lives in the penthouse."

Things were getting stranger.

Next, a friend came to visit from St. Louis. He said bluntly, "There is something really weird about this apartment."

"Oh, we just moved in. It doesn't scare us." Then Carol started to tell me that she felt like someone was watching her all the time.

And then one night, as we were sitting in the apartment, for some reason we paid special attention to a painting which was hanging on the wall next to a window. Carol said, "Go stand at the window. Now look in the room and tell me what you see." I described what I saw.

She then said, "Now come here and look at that painting. That painting is of this room!" The painting was of a man dressed in black, standing around the table in our apartment. On the table were a pair of scissors, two Bibles, and blood.

We started freaking out. She said, "Take it down!" We took it down. Where the painting had once hung was now black candle wax. A pentagram was carved into the wax on the wall. Having read *Rosemary's Baby* and *The Exorcist*, I immediately got it. All of a sudden, I understood why all the furniture was painted red.

We decided that we had to get out of there. We went to find the number of the lady who had rented us the apartment. We got the yellow pages and turned to the page where her rental agency would have been listed. The page was ripped out.

I went to the doorman and told him that there was something weird going on. I said that we had paid our month's rent and we were just going to leave.

He said, "I think it's best that you do leave."

We frantically started throwing our things into our suitcases. It was eleven thirty at night and we were out on the streets of New York. Thank God we had a friend to stay with. It was one of those experiences that you only have when you first come to New York.

Ken Page. *Cats* (Old Deuteronomy) [O], *Guys and Dolls* (Nicely-Nicely Johnson) [O], *Ain't Misbehavin'* [O], *The Wiz* (Lion), *Purlie**

Leaks, Freaks, and Gregory Hines

I found a really cool apartment in a brownstone on 85th Street between West End and Riverside. It was a beautiful, high-ceiling, one-bedroom apartment, which had a beautiful terrace covered with Astroturf. It was great for parties.

One January morning, as I was getting up early to do my aerobics tape, someone knocked on my door. I opened the door in my sweats, and it was John Lithgow.

He said, "Hello, let me introduce myself."

Before he could say anything, I said, "You're John Lithgow!"

He said, "Yes, I am!" And we stood there and just stared at each other. I asked, "Can I help you?"

And he said, "Well, actually you can. We have a little problem. Your terrace is dripping into my kitchen. Do you mind if we go take a look?"

On my terrace, there was a huge ice block that was melting. Gallons and gallons of water were spewing down into his kitchen. We needed to find some way to contain the flood.

He asked, "Do you have a bucket by any chance?"

I said, "No, but we could use a wastebasket."

"Oh, that's lovely. That's a great idea. I'll be right back."

He went down and got a wastebasket. Then he came out on my balcony and we started having this Spencer Tracy/Katharine Hepburn moment. We were throwing banter back and forth, cracking each other up, and just having a wonderful time.

Ten minutes into it, there was a loud rapping on his window downstairs. I looked over and saw the very angry eyes of John's wife.

He said, "I have to go now, but it's been lovely meeting you."

Pamela Winslow. *Into the Woods* (Rapunzel) [O], *Beauty and the Beast* (Babette)

I had a crazy neighbor who lived downstairs. We called him "The Bald-Headed Fuck." He was the quintessential hellish neighbor.

We were pretty quiet. We didn't have parties, and we didn't have screaming fights or anything. Yet if we dropped the remote or something, you'd hear him pounding up the stairs. Slam. Boom. Boom. Boom.

We would open up the door and he'd hit us with a stream of obscenities.

"You people are white trash. We didn't have cockroaches until you moved in. Who the fuck are you?"

I'd say, "Hey, I dropped the remote, relax."

Alice Ripley. *Side Show* (Violet Hilton) [O][t], *The Rocky Horror Show* (Janet Weiss) [O], *Sunset Boulevard* (Betty Schaefer) [O], *King David* (Bathsheba) [O], *James Joyce's The Dead* (Mrs. Molly Ivors) [O], *The Who's Tommy* [O], *Les Misérables* (Fantine), *Little Shop of Horrors** (Audrey)

I was hanging out with some kids from HB Studio and we got free tickets to *Les Misérables*. After the show, we went next door to Sam's for coffee and drinks. Suddenly, Gregory Hines walked by. He was doing *Jelly's Last Jam* at the time. One of the girls said, "That was Gregory Hines! My friend Cee-Cee Harshaw is in *Jelly's Last Jam* with him. I'm going to say something when he passes by."

When Gregory Hines passed by the table again, she said, "Hello, Mr. Hines. I'm friends with Cee-Cee."

He said, "Oh, really?"

She said, "We are all actors and students down at HB Studio."

He said, "Oh, really?"

He pulled up a chair and sat down. He then started talking and asking questions of everybody. I was fresh to New York City, so I was still trying to be very quiet and polite. Everybody was talking to Gregory Hines about *Jelly's Last Jam* and about theater and art.

Gregory Hines ordered a round of drinks. I was sitting right next to him. Suddenly, there was a lull in the conversation. I thought, "I cannot sit here with Gregory Hines and not say anything. He is the first celebrity I've ever seen in New York. I've got to say something."

So, in the lull in the conversation, I said, "Well, you know, I haven't seen *Jelly's Last Jam,* but I really liked you in that movie *White Nights!*" And at that point, a big "L" materialized above my head for capital Loser. I just shrank back into my chair.

Doug Storm. *Dance of the Vampires* [O], *The Scarlet Pimpernel* (Leggett), *Les Misérables* (Feuilly)

CHAPTER 6

Survival Jobs

Many actors arrive in New York City with as little as a few thousand dollars in their pocket. Within weeks, the money is gone, and it is time to find a "survival job." Many actors work as waiters before getting their lucky break. But finding a job as a waiter can be difficult, and sometimes undesirable.

As a result, actors are often willing to do just about anything to support their dreams of living in New York City, from scrubbing toilets to spraying perfume to posing as a human ice sculpture. Once they are cast in their first Broadway show, they will never have to work such jobs again—or so they believe.

The Toilet Scrubber

I had a gig one night at a club called Flamingo East. It was one of my favorite places to perform. Before the gig, however, I was in a bathroom scrubbing a woman's toilet. It was my job.

I thought, "This sucks. I feel like Cinderella, only it's not that cute! Am I going to do this my whole life?"

I had this incredible moment of self-pity.

Then I had an epiphany. "If you really want to be good at being a performer, then you had better scrub this toilet really good." That was what the voice said. "If you want to be good at anything, scrub this toilet and make it clean. Clean this toilet with as much tenacity as you would turn out a song."

It was so real for me. The voice said, "Do everything with incredible love and with incredible caring." It was about being in the present.

Daphne Rubin-Vega. *Rent* (Mimi) [O][t], *The Rocky Horror Show* (Magenta) [O], *Anna in the Tropics* (Conchita) [O]

The Fitness Instructor

I taught aerobics in an Upper East Side studio. It was a joke. I would just try to make the ladies laugh. I would teach them the Ivana Trump step—the "Take the Money and Run!" However, teaching aerobics was not the wisest thing, especially when I had to yell over the music before an audition. But, I was getting paid to stay in shape.

I also sprayed people with cologne at Bloomingdale's. It was hateful. Nobody wants to be sprayed. They just don't. I had to ask people if I could spray them—as if I didn't get enough rejection in the theater.

I got kooky with that job. When I had the Perry Ellis spray, I would say, "Try Perry Ellis. The man is gone, but his fragrance lingers." It was uncalled-for and tacky.

I would come home reeking. Reeking. Like a cheap prostitute. Awful. It turned me off from cologne. I had my fill.

Bryan Batt. *Seussical* (The Cat in the Hat s/b) [O], *Saturday Night Fever* (Monty) [O], *Sunset Boulevard* (Joe Gillis u/s) [O], *Cats* (Munkustrap), *Beauty and the Beast* (Lumiere), *Starlight Express* (Rocky One), *The Scarlet Pimpernel* (Percy s/b), *Joseph and the Amazing Technicolor® Dreamcoat* (Reuben)

Welcome to Macy's

When I came to New York, I moved in with a friend who lived on 15th Street. I was subletting his couch. It was a tiny one-bedroom apartment and it was hot. I came from Cincinnati with two suitcases and maybe two thousand bucks. I thought that within a month I would be a Broadway star.

In a month, I had no money and not a lot of clothes. I had to get a real job. I went to a temp agency. They offered me a job at Macy's as a fragrance model.

They asked, "Do you have a nice pair of black pants, a nice white shirt, and some nice black shoes?"

I said, "Yeah, I do." But I didn't have any of that.

The only black pants I had were a pair of genie pants that ballooned out and snapped around the ankles. I didn't own a pair of black shoes. My friend had a pair of red tap shoes—with witch heels. We spray-painted them black and took off the taps. However, I kept getting red scuffmarks on them.

Also, the only nice white shirt I owned was made of silk and was as thin as Kleenex. You could see right through it.

All dressed up, I showed up at Macy's and said, "Hi, I'm here, and I am ready to fragrance model."

They looked at me, absolutely horrified. They gave me an apron, so all anyone could really see were my black genie pants that snapped around the ankles and the huge high-heeled and scuffed black-red shoes.

I would say "Ah, fra-fragrance, fragrance." I was supposed to be gregarious. I was supposed to say, "Hey, try some Hermès!" I, however, would lean against the counter and say, "Uh, does anyone want to try some Hermès?"

They fired me that day. It was humiliating.

Robert DuSold. *Les Misérables* (Javert), *Jekyll & Hyde* (Archbishop of Basingstoke), *Kiss of the Spider Woman* (Marcos), *Cats** (Deuteronomy), *The Phantom of the Opera** (André), *Chicago** (Little Mary Sunshine s/b), *Showboat** (Pete)

The Ice Sculpture

I did entertainment catering with a group called Shazam! Mostly, we worked bar and bat mitzvahs. I would put on costumes and do a couple minutes of choreography. I would then dance with the guests.

The people who ran the company watched us like hawks. If I wasn't jumping around on a table, or if I didn't have little Jewish girls dancing around me, they would tap me on the shoulder.

We used to do this thing called "table setting." Once the banquet was set up, we would have to sit on a table in a crazy outfit. When we did Amadeus, we all looked like Mozart. When we did Tiger World, we were all tigers. When we did Ice World, we were all dressed in this silver shit. We would sit on the table and pose for forty-five minutes. It was painful. I would cry. People would come and poke me. It was bad.

Ray Walker. *Jesus Christ Superstar* (Annas) [O], *Grease!* (Doody), *Les Misérables* (Marius), *Whistle Down the Wind** (Preacher), *Music of the Night** (Principal Soloist), *Joseph and the Amazing Technicolor® Dreamcoat** (Joseph u/s), *Falsettos** (Whizzer)

The Telemarketer

I had a job telemarketing. I sold *The American Lawyer* magazine to first-year lawyers. We had this great campaign where we'd call first-year associates and say, "I know you've read *The American Lawyer* magazine, and we are going to give it to you for a great price." The idea was to get them into the magazine and then raise the price. All things considered, not a bad deal. And, if you are halfway good at telemarketing, you say, "Forget the script. I'll just talk and sell the thing."

Once, I called a guy from San Francisco. As far as his speech pattern was concerned, he was as gay as a Mexican tablecloth. It was a commission-based job, so I put on my best gay voice. We ended up chatting. I flirted with him and told him that I was an actor in New York. I made the sale. I thought I had sunk so low. That was, until the next call.

A woman picked up the phone. I gave her the pitch.

She said, "I'm a single mother and I didn't go to law school until my thirties. I just finished and I'm trying to raise one kid by myself. I have tons of loans to pay." She was going on and on.

In telemarketing mode, I said, "I understand, but you can't afford to turn this down." I went on and on until I almost had the woman's credit card number.

Finally, I said, "You know what, you don't need this. You've given me about a thousand reasons why you shouldn't order the magazine. If you don't want it, I am not going to try to sell it to you." I hung up the phone, went into my boss's office, and quit.

Jeff Gurner. *The Lion King* (Ed the Hyena)

The Waiters

I waited tables. It was bad because I became a professional waiter instead of pursuing my craft. I got a job at Lindy's—next to Radio City Music Hall. I would work in the mornings from 7:00 A.M. until 5:00 P.M. Then, from 5:00 P.M. to midnight I worked at a Mexican restaurant in Times Square. I had no time to audition. I had no time for anything else. I had to pay the rent. In an effort to cut costs, we ended up putting four people in a one-bedroom apartment.

Dave Clemmons. *The Scarlet Pimpernel* (Ben) [O], *The Civil War* (Sergeant Virgil Frank/Auctioneer's Assistant) [O], *Les Misérables* (Jean Valjean), *Whistle Down the Wind**, *Jekyll & Hyde** (Bishop)

A friend of mine worked at a Mexican restaurant. I went in for the job.

They asked, "Do you have any experience?"

"Yeah, I have tons of experience." I had never waited tables or bartended.

Within a week, I was bartending, hosting, and waiting tables. At eleven o'clock brunch, everyone got a free margarita. The margaritas were strong, and people would get sick all the time.

"The lady at table twelve is going to barf," the manager would say. "Could you get a tin and put it underneath her?"

I said, "No. I can't."

One day, someone puked over the balcony into another person's food. I thought I was in Babylon. I couldn't believe it. There would be people passed out on the way to the bathroom. It freaked me out.

The other people I worked with were all struggling actors. I didn't tell anyone when I got cast in *Les Misérables*. I just said, "I'm leaving."

Robert DuSold. *Les Misérables* (Javert), *Jekyll & Hyde* (Archbishop of Basingstoke), *Kiss of the Spider Woman* (Marcos), *Cats** (Deuteronomy), *The Phantom of the Opera** (André), *Chicago** (Little Mary Sunshine s/b), *Showboat** (Pete)

I worked at The Polo Grounds, a sports bar on 83rd Street and Third Avenue. My advice: "If you don't like sports, don't work at a sports bar."

I had done a commercial for Prudential Life Insurance. They used to play it, without fail, during halftime of every college football game. The bar had over ten television screens. Whenever it was halftime, everyone would yell, "Be quiet. Be quiet." The commercial would come on, and everyone would yell, "It's the waitress!"

Kelli Rabke. *Joseph and the Amazing Technicolor® Dreamcoat* (Narrator) [O], *Les Misérables* (Eponine)

I worked as a waiter in an Italian restaurant on 72nd Street. This old lady would come in several times a week, and she would always order a bowl of minestrone soup.

One day, about ten minutes after she placed her order, she yelled, "Waiter!" When I came over, she picked out a piece of broken glass from her bowl of soup.

I said, "I'm so sorry."

"That's all right," she said, and I brought her another bowl. No charge.

Two days later, once again, she yelled, "Waiter!" When I came over, she pulled a piece of hair from her bowl of soup.

"I'm so sorry."

"That's all right," she said, and I brought her another bowl. Once again, no charge.

That week, she came in on Monday, Wednesday, and Friday. On Friday, I started keeping an eye on her. Sure enough, when she thought I was not looking, she put something new in her food.

When I told the manager, he said, "Just give her the soup." It was the neighborhood.

Terrence Mann. *Les Misérables* (Javert) [O] [t], *Beauty and the Beast* (Beast) [O][t], *Cats* (Rum Tum Tugger) [O], *The Scarlet Pimpernel* (Chauvelin) [O], *Barnum* (Chester Lyman) [O], *Rags* (Saul) [O], *Getting Away with Murder* (Gregory Reed) [O], *Jerome Robbins' Broadway* (Emcee), *The Rocky Horror Show* (Dr. Frank N. Furter)

Pebbles, Winnie, and The Count

I played Pebbles Flintstone in a children's theater show. Once in a while, I also played Smurfette. It was one of the best survival jobs you could have because I only had to work on the weekends. I would do twenty-minute children's shows at malls across the United States. I would fly out on a Friday and be back in New York by Sunday night.

I would dress up as Pebbles Flintstone, with a bone in my hair. I performed alongside three dancers who were inside huge animal costumes with mesh eye peepholes—the kind you see at theme parks. They would be dressed as Fred, Barney, and Dino. I would teach them the show on Friday night, and then on Saturday we would do three or four shows. I had a microphone, and the Barney and Fred voices were on tape.

One afternoon, during a Smurf show, one of the dancers fainted inside his costume. He got sick, and just fell off the stage. When he fell, the huge head of the costume suddenly popped off. It looked like he had been decapitated. The kids all screamed and started to cry.

Ana Maria Andricain. *Marie Christine* (Dakota/Emma Parker) [O], *Les Misérables* (Fantine u/s), *Beauty and the Beast* (Belle), *By Jeeves* (Stiffy Byng), *Evita** (Eva Alternate), *Annie Get Your Gun** (Annie u/s)

I used to dress up as various characters and go to homes for birthday parties. One of the characters was Winnie the Pooh. I would put on a big yellow bear suit which was constructed out of large hula hoops. The costume also consisted of enormous gloves and a huge hat with a bowl of honey attached. I would play games with the kids, do magic tricks, and make animal balloons.

One afternoon, five minutes into the party, I realized that there was something wrong with my costume. One of the hula hoops broke, revealing a large pin, which started poking my ass. The party had just started, and there was no way for me to fix the costume. It was very painful, and I grew rather irritated. Even worse, the family had paid for a happy Winnie the Pooh, and I gave them Winnie the Pooh on a bad day with a bad attitude. I was short with the kids. The parents called my boss and complained.

Kevin Loreque. *Cats** (Rum Tum Tugger), *Hot Shoe Shuffle**

I was introduced to an agent who booked actors for toy presentations. That year, there was a new board game for Halloween at the toy store FAO Schwartz. It was about Transylvania. She said, "Why don't you do that?" And I did.

I dressed up in a wild Dracula costume, applied my own make-up, and spent three hours yelling "Whoa ho ho ho" and stuff like that. I kid you not. I would stand in the window and scare the piss out of little kids.

Geoffrey Blaisdell. *Jekyll & Hyde* (Lord Glossop) [O], *Cyrano—The Musical* (Captain De Castel Jaloux) [O], *Amadeus* (Servant) [O], *Les Misérables** (Javert), *The Phantom of the Opera** (The Auctioneer)

CHAPTER 7

Singing for Supper

Dressing up as Pebbles, Winnie, or The Count is not the only way for an actor to both make money and perform before "making it" on Broadway. Piano bars, bar mitzvahs, cruise ships, non-Equity productions, and Las Vegas all provide opportunities for actors to both express themselves and pay the rent.

However, there are costs involved. Once an actor leaves New York, dreams of Broadway can quickly become buried in cheap hotel rooms and long hours. The work can be demeaning, and the experiences can be horrific. Self-esteem and self-respect are often the first things to go.

Bar Hopping

The first night my sister was in New York, I said, "Let's go out and celebrate this dream we have." We walked around the corner and sat down at a little piano bar. Somebody asked for the song "Sometimes When We Touch." The pianist didn't know it.

I said, "I know it."

He said, "Well, I can't play it."

I said, "I can play it."

He said, "Fine."

I sat down at the piano and played. Not only did I get a standing ovation, but I was offered my first singing job. It was only three days after I moved to New York City. When I would play, often people would ask, "Why aren't you a star?"

I would say, "Oh, in a few years I will hone my craft. I'll audition and I'll probably be a star on Broadway."

If someone would have said, "Oh no, it will take you twenty years," I would have said, "You are out of your mind!"

Ann Hampton Callaway. *Swing!* [O][t]

Hava Nagila

I sang at weddings and bar and bat mitzvahs on the weekends. I was your typical wedding singer in a black sequined dress.

Once, a guy died on the floor during the cha-cha. The bandleader said, "Keep playing, keep playing." While the paramedics were on the floor trying to revive this guy, the bride came over and told us to stop playing. The guy was her uncle.

I always had this "holier-than-thou" attitude. I really believed I was going to do something better. I had to keep telling myself that. Doing weddings was a creative void. I never wanted to follow all the rules and do all the choreography. If I gave in, I would lose myself forever. I always thought, "I'm gonna get out of here."

During one bar mitzvah, they kept turning my microphone down. The bandleader's girlfriend was the other singer. Although she couldn't sing very well, he always had her microphone pumped up and mine turned down. I had to sing all the high C&C Music Factory stuff. I had just lost my voice and was returning back from a week of laryngitis. I kept asking him to pump up the volume on my microphone. He wouldn't.

Finally, he said, "Get back over here and just dance."

He threw his microphone down at his feet. It hit my foot.

I said, "I'm out of here. I'm not singing another word."

As I walked across the dance floor, the people saw that their singer was leaving. I got my big coat, bundled myself up, and dragged my microphone stand and wire through the crowd. I made a scene so the bandleader would get in trouble.

When I got in my car, I started to cry. I started to shake. I wasn't going to be treated like crap.

Idina Menzel. *Rent* (Maureen Johnson) [O][**t**], *Wicked* (Elphaba) [O], *Aida* (Amneris)

All Aboard

When I was doing a show on a cruise ship, we had to wear silver jumpsuits. Mine was a little small. The costume designer really liked me. His name was Oscar. He thought I was so very cute, so he made mine kinda tight.

So, with the midnight buffets, I was giving you full camel toe. It was one of the worst experiences of my life. There I was, with a sequined top hat, singing, "Hats off, here they come, those beautiful girls"—camel toe—"That's what you've been waiting for."

It was horrible. At one point in the show, I came out on stage in a ruffled-sleeve thing. It was an olive-green polka-dot crop top. It was tight in the middle. I looked like Chiquita Banana's gay nephew. I came out singing, "Feel the beat of the rhythm of the night, dance until the morning light." Simply horrific.

> **Davis Kirby.** *The Boys from Syracuse* (Soldier) [O], *Thou Shalt Not* (Sugar Hips) [O], *Thoroughly Modern Millie, Cats** (Swing)

When I was a senior in college, I got an offer to work on a cruise ship during Christmas break. It was a one-month contract and it would help me get my Equity card. For any college senior, it was a dream come true. At first, it seemed so easy. Only three shows in ten days.

One night, there was a horrible storm. Twenty-foot swells. Almost everyone on the ship was in his or her room—puking. However, some people couldn't even get to their cabin because they were so ill. People started to puke in the hallways. It was everywhere.

I was feeling sick too, but I had to perform. There were no understudies. I left my cabin an hour before the show in order to have enough time to get to the theater. Usually, the trip would only take a few minutes. Not that night. I remember walking from the Lido Deck to the theater and seeing old people holding onto the railings. Another girl in the show was stuck in a tiny hallway with a seventy-year-old woman who was sick and making a rather large mess on the walls and carpet. The girl was trapped. She had no choice but to get a running start and try to jump over the old woman. When we finally arrived at the theater, we couldn't believe that we had to perform.

> **Jodie Langel.** *Les Misérables* (Cosette/Eponine), *Martin Guerre** (Bertrande Alternate), *Cats** (Grizabella), *Joseph and the Amazing Technicolor® Dreamcoat** (Narrator)

On Guard

I moved to New York in 1991. I didn't really know anybody. I was subletting an apartment that was smaller than a dressing room. For a job, I carried a spear in *Richard III* in Central Park.

I never felt bad about it. I got to watch great people perform. You've got to carry the spear every once in a while.

> **Tom Hewitt.** *The Rocky Horror Show* (Dr. Frank N. Furter) [O][t], *The Boys from Syracuse* (Antipholus of Ephesus) [O], *Art* (Serge u/s) [O], *The Lion King* (Scar), *School for Scandal* (Charles Surface), *Sisters Rosensweig* (Geoffrey), *Urinetown** (Officer Lockstock)

Before I made it to Broadway, I was cast in a production of *South Pacific.* I played Lieutenant Cable. I was so nervous for the first show that I couldn't even make a face because my eyebrows were shaking so hard.

In the fourth performance, they made a decision to show Lieutenant

Cable getting killed on stage. They gave me a T-shirt which contained a packet of fake blood. During the death scene, my new direction was to turn around, get shot, and let the blood spread around my chest. But the producer, about ten minutes before I was to go on, said, "We forgot to tell you this. We can't see enough blood through your T-shirt. Take the blood pack out from your shirt and smack it on your face during the death scene."

Well, during the death scene, once again I got that nervous tension. This time, however, I had the blood pack in my right hand. I didn't even have my hand on the trigger of the gun. Well, all of the sudden, gunshots go off, and I scream. Wham. I whack this thing the size of my fist onto my head.

From behind, it looked as if my head was blown off. The whole audience screamed. Even worse, the blood was made from colored shampoo. And it was not Johnson & Johnson. My eyes quickly started to sting. The stuff was in my mouth, and it got all over the audience.

When I screamed, my gun accidentally fell into the audience, and the lights went out. Everything was completely black. I had to exit up the aisle, but because I was now blind, I bumped into people in the audience, covering them in blood.

When the lights went out, the actor who played Emile de Beque saw my gun go into the aisle. During the blackout, he reached into the audience and grabbed the strap of the gun. He was also covered in my blood. To his eventual horror, he mistook a lady's white leather purse for the gun, covering the purse in blood. When the lights came up, she grabbed for her purse. We had a great time with that one.

Steven Buntrock. *Jane Eyre* (Mr. Eshton) [O], *Oklahoma!* (Joe/Curley) [O], *Titanic* (Frederick Barrett), *Les Misérables* (Enjolras), *Martin Guerre** (Arnaud), *Joseph and the Amazing Technicolor® Dreamcoat** (Reuben)

I was cast in a non-Equity performance of *Gypsy*. I played Louise. I was the lead in the show. It was so exciting. There was a part in the show where Mamma Rose gave Louise a lamb as a gift for her birthday, and Louise sang the song, "Little Lamb." However, since it was a non-Equity show, they couldn't afford a real lamb. It was also not the season for lamb. The show was in the fall. Apparently, in the fall, there are no lambs. So they got a sheep instead. They put a huge diaper on it, with a pink bow on the butt.

In the Broadway production, the animal was supposed to be a little lamb that Louise would coddle in her arms. My sheep was up to my waist. It was a monster of an animal, a petting-zoo thing, with a big cloth diaper that sagged.

When I would sing "Little Lamb" to this thing, it would start *baa*-ing directly into my microphone.

"Little lamb, little lamb."

"*Baa.*"

It would always *baa* right there.

The audience would be hysterical. And then the thing would shit onstage, and little turds would fall out of the diaper. It was a mess. This sweet, tender ballad became the comic relief of the show.

Rena Strober. *Les Misérables* (Cosette u/s)

Carrots and Hamburgers

I was fortunate enough to play the role of Peter in *Peter Rabbit*, a Theater Works USA production.

We traveled in one small van with six people—three in the front and three in the back. We had to sit next to each other for long distances, like from Chicago to New York. Every time we stopped short, the set would hit the back of my head. It was ridiculous.

We would get up at seven in the morning, get in the van, and drive to a school or performing arts center. We had to help unload the van, sometimes in the pouring rain. After the show, we would dismantle the set, put it back in the van, and drive off.

We would drive by a Holiday Inn and cry because we couldn't afford to stay there. That's how pathetic it was. It was a real treat to stay in a classy place such as a Super 8. We would stay at a classy place about once a month. And, because I don't eat fast food, life was difficult. Finally, I put my foot down and said, "I am not eating at another restaurant with the word 'family,' 'grandmother,' 'home-style,' or 'buffet' in the title." That didn't leave me with too many options.

My big eleven o'clock number in the show was a song called "Endless Salad." It was about how Peter Rabbit loved vegetables. I would go through a list of all the vegetables I liked to eat. I would sing the song to a prerecorded click track. One night, the click track didn't start. Three thousand kids started rustling in their seats. We all started laughing on stage. We couldn't even begin to pretend that we cared or that anyone was paying attention. Suddenly, a girl dressed in bunny ears and a big fluffy skirt with carrots on it screamed, at the top of her lungs: "I can't take it anymore." She was replaced.

Lee Zarrett. *Jane Eyre* (Young John Reed) [O]

Before making it to Broadway, I did children's theater. In the show, I played the dancing Fiber Girl. I was a dancing piece of shit —with a hard hat. I taught children about why they needed fiber in their diet. While break dancing, I had to sing a song about how you need to eat fiber because it helps your body "move."

In the same show, I also played "Okra Winfrey." Okra's role in the show was to interview Carrot and Broccoli about why they are good for you.

Marissa Jaret Winokur. *Hairspray* (Tracy Turnblad) [O][**T**], *Grease!* (Jan)

I went to Las Vegas and opened a show. I was miserable. I was dancing full-time in two shows. It was hot and, because I had just come from college, I was a little chunky. I was in a fraternity—chunky-chunky two-by-four. So when I went out to Las Vegas, I just stopped eating. It was so hot that we couldn't even really tap because the stops on our shoes would melt on the cement. Ridiculous.

My day consisted of waking up at 8:00 A.M., getting to my show at 9:00 A.M., and doing the opening ceremony by 9:30 A.M. I would do shows until 5:00 P.M.

Then, I would get in my car and drive three big blocks to the Flamingo Hilton. I would go into the girls' dressing room and fall asleep under the dresses. When they came in, I knew it was time for me to wake up.

After waking up, I would get myself a McDonald's dinner. I inhaled it.

Then I would go back upstairs and get in the shower for thirty minutes. I showered by candlelight because I hated the sight of my body. And I would make myself throw up all the food. I had eaten it so quickly that huge chunks would come out. I would literally pound pieces of cheeseburger down the drain. I can't make this shit up!

And the worst thing is, everybody thought I was in there jerking off. So I got no sympathy. Did I say my name was Davis Kirby? I meant Kavis Dirby.

Davis Kirby. *The Boys from Syracuse* (Soldier) [O], *Thou Shalt Not* (Sugar Hips) [O], *Thoroughly Modern Millie*, *Cats** (Swing)

Life before the Union

Before I got my Equity card, I was doing summer stock at Wagon Wheel Playhouse. I was in a production of *Pippin* with Faith Prince. She played the grandma and I was Catherine. We made very little money. It was hard-core summer stock. We would do *Pippin* during the day and *Camelot* at night—back-to-back. I also did chorus in another show.

We were all assigned a "strike duty" after every show. Cleaning out men's urinals was one of my duties. I don't like to think about the details.

Barbara Walsh. *Falsettos* (Trina) [O][t], *Blood Brothers* (Mrs. Lyons) [O], *Big* (Mrs. Baskin) [O], *Rock 'N Roll! The First 5,000 Years* [O], *Hairspray* (Velma Von Tussle), *Ragtime** (Mother), *Les Misérables** (Fantine/Cosette u/s), *Chess** (Svetlana), *Oklahoma!**, *Nine**

I was cast in a non-Equity tour of *Tommy*. I played Tommy. We would get up at 6:00 A.M., get on a bus, and would literally lie on top of each other. Regularly, we would rotate positions with our "bus partner." Sometimes you got the floor, and sometimes you got the seat. The floor was great because it was warm, but it was usually wet. The seat was great because it was dry, but it was usually cold. It was pretty horrific. We would fall on each other when the bus stopped short.

I would try to sleep on the bus until lunchtime. They would wake us up for lunch, and then we would get back on the bus and arrive at a new city by 3:00 P.M. I would put my bags in my room, get dressed, go to a television station, do an interview, and go straight to the theater.

After the sound check I would have thirty minutes to get something to eat, get into costume, and do the show. I would get home at 11:00 P.M., be in bed by 1:00 A.M., wake up at 6:00 A.M., get on the bus, drive to a new city, and start the whole thing all over again.

Davis Kirby. *The Boys from Syracuse* (Soldier) [O], *Thou Shalt Not* (Sugar Hips) [O], *Thoroughly Modern Millie*, *Cats** (Swing)

PART THREE

TRANSITION TO STARDOM

CHAPTER 8

The Audition Room

In the previous two chapters, actors have told stories of jobs they needed to take before making it to Broadway. Their experiences have been diverse. However, there is one job that all actors who dream of starring on Broadway must do. It is possibly the most difficult and demeaning job of them all. It is the job of auditioning.

Even with an agent, simply getting into a Broadway audition can be difficult. And, for those without representation and who are not members of the actors' union, waiting on long lines at open calls is often their only chance to be seen. Once in the audition room, actors usually have only a few seconds to show their stuff. Anything can happen once an audition has begun, and some actors audition for many years before being invited onto a Broadway stage. Most never are. With hundreds of people auditioning for each role, it is important to find a way to be remembered. Sometimes, being remembered is simply not enough.

However, dreams of Broadway can come true, and often do in a spectacular fashion. While some believe in destiny, others are willing to pull out all stops in order to get cast—including crossing oceans. Sometimes persistence and perhaps a little consistency can make the difference between waiting tables and signing autographs.

The feeling of getting cast in a Broadway show is like none other. It is a rebirth of sorts. Life starts to make sense again as all the years of struggle and hard work finally begin to pay off. Soon, the actor will be standing on a Broadway stage with the best of the best, pursuing his or her childhood love of theater.

The Life

I honestly wonder what I would have done if someone had told me that my real job as an actor will be looking for work—bringing together all of my skills for a few seconds when I am in that room. Looking for work, time after time after time, professionally.

If somebody had said that, as an actor, most of my life would be comprised of looking for work, maybe I wouldn't have been able to appreciate or even understand what they meant. But that's what it is.

Steve Pudenz. *Hello, Dolly!* (Rudolph) [O], *Joseph and the Amazing Technicolor®*
*Dreamcoat** (Jacob), *The Sound of Music**

The Open Call

Here's how it can work when you start auditioning for Broadway. You buy a *Back Stage* magazine like everybody else, go through it, and go to an open call. There are hundreds of people in dance clothes, stretching, legs up on the wall. You wait a long time and finally get a number, like number 456. Then, much later that day, the next day, or the next week, you go back to the call. You wait the whole day, and possibly aren't even seen.

Sean McDermott. *Starlight Express* (Prince of Wales) [O], *Miss Saigon* (Chris u/s)
[O], *Falsettos* (Whizzer), *Grease!* (Danny Zuko)

I remember going to an open call for the role of Cosette in *Les Misérables.* I woke up at 4:30 A.M. in my tiny little house. My two friends and I stood outside in the rain—crazy cold rain—signed up, got our time, went home, and got our hair done.

At 2:30 in the afternoon, the second we stepped forward at the audition, we were immediately "typed out" because of the way we looked. We went to the Olive Garden and laughed about it. It never dampened my spirits.

Next, there was an audition for the road company of *Jesus Christ Superstar*—a real crazy boobs-and-g-string production. Jesus was in leather. I didn't know that.

I showed up looking like Pollyanna in a blue jumper. The audition song was "I Don't Know How to Love Him." Every other girl was in a crazy bustier, wicked make-up, and stiletto heals. I was in loafers.

One after another, each girl went in.

"*I don't know how to . . .*"

"Thank you."

"*I don't know how to . . .*"

"Thank you."

I was the last one to go down that day. I knew I was wrong, but I had to be heard.

Erin Dilly. *Follies* (Young Phyllis) [O], *The Boys from Syracuse* (Luciana) [O], *Into*
the Woods (Cinderella), *Martin Guerre** (Bertrande), *Beauty and the Beast** (Belle),
*South Pacific** (Nellie)

I had nineteen auditions for *Jerome Robbins' Broadway.* I didn't get a callback after the first audition, so I went to the next open call and got a callback. They seemed to want me for a part. But on the fourth callback, I didn't get in.

I went back to the next open call, and got right back down to the final cut. This happened three or four times.

Finally, on the nineteenth open call, I showed up thinking, "I want this show."

They said, "Cory, go home. Just go home. We know you. You don't have to be here. When there is a spot open, we will call you."

"Are you sure?"

"Yes, Cory."

So I left and I didn't audition that nineteenth time—but I was all warmed up and ready to go. I wore the exact same shirt to every audition so that they would remember me.

Cory English. *A Funny Thing Happened on the Way to the Forum* (Protean) [O], *Guys & Dolls* (Brandy Bottle Bates) [O], *Hello, Dolly!* (Barnaby Tucker) [O], *Damn Yankees* (Bubba) [O], *Gypsy* (St. Paul)

I arrived in New York City on April 1, 1991—April Fools' Day. I had a *Back Stage* magazine and I stayed with my cousin on his couch. The first day I arrived, I went to Musical Theater Works and auditioned for an open call for *Jesus Christ Superstar*. There was a long line outside the door, and I thought it couldn't be for the auditions. It was. Tons and tons of guys. Not knowing any better, I got in line and waited. I sang my song, and I got a callback.

When I moved out of my cousin's place, I didn't have a phone service. A week went by, and I thought I had a chance of getting the job.

I called back and said, "I am just checking to see if you have cast *Jesus Christ Superstar*."

"Who is this?"

"Brian d'Arcy James."

"We wanted to hire you. You got the job but we couldn't find you. There was no one at the number we called." It was a perfect way to start my time here in New York.

Brian d'Arcy James. *Sweet Smell of Success* (Sidney) [O][t], *Titanic* (Frederick Barrett) [O], *Carousel* (Captain) [O], *Blood Brothers*

Growing Pains

A friend of mine, Barry Moss, was a graduate student at UCLA. He had all kinds of chutzpa, and called up Shirley Rich, who worked for Hal Prince, and got me an audition for *Cabaret*. They thought that he was Barry Morse, who was a well-known actor at the time. Although he didn't lie, he didn't correct them. He just said, "I have this wonderful actor," and they made an appointment for me. They had never heard of me before.

When I flew to New York, Shirley Rich said, "Well, you know your audition is set, but you look mighty young. Your part is supposed to be a decadent fellow."

I said, "Yeah, but at that time in Germany, he could have been anybody. He could have been a horrible young boy who was weird, dirty, and sexually promiscuous."

She said, "Yeah, but there is a youngness about you." And I did look young. I was very skinny, with a long neck.

I asked, "Should I wear the make-up the character wears in the actual show?"

"That might be a good idea," she said.

I went to Max Factor and got white make-up. I put it all over my face. I basically copied what Joel Grey had on in the original production, even the little lips. I looked good. I worked on the songs, got a cane, and went to the theater.

At the audition, there were lots of guys singing with huge voices. I was terrified, but confident. I walked in, played my part, sang it well, and that was that. They called me back two days later. I didn't realize that they had cut two hundred people and I was in the last group. Once again, I did the callback audition in make-up.

After the audition, I flew back to Los Angeles. Two weeks later, I received a letter from Hal Prince. It said something like, "You were possibly the best person who auditioned for this role, and I have been going through a lot of decision-making. I want to give you this part. But you are just too young-looking for me to believe you in the part. Good luck, you're great, and I am sad that I don't get to have you."

Although I thought the letter was pretty neat, I was disappointed. I should have worn the costume. I should have worn a suit with black tails. In those days, people wore tighter pants than they do now. I looked like a skinny kid with make-up. But if I had worn a full costume with make-up, it would have been nearly impossible to guess my age. I would have gotten the damn part. That was my first Broadway audition.

John Rubinstein. *Children of a Lesser God* (James Leeds) [O] [**T**], *Pippin* (Pippin) [O], *Fools* (Leon) [O], *Getting Away with Murder* (Martin Chisholm) [O], *The Caine Mutiny Court-Martial* (Lt. Barney Greenwald) [O], *Ragtime* (Tateh), *Hurlyburly* (Eddie), *Love Letters* (Andrew), *M. Butterfly* (Rene)

I auditioned for *Grease!* on Broadway. I am a musician, so I arranged the song "Johnny B. Goode" to last for thirty-two bars. The piano player, who shall remain nameless, but who is a hideous monster, rolled his eyes when he saw the music. He huffed and puffed.

At the end of the arrangement, he stood up and announced, "You cut this song inappropriately. I don't know what you were thinking." He just lambasted me in front of all the audition people. The accompanist!

I shrank down to the size of a grain of rice. I crept out of the room, feeling miserable. If somebody did that to me now, I would have a fit. I would probably call the union. Back then, I was a child. I didn't understand my place.

I will never forgive him for doing that. Oftentimes, you put your entire well-being into the hands of a person who pushes a broom. They are not even the real casting people. It is just ridiculous.

Marsh Hanson. *Les Misérables* (Marius), *Joseph and the Amazing Technicolor®
Dreamcoat** (Brother)

Destiny Calling

The minute you walk into an audition, it's basically over. You are either "it" or you're "not it." I did a Broadway show that ran one night only. It was called *The Moony Shapiro Song Book.* My point in telling you this is that as soon as I walked into the audition, they wanted me. I could do no wrong.

"Do you play the guitar?"

I said, "No."

"He'll learn. Do you tap?"

"No."

"That's okay, it's easy." It made no difference. I had something they wanted. Early on, it was valuable to learn that it's just out of your hands.

Gary Beach. *The Producers* (Roger DeBris) [O][**T**], *Beauty and the Beast* (Lumiere)
[O][t], *The Moony Shapiro Songbook* [O], *Doonesbury* (Duke) [O], *Something's
Afoot* (Nigel) [O], *Sweet Adeline* (Dan Ward) [O], *Annie* (Rooster Hannigan), *1776*
(Edward Rutledge), *Les Misérables** (Thénardier), *Of Thee I Sing**

In 1986, I went to New York City and auditioned for *Starlight Express.* I had never been to New York, I had never done any professional theater, and I didn't know how to skate. There were probably a thousand men at the audition. During the first two rounds, all I had to do was sing. I made it through to the final round. On the last day of auditions, I had to audition before Trevor Nunn, Andrew Lloyd Webber, and all of the powers that be.

During the final round, not only were people skating well, but they were doing back flips and front flips.

The choreographer turned to me and said, "Okay, skate forward."

So I skated forward. That I could do. Barely.

Then she said, "Skate backwards." I kept skating forward.

"I'm sorry. You didn't hear me," she said, "Skate backwards."

A Chorus Line. Photo credit: Photofest

I sighed and said, "This *is* backwards! It's all I've got." I then started to skate from one side of the room to the other as fast as I could. I took out some chairs. I purposely tried to have an accident.

The director stopped me and said, "Do you have a problem?"

Two days later, I got the job.

Robert Torti. *Starlight Express* (Greaseball) [O][t], *Joseph and the Amazing Technicolor® Dreamcoat* (Pharaoh) [O]

I went to college for accounting. I didn't enjoy it at all. It was not what I wanted to do, so I started studying ballet—eight-hour classes, seven days a week. I was working constantly. I always felt like I was behind.

On a dare from a couple of guys, I went to an open call for *A Chorus Line.* Because I had no money, my friends bought me a ticket to see the show. I'd never seen anything like that. I thought, "How do people do that?" I was mesmerized.

I auditioned for the heck of it, and they kept calling me back. I had only sung a little in high school, and I didn't have a song prepared for the audition. I sang "Cool" from *West Side Story.* It's not even a song. It's like a rap.

Next, they needed an 8 × 10 headshot. I didn't have one, so I went to one of those guys in Times Square who takes Polaroid photos. That was my 8 × 10—a Polaroid of me in Times Square.

Amazingly, I got the part. Everything fit. I had a revelation. I knew Broadway was where I belonged. It was overwhelming.

Scott Wise. *Jerome Robbins' Broadway* [O][**T**], *Fosse* [O][**t**], *State Fair* (Pat Gilbert) [O][**t**], *Movin' Out* (Sergeant O'Leary) [O], *Goodbye Girl* (Billy) [O], *Damn Yankees* (Rocky) [O], *Carrie* (Scott) [O], *Guys and Dolls* (Guy) [O], *Song and Dance* (Man) [O], *A Chorus Line* (Mike), *Cats* (Plato/Macavity), *Victor Victoria* (Jazz Hot Ensemble)

Crossing the Atlantic

In the spring of 1982, I told my agents, "I'd love to get an audition for *Cats*."

My agent said, "They don't want to see you for the role."

I said, "Really? Well, call again. I'd love to get in."

He called me back about two hours later and said, "Terry, they don't want to see you. They want a Rex Smith or a John Travolta type. They want someone like that."

"Oh man, are you kidding me? I can't even get seen?"

This was my first lesson in the power of casting directors, and why some people have careers and others don't. My wife at the time, Juliet, was English, and we were going on vacation in London. I brought some résumés on the plane ride over.

I said to Juliet, "I wish I could get in for an audition in London."

She said, "Why don't I call up my friend Miriam? I think she has money in *Cats*. Let me call her up and see what we can do."

She called Miriam, who made a phone call to the producers, who made a phone call to the stage manager. They happened to be doing a put-in rehearsal at the New London Theater the Monday afternoon that I was in town.

I went over to the theater with my résumé in hand and knocked on the door.

The doorman opened up and asked, "What can I do for you?"

I said, "I'm here to see Gillian Lynne."

"Yeah, right." Slam.

Two minutes later, the stage manager came out and said, "Terry, let me see what mood she's in."

She came back and said, "They are on a lunch break. Go over, I will prep her, and take it from there."

As I walked into the New London Theater, I thought, "I just saw the show two nights ago. It's no problem. I can do the role. It's right up my alley." I walked over. Gillian was sitting there eating a tuna fish sandwich with her legs crossed. Everybody else was just hanging out on stage, eating lunch.

Gillian said, "Yes, darling? What can I do for you?"

"I'd like to audition for the show."

She replied, "Well, I'm afraid we are all cast here. These people have jobs."

"No. For the New York production."

She stuttered, "Ah, well, yes, um, why?"

"Well, I'm over here and I'd like to audition." I didn't want to say that the casting director in New York didn't want to see me. I was trying to be political.

She said, "Well, what do you want to do? Our piano player is off to lunch."

"That's okay," I said. "I can play for myself."

"Oh. Well, go ahead."

I sat down at the piano and started playing Elton John's "Take Me to the Pilot." I finish with a big rock-and-roll wail. After I finished playing, Gillian came over and said, "You know, you remind me of a very good friend of mine."

"Tim Curry?" I asked.

She exclaimed, "Yes! Tim Curry. Why didn't I see you at the auditions?"

"They didn't think I was right for the role."

"Ah yes, well, I will see you at the callbacks."

Sure enough, I got the role.

Terrence Mann. *Les Misérables* (Javert) [O][t], *Beauty and the Beast* (Beast) [O] [t], *Cats* (Rum Tum Tugger) [O], *The Scarlet Pimpernel* (Chauvelin) [O], *Barnum* (Chester Lyman) [O], *Rags* (Saul) [O], *Getting Away with Murder* (Gregory Reed) [O], *Jerome Robbins' Broadway* (Emcee), *The Rocky Horror Show* (Dr. Frank N. Furter)

Fashion Statement

I was doing *Night of a Hundred Stars* at Radio City Music Hall. We were at the Minskoff rehearsal studios. Often, when I would walk through the halls during break, there would be an old guy with gray hair, kneepads around his ankles, all in black, checking me out.

One day he said hello when I was on my way to the bathroom. I totally snubbed him. Another day, when I was feeling sick and lying on a couch, he walked by and gave me the big "up and down" with his eyes. I thought, "I can't believe this guy."

As he walked away, somebody said, "Oh, my God. With Fosse checking you out like that, you will be the next Reinking."

I thought, "That's Bob Fosse? The guy I have been snubbing the whole time?"

Later, I went to an audition for *Sweet Charity*. I wore the same leotard I had on the day I found out it was Bob Fosse. There were approximately three hundred and fifty girls at the Equity call and three hundred and fifty girls at the non-Equity call. Bob came right up to my face and said, "Same leotard. Smart."

Jane Lanier. *Jerome Robbins' Broadway* [O][t], *Anything Goes* (Virtue) [O], *Sweet Charity* (Frenchy) [O], *Fosse* [O]

Cinderella Stories

As we were nearing the end of the run for *The Wizard of Oz* at Paper Mill Playhouse, I got an audition for *Joseph and the Amazing Technicolor® Dreamcoat.* The only reason I got the audition was because I had a friend who worked for Johnson-Liff Casting, and she noticed there was a last-minute cancellation. She told Vinnie Liff, "You should really see my friend Kelli." She mentioned my name a couple of times, and I guess he finally gave in and said, "Whatever. Bring her in for this."

I had never seen the show. I had never heard the music. I knew nothing about it. The audition was on the actual stage of the Broadhurst Theater. I sang "Jacob and Sons" and "Pharaoh's Story." After I finished singing, I left the theater and went about my day.

I remember thinking that the audition went well, so that afternoon, I checked my answering machine. I didn't have any messages, so I went to my chiropractor as previously planned. I had an injury from carrying that damn dog around in *The Wizard of Oz.* When I got home at 6:00 P.M. there was a message on my answering machine from my friend at the casting agency.

"Get your ass back down to the Broadhurst immediately. Andrew Lloyd Webber is there and he wants to see you again." The message was now almost an hour old.

I called back frantically and said, "I am on my way! I am on my way!" Meanwhile, at the chiropractor, my face had been in a cradle. I was a mess. Even worse, I was on the Upper West Side and I had to get to midtown. There was traffic. I decided to take a cab, but I only had four dollars in my wallet. So I had to run to the bank machine and get money. I put on my make-up in the cab, ran into the Broadhurst, and was the picture of chaos. "I'm here! I'm here!"

They were all still sitting in the house having a little powwow. Someone came over and said, "Calm down. Andrew has gone back to his apartment in the Trump Tower. We are going to take you over there for your callback."

We piled into two cabs. The choreographer patted my knee and said, "Don't worry, darling. Just think of it as an adventure." We arrived at Trump Tower, stumbled out of the cabs, and went up to the sixtieth floor.

As I walked in, Andrew apologized for ruining my plans for the evening and rushing me about. I thought, "It's okay with me."

He brought me into the living room, which had floor-to-ceiling windows looking out over the city. I could probably see my house in New Jersey. It was unbelievable. He told everyone to go into another wing of the apartment, leaving only Paul Bogaev at the piano.

He said, "I want you to sing 'Pharaoh's Story' to me, but with your views of the recent presidential election." It was November 11, 1992, so the Pharaoh was Clinton, Bush, or Perot. As I was singing, he stood less than two feet from my face.

When I finished, he brought everybody back in the room. He asked me to sing the song one more time. Then he stood up and said, "Well, I guess I speak for everyone when I say we would very much like for you to be our Narrator."

I just stood there. He asked, "Would you like to sit down?"

"Yes, please."

"Would you like a glass of wine?"

"Yes, please."

"Would you like to make a phone call?"

"Yeah. That would be great."

Kelli Rabke. *Joseph and the Amazing Technicolor® Dreamcoat* (Narrator) [O], *Les Misérables* (Eponine)

I was a senior at Carnegie Mellon University and I had just been cast as the lead in the summer production. It was a Gershwin musical. At the time, I was still non-Equity. I had never done a show in New York City. I was freelancing with an agent, and going back and forth to New York City for auditions. I had just graduated. I was confident. I got an audition for *Into the Woods*, and made it to the final callbacks.

The final callbacks were at the Martin Beck Theater. I had prepared a monologue. Twelve rows back, I heard hysterical laughter. It was Stephen Sondheim. Before the callback, I knew that they were excited about my singing. Now I knew they were very excited about my performance as Rapunzel as well. I felt like the part was mine. My whole body was electrified. I was twenty years old.

I left the theater and went to the first payphone I could find. I called my agent and said, "I think I got it."

"Oh, Pamela, there are a lot of auditions ahead. I am glad you did well, but just wait and see."

I said, "Okay, but I am telling you, I really think I got it." I was right.

Then, no one could believe what I did. I turned down the Broadway workshop because I didn't want to snub my school. A two-week workshop was to take place six weeks before the rehearsals started for the actual Broadway show. I didn't want to tell my school, "To hell with you! I got a Broadway show." Although I had graduated, I was scheduled to stay in Pittsburgh to do summer repertory theater. I would have left them completely high and dry.

So, I told my agents that I didn't want to do the workshop because it conflicted. They were flabbergasted.

"Do you realize what you are doing?"

"Yeah, but I can't let my school down."

They explained, "Well, you may get fired. They may be so angry that they won't give you the part."

I said "I hope that's not true, but what else can I do?"

Pamela Winslow. *Into the Woods* (Rapunzel) [O], *Beauty and the Beast* (Babette)

Truth Be Told

I auditioned in front of Stephen Sondheim and Hal Prince for *Merrily We Roll Along*. I remember being aware of them while I was singing. I was twenty-five years old, but I looked sixteen. I read a scene or two, and did fine. Then Hal Prince asked me how old I was. I wondered if I should lie and take off a couple of years. I decided against it, and told them my real age. I knew I was too old. They cast me anyway.

Jim Walton. *The Music Man* (Harold Hill s/b) [O], *Merrily We Roll Along* (Franklin Shepard) [O], *Sweeney Todd* (Anthony Hope) [O], *Perfectly Frank* [O], *Stardust* [O], *42nd Street* (Billy Lawlor)

While I was still in school, I started auditioning for regional theater. I was offered the part of Lun Tha in *The King And I*. At the callback, I bumped into a friend who said, "You're going in for *The King and I* on Broadway too, right?"

I asked, "They're doing *The King and I* on Broadway?" I had no idea.

She said, "They are doing the first round of Equity auditions tomorrow. If you can, skip school, pack a lunch, and go and wait all day. Sometimes they see non-Equity actors at the end of the day. You're better off going during an agent submission day than during an open call day with five hundred other non-Equity actors."

So I skipped school, packed a lunch, arrived at noon, and expected to wait until 5:30 P.M. At around 2:00 P.M., some actor didn't show up for his time slot. His name was Robert. They kept calling his name. I kept looking around.

Finally I said, "That's me." The guy's headshot and résumé were on the table face down. Mark Simon, who was running the audition, didn't see them. I sang a song, scared shitless that he was going to throw me out. After my audition, he said, "You'll be getting a callback, Robert. I'll see you soon." I was literally shaking in my pants.

"Excuse me," I said. "My name is Jose Llana. That's not me. I'm still in school and I just came for the experience. I totally understand if you want to throw me out." He gave me a look of disbelief I will never forget, and then said, "Give me your résumé." That was March.

They kept calling me back throughout the summer. It was clear that they liked me. I went in at least fifteen times, but they never offered me the part. The whole summer, I was losing my hair. I was broke, and I was waiting tables. Finally, at the end of the summer, they said, "You have a job. Whether you are in the ensemble, an understudy, or the lead, is undecided."

Then one night, Jay Binder called. "What are you doing in November?"

"Why?"

"Because we are going to be rehearsing in November and we'd like you to play the lead role of Lun Tha, the young lover." It was inconceivable. To this day, nothing has matched that sense of disbelief.

Jose Llana. *Flower Drum Song* (Ta) [O], *The King and I* (Lun Tha) [O], *Street Corner Symphony* (Jessie-Lee) [O], *Rent* (Angel), *Martin Guerre** (Guillaume)

Patience Is a Virtue

One day, I decided to call the casting director of *Les Misérables* on the phone. "Hi, you don't know me. My name is Joe Paparella and I want to be in *Les Misérables.*"

"You and the rest of New York!"

I said, "Well, I am not the rest of New York. I'm sorry to be so forward, but I have some friends who are on the national tour, and they think I am perfect for the show. Besides, I really want to do it."

He said, "Look, we don't have anything available now. Furthermore, I don't know you. Call me later and we can talk about it."

I ended up taking a workshop with him that summer. I showed him what I thought he wanted to see as opposed to just being myself. I didn't get any auditions that year.

When they were casting the tenth-anniversary production of *Les Misérables*, they called me in to audition. Again, I did what I thought they wanted to see. I didn't get the job.

Two years passed and I had gone on many other auditions for the casting agency. Casting agencies like to see actors improve, and they like to see actors who are eager. They called me in for *Les Misérables.* I decided I was going to get the job. The audition was amazing. I was connected. I made them laugh. I didn't try to be someone else. It worked. The casting agent said, "You've really come a long way. You've really focused on this material. How would you like to swing the show?"

I said, "No thanks." I wanted to be cast in a role. I felt like I had planted seeds.

Two more months passed, and after about seven months of unemployment, I was dead broke. I had been auditioning, callback after callback. Nothing.

The day before Thanksgiving, I started to sob in my bathtub. I called my best friend and said, "I can't do this anymore. This isn't worth all of this effort. I hate this constant fight. I'm doing all my work and it's not going to happen!"

Call waiting.

"Hello?"

"Hi, this is Jamibeth Margolis from Johnson-Liff Casting. We'd like to offer you *Les Misérables*."

"Hold on."

I felt like it was a dream. It was my dream. I started to cry again. I said, "Please let me call you back. I've had a really bad day."

I got myself together and called back. They told me I had been cast in the national tour. Three days later they called back.

"We've had a change of plans. We don't know how you would feel about this, but would you rather do the role on Broadway?"

"Of course I would!"

Joe Paparella. *Jesus Christ Superstar* (Swing), *Les Misérables* (Thénardier u/s), *Martin Guerre** (Martin u/s), *Mamma Mia!** (Eddie), *Joseph and the Amazing Technicolor® Dreamcoat** (Swing), *Ragtime**, *Big**

Weighing In

I could not get an audition for *Beauty and the Beast*. One day when I went in for a voice lesson, my teacher told me that they were looking for a Belle understudy. She made a phone call to the music supervisor, and somehow got me an audition.

I showed up at the studios, and there were only seven girls. One girl was on the floor, and the other six had their legs straight up over their heads. I dance well, but I am not one of those dancers. I looked at the girl on the floor, who was Kristin Chenoweth, and said, "You're a singer, aren't you?"

"Yes."

"So am I." I sat on the floor with her, and we did our singer stretches and watched the girls with their legs over their heads. I was very nervous and intimidated. They paired me with Kristin to dance, so we both looked good.

After we read the scenes, they asked us to go to the theater and sing. They brought us in, one at a time, onto the stage. Before that moment, I had never stood on a Broadway stage. There I was, at the Palace Theater, standing on the stage, auditioning for my first Broadway show. After I finished singing, they thanked us all, and kept Kristin.

I went home and called my parents. "Well, I don't think I got it, but it went really well. Maybe they will put me on file. A really nice girl got the part."

As I was on the phone, my call waiting came on. I flipped over, and it was my agent. He said they wanted me to come back to do a work session with the dance captain before the show that evening. I had no idea what it meant to do a work session.

When I made it back to the theater, I was scared to death. The dance captain was so focused, and she put me through the ringer. They offered me the job the next day. I screamed. I couldn't believe that I got a Broadway show. I was so excited.

My agent went back and forth with the terms of the contract. After the negotiations, on Friday, my agent called and said everything was good. The last thing she said to me was, "They want you to lose ten pounds."

I said, "What?"

"They want you to lose ten pounds."

Now, at the time I got the offer, I was 5'2" and I weighed 110 pounds. And they wanted me to lose ten pounds!

I said to my agent, "There is no way I can physically do that. I have never weighed a hundred pounds as an adult in my whole life. I can't sign a contract that says I have to do this when I know I can't."

My agent said, "Don't worry about it. I'll take care of it."

On Saturday morning, I got a call from the stage manager. He wanted me to come in for a costume fitting. I showed up at the theater. I did my costume fitting. I got my wig. I got the script. I was so excited. My dream of making it to Broadway had finally come true. Then, he pulled out a scale from under his desk and put it on the floor.

"I am really sorry I have to do this, but I have to weigh you."

I was about to cry. I was so embarrassed. I got on the scale. It read 111 pounds, and I got out of there.

I called my agent and left a message. "You have to turn this down. I can't do this job."

Two weeks passed. I told them, "I can't ever weigh a hundred pounds. I simply can't." I had just been cast in my first Broadway show, and I was going to have to turn it down.

Finally, they came back and dropped the issue. It was a tainted beginning to my time on Broadway.

That said, the first time I went on for the lead was probably the most incredible moment of my life. It was what I had dreamed about as a child. I had made it to Broadway.

Ana Maria Andricain. *Marie Christine* (Dakota/Emma Parker) [O], *Les Misérables* (Fantine u/s), *Beauty and the Beast* (Belle), *By Jeeves* (Stiffy Byng), *Evita** (Eva Alternate), *Annie Get Your Gun** (Annie u/s)

PART FOUR

THE THRILL OF LIVE THEATER

CHAPTER 9

Take Two

Wander into a bar in the theater district after eleven o'clock at night, and you are likely to find groups of Broadway actors relaxing after a long show. Sit down next to them, and if you are lucky, you just might hear an actor tell a story of something that went wrong during the show that night.

These are the stories actors cherish, which remind them that anything can happen on a Broadway stage, and just about everything has—from forgetting one's lyrics to forgetting where the stage ends. As the saying goes, the show must go on. However, once in a while, things get so crazy that everything comes to a halt.

Sometimes human failure is to blame. Other times, technical failures are responsible. Once in a while, you can blame it on your dog. And occasionally, actors make choices before the curtain goes up which they are forced to contend with throughout the show. While such experiences can be humorous and entertaining, they can also be humiliating and terrifying for the actors involved. Regardless, they are moments an actor will never forget.

Once the unexpected occurs, for a moment, actors are free from their blocking and the constraints imposed by directors and stage managers. Life seems to stand still as actors are often asked to improvise with hundreds of people watching. Sometimes, the audience has no idea things are going wrong. Other times, it is painfully clear that something, or someone, is out of line. In this chapter, actors tell the stories that add texture to Broadway, and that usually never drift beyond the crowded theater bars on New York's Restaurant Row.

Unexpected Transformations

So I'm doing *Jekyll & Hyde*. It's Friday night. The audience is packed. I go out to sing the song "This is the Moment." I'm in a tuxedo—tails and everything. I'm singing the song and I'm in great voice. It's really going well, but I'm kind of feeling weird about the audience's reaction. I hear people talking while I'm singing. That had never happened before. I sing the big note at the end of the song and put my hand up in the air. There is a mixed response. I really felt like I nailed it.

Then I hear, "You go, brother!"

I start the lab scene right before I take the formula. I hear somebody in the audience say something like, "Da da da . . . undone." I can't understand what he's saying. I'm doing the scene and I don't know what's going on. There's giggling in the audience. I can't figure out what's happening. I do the scene and transform into the creature.

I stand up. I look in the mirror. My fly is not only down, it's gaping down. And my shirttail is hanging out of my fly, totally flopping out. It's a huge fly, just huge. It's just gaping down. I am mortified. I zip it up, and the audience goes nuts.

Robert Evan. *Jekyll & Hyde* (Dr. Jekyll) [O], *Dance of the Vampires* (Count von Krolock s/b) [O], *Les Misérables* (Jean Valjean)

During *Annie*, there was a clause in our contracts which said that we could not sit in the sun and get a tan. I wanted a tan, so I started looking for a loophole. I found one. I went to a store and bought one of the first aerosol spray-on tanning foams ever sold. A day before the show, I applied the stuff all over my body.

That night, Annie didn't look so good. As usual, I wore my red dress, my red wig, and my white socks. However, the tanning foam had turned my skin bright orange. I was thirteen years old and didn't have much facial hair, but the stuff gave me an orange moustache. I looked like Annie the werewolf.

Andrea McArdle. *Annie* (Annie) [O][t], *Starlight Express* (Ashley) [O], *State Fair* (Margy Frake) [O], *Les Misérables* (Fantine), *Beauty and the Beast* (Belle), *Cabaret** (Sally Bowles), *Jerry's Girls**

Look Out Below!

After I sang the "Starlight Express" song, the conductor, Paul Bogaev, came to me and said, "Sean, you are taking it too fast. You have to watch me on the monitor." There was no orchestra pit in the theater. The orchestra was on the third floor, up near the lobby, behind the men's room. It was a big sound studio. We had television monitors all over.

It was my second night on for the lead role of Rusty. There was a part in the middle of the song where I would roll backwards, and then roll forwards in a spotlight. The words were, "And if you're there, and if you know, then show me which way I should go. Starlight Express, Starlight Express." As directed, I started rolling forward in the pin spot. That night, I was watching the guy on the monitor very closely.

When you are on roller skates, and in total blackness, you feel as if you are floating. It's a weird sensation. As I was rolling forward, I sang, "And if you're there, and if you know, then show me which way I should gooooo."

I was going down. I thought, "My God, I've hit a seam. A snag. I'm going to hit the floor." I went down, thinking I would hit the stage hard. Unfortunately, I was wrong.

Suddenly, I realized, "There are people. I am on top of people. I have fallen into the audience." The people turned me around and pushed me back on stage. I barely missed a beat.

"Starlight Express, Starlight Express."

And, because I was in a pin spot, very few people could see what had happened. Most of the audience didn't even know. It looked like I fell into a trap door, and suddenly reemerged. Even the sound man looked up and thought, "where did he go?"

Sean McDermott. *Starlight Express* (Prince of Wales) [O], *Miss Saigon* (Chris u/s) [O], *Falsettos* (Whizzer), *Grease!* (Danny Zuko)

I played Madame Thénardier in *Les Misérables.* We were doing the scene with Jean Valjean in the Thénardier Inn. At the end of the scene, Thénardier and I would get money for selling Cosette. Thénardier would lean over a table, ogling the money, and I would say, "Ah, you son of a bitch," and jump on top of him. It always got a huge laugh. The turntable would go around and we would exit.

I had been performing the role with an understudy for a while. He was quite a bit taller than the usual Thénardier. I really had to jump up on his back to get him flat. One night, the table felt a little loose. I jumped on his back and heard a "crack." The table legs fell out and I flew head-first into the orchestra pit. I did a tuck and a roll and heard the audience gasp.

I landed on the thin netting over the orchestra pit, which is usually used to block silverware and other small objects. Of course, I was a bit heavier than a fork. I went right through the netting and onto the drum set.

Some of the audience leaned over and looked at me in the pit. They must have thought it was a part of the show. The show was still going on, so they eventually sat down. The drummer was reading a magazine.

He looked up and said, "Are you all right, Gina?"

I asked, "Did I just fall into the pit?"

To make things worse, when I got off the drums, I tripped on the cymbals. The conductor looked at me, horrified. Meanwhile, the young actress who played Little Cosette was on stage in tears. She saw me go into the pit. She thought I was dead. People were running around backstage thinking that I had died.

Annie. Photo credit: Photofest

Suddenly, I remembered that I had a cue to make. However, I was so cramped that I couldn't get out of the pit by myself. Some of the musicians finally helped me out. The entire cast was looking at me. "Get out of my way. I have an entrance!"

I made it on stage without a scratch. Most of the audience had no idea.

Gina Ferrall. *Big River* (Widow Douglas) [O], *Jane Eyre* (Mrs. Reed) [O], *The Sound of Music* (Sister Berthe) [O], *Les Misérables* (Madame Thénardier)

Unleashed

Peter Howard, the conductor of *Annie*, used to use a pencil while he was conducting. Once the show became a big hit, he decided to get a proper baton.

I remember the first night Peter had his new baton. During the song "Tomorrow," I was dead-center with my dog. When the dog saw the real baton in Peter's hand instead of the usual pencil, he started making growling noises.

As I made my way through the song, the dog got more and more ticked off. He began to go crazy. The conductor looked at the dog, thinking, "What is he doing?" I tried to calm him down while I was singing

"Tomorrow." I was totally out of control. There I was, singing the biggest number in the show, and the dog was simply going berserk.

When the dog started going into a full bark, Peter Howard looked terrified. Meanwhile, the audience came to see *Annie* and hear the song "Tomorrow," and all they heard was barking. Needless to say, the baton went away after that.

Andrea McArdle. *Annie* (Annie) [O][**t**], *Starlight Express* (Ashley) [O], *State Fair* (Margy Frake) [O], *Les Misérables* (Fantine), *Beauty and the Beast* (Belle), *Cabaret** (Sally Bowles), *Jerry's Girls**

I went to a pet store with Mary Ann Lamb, my best friend. We found a dog that we thought was the cutest thing in the world. It was a pointer. Because no one wanted him, they were going to put him to sleep. Since we were making money in *Jerome Robbins' Broadway*, we thought that we should buy the dog and give it to somebody. Each of us already had two dogs and we couldn't take a third. We bought the dog for $400 and gave him to the follow-spot operator in our show. He had a great house in the country.

Eight months passed.

One day, the operator said, "Hey, I am going to bring Blue into the city." I asked, "Can we take the dog in between shows?"

He said yes. Mind you, the dog was now huge. We took the dog and put him in Mary Ann's dressing room. Her dressing room was five flights up in the theater, and he would be safe there. Of course, no dogs were allowed in the theater.

I was about to come out for the *Peter Pan* number and was waiting in the wings. Mary Ann was doing *Gypsy*, and was sitting in a chair on stage. Out of nowhere, the dog walked out on stage. He managed to get down four flights of stairs, through a packed theater, through the wings, between Terrence Mann's legs, and out onto the stage to visit Mary Ann, who was sitting all the way across the stage. She was in the middle of singing her song. The audience broke down laughing.

The dog simply walked out, wiggled, turned around, and walked back off stage. I still don't know how it happened. The dog was as big as a table, and there were more than sixty cast members in the company.

Charlotte d'Amboise. *Jerome Robbins' Broadway* (Anita/Peter Pan) [O][**t**], *Carrie* (Chris) [O], *Company* (Cathy) [O], *Song & Dance* [O], *Contact* (Wife), *Damn Yankees* (Lola), *Chicago* (Roxie Hart), *Cats* (Cassandra)

Left Hanging

During one performance of *The Full Monty*, we could all sense that something was wrong with the lights. It terrified us. Usually, the strip scene at the end of the show had a great lighting effect where you could kind of see, but you really couldn't see. In sixteen bars, we were going to be naked. We took off our clothes and walked upstage. We looked around at each other.

"What do we do?"

We had been doing the show for two hours and forty-five minutes. We had to go "The Full Monty." We did our thing and put our hats in front of us, hoping that somehow, the lights would work properly. We had a full thirty seconds knowing something disastrous was about to happen.

Sure enough, we took it all off, and stood completely naked in front of hundreds of people. And, sure enough, that night, there was no "great lighting effect." The lights just stayed on.

Some people were in awe. Some people were terrified. Some of the guys had their arms down. For some reason, my arms were up in the air. We ran off stage completely naked. That night, everybody in the theater saw everything we had. It was terrifying.

Patrick Wilson. *The Full Monty* (Jerry Lukowski) [O][t], *Oklahoma!* (Curley) [O][t], *The Gershwin's Fascinating Rhythm* [O], *Carousel** (Billy Bigelow), *Miss Saigon**

While I was performing *Les Misérables*, there was often a problem during my solo, "I Dreamed a Dream."

One night, while I was singing my song, I looked up at the balcony and rows and rows of people were emptying out.

They said, "Randy! Get off the stage! There is a fire!" The entire building was evacuated. The whole cast stood in their costumes outside the stage door. Luckily, it was a false alarm. Everyone came back into the theater and I sang the song again.

Another time, while I was singing my song, the turntable kept jolting. Once again, someone yelled, "Randy! Get off the stage!" They stopped the show for forty-five minutes to fix it. That was the first time there were gremlins in the turntable. Then it happened again.

Another night, during my big song, someone had some kind of seizure. While I was singing "I Dreamed a Dream," someone started yelling, "Is there a doctor in the house?"

And then there was the night that Colm Wilkinson, who played Jean Valjean, never came out on stage to sing my last number with me, when I die in his arms. I was out there dying by myself. I had to drag myself into my deathbed without his help. Then I had to sing my part of the song, let his phrase go by, sing my part, and then let his phrase go by again.

Over the monitor, you could hear, "Oh, shit!" So they turned him off. By the time he finally came out, I was already in bed. He started hugging me and saying in my ear, "I'm so sorry. I'm so sorry."

Randy Graff. *City of Angels* (Oolie) [O][T], *A Class Act* (Sophie) [O][t], *Les Misérables* (Fantine) [O], *Moon over Buffalo* (Rosalind) [O], *High Society* (Liz Imbrie) [O], *Laughter on the 23rd Floor* (Carol) [O], *Saravà* (Rosalia), *Fiddler on the Roof* (Golde) [O], *Grease!* (Rizzo u/s), *Falsettos* (Trina)

The Rest of the Story

I was doing *Les Misérables* with Colm Wilkinson and Leo Burmester. In the show, the exits and entrances off stage were like choreography. There was a routine. During the show, there were two times that the three of us walked off stage together. Usually, we would walk to Colm's dressing room.

The first time we walked off together, we would stand and talk until Colm would go out on stage and perform the Fantine dying number, where he would put her back into bed. The second time, he had more time. He would go into his dressing room and change his costume.

So, we were several months into the show. We finished the first scene and the three of us walked off stage. We started talking about Irish whiskey.

Leo said, "I had some really good Irish whiskey the other night."

Colm, who doesn't drink, but who is Irish and knows everything there is to know about Irish whiskey, started talking in his Irish brogue. "Well, you know, the single malt, it depends on where it comes from. You know, the really good one is Oban." He was going on and on.

Caught up in conversation, we all walked into his dressing room and Colm started taking off his clothes as if it was the second change. In reality, he had only about thirty seconds until he was supposed to go out on stage to save Fantine. He started unbuttoning his sailor pants and pulled them down. He pulled off one shoe. He took off his shirt. He was still talking about Irish whiskey. This must have gone on for over a minute.

All of a sudden, he heard Fantine sing, "Oh, Cosette, I don't know . . ." She was making up words. Colm said, "Oh, my God! Oh, ya fucks! Oh, ya fucks!" He started putting on his pants and ran out. Fantine, played by Randy Graff, had crawled all the way down to the edge of the stage and was looking at the conductor, who was just vamping. Colm ran out, gently picked her up, and put her into bed.

Terrence Mann. *Les Misérables* (Javert) [O][t], *Beauty and the Beast* (Beast) [O] [t], *Cats* (Rum Tum Tugger) [O], *The Scarlet Pimpernel* (Chauvelin) [O], *Barnum* (Chester Lyman) [O], *Rags* (Saul) [O], *Getting Away with Murder* (Gregory Reed) [O], *Jerome Robbins' Broadway* (Emcee), *The Rocky Horror Show* (Dr. Frank N. Furter)

This is the way I remember the story. We had just opened *Les Misérables* on Broadway on March 12, 1987. Now, I don't drink, but people had sent me bottles of all kinds of alcohol as opening night presents. On the 17th of March, St. Patrick's Day, Leo Burmester and Terry Mann were in my dressing room. They were asking me if I would have a drink because it was St. Patrick's Day. We were joking around, having a laugh about it. I had just finished the "Who Am I" scene and must have been distracted by all the banter that was going on. I started to change costumes.

It was only when I was down to my underpants that I realized I was due on stage for the hospital scene with Randy Graff. When I heard my entrance music being played, I started to frantically throw my clothes back on, and of course, like the true artists that they are, Mann and Burmester ran in a panic out of the dressing room, with me a close third.

We wore radio microphones for that show, and the sound person, who was totally oblivious to what was going on, had put the volume up on my microphone for my entrance. I was still struggling to get on stage. Not knowing the microphone was on, I was swearing and cursing, and all of this was coming out into the house.

The girl who played the nun in the hospital scene had gone on stage and was reassuring Randy Graff by improvising lines like, "Monsieur Le Mayor has been detained but he will be here soon . . ."

I finally arrived on stage with my clothes all over the place. Poor Randy Graff was the color of the sheets on the bed. I don't remember what I sang or did, but I know it didn't make much sense. The next night, Randy knocked on my dressing-room door and said, "I'm going out for the hospital scene now, Colm. You will be there tonight, won't you?" That was the only time I was ever "off," as they say, in the theater.

Colm Wilkinson. *Les Misérables* (Jean Valjean) [O][t]

A Bit Behind Schedule

One night, when I was the dance captain in *Cats*, the understudy for Grizabella was on for the role. I was sitting in the back of the audience with all the important people. It finally came time for Grizabella to make her final entrance. It was time to sing "Memory."

The music started, and there was no Grizabella. At this point in the show, all the cats were supposed to react to Grizabella by turning and walking away. Time was passing, and there was still no Grizabella. Now, it was getting to the point where the actors were vamping for her song. One of the cats came to the center of the stage and tried to postpone the inevitable. There was only so long that he could improvise. He moved away.

Next, they all looked to the actress who played the little cat Sillabub. In the show, she sang a tiny version of "Memory." They looked at her, thinking, "Can you sing it?" She turned upstage with this look on her face of, "No way." Normally, there was a Grizabella understudy on stage, but that evening she was out of the show. There was no one.

Nothing was happening. I ran down the side aisle to the door that led backstage. I said, "Where is she?" It was so odd. No one seemed to know and no one seemed to care. I ran to her dressing room. She was totally disoriented. She had just woken up from a nap. Her dresser was sort of helping her into her costume. I said, "Come on!"

I grabbed her, and we started running.

She said, "I forgot my coat and my gloves."

"Forget the coat," I said. Normally she entered from stage right, but there was no time to get her there. She was still kind of waffling. I gave her a shove onto stage left. All the cats looked at her. They had been vamping her song for about three minutes.

She just started to cry. It was one of the most heartfelt performances of "Memory" I have ever seen. She later told me that she was thinking that it was the last time she would sing "Memory" on a Broadway stage. It was beautiful. Her dress was unzipped. She had no coat and was without her gloves. She was also missing her tail.

After the show, she went into the office. She thought that management would have a plane ticket waiting for her. They didn't. They said, "Well, you've got your David Letterman story now. I'm sure you are punishing yourself more than we could ever punish you." They let it go at that.

James Hadley. *Thou Shalt Not* (Swing) [O], *Bells Are Ringing* (Swing) [O], *The Red Shoes* (Swing) [O], *Cats* (Coricopat), *Chicago* (Swing), *The Producers**

In *The Scarlet Pimpernel,* we had to make a big human pinwheel in "The Creation of Man" number. The Pimpernel was at the center and we were like Radio City Rockettes around him. We used handkerchiefs in the number. We were told to pick up our silk handkerchiefs if we dropped them because someone might slip.

I was positioned on the end of the pinwheel, so I had the most ground to cover. One night, before the pinwheel started, I dropped my handkerchief. As I went to grab it, the pinwheel started. I was wearing two-inch heels. Trying to catch up, I chased the pinwheel around, saying, "Wait for me! I'm coming. Wait for me!"

As I was chasing these men around in a circle, I kept thinking, "I'm in a Broadway show. I could be fired right now. I am screwing up a Broadway show." No one could get through the rest of the scene. They were all laughing. I was mortified. At intermission, stage management made an announcement thanking me for my new and intriguing staging.

Danny Gurwin. *The Scarlet Pimpernel* (Hal), *The Full Monty* (Malcolm MacGregor), *Urinetown* (Mr. McQueen)

Say What?

My first night on a Broadway stage was a classic moment in musical theater history. The tour of *Les Misérables* was in the Jackie Gleason Theater in Miami Beach. My first line in the beginning of the play was, "Why should you get the same as honest men like me?"

I said it wrong.

I said, "Why don't you get the same as other people like me?"

It was totally wrong. And then, to make things even worse, Paul Ainsley looked up at me and said, "First line—new line!" The turntable started spinning, and I was mortified.

Geoffrey Blaisdell. *Jekyll & Hyde* (Lord Glossop) [O], *Cyrano—The Musical* (Captain De Castel Jaloux) [O], *Amadeus* (Servant) [O], *Les Misérables** (Javert), *The Phantom of the Opera** (The Auctioneer)

In *Cabaret*, I forgot my lines to my songs a couple of times. "I am a perfectly marvelous girl, in this perfectly marvelous place, I'm a do bada do bada do." That happened a few times. It is terrifying because it comes out of nowhere. You are just fine. It's your sixtieth performance, and you're fine. You had a good meal, slept well, you're not hung over, and all of a sudden your mind just goes.

But one thing I am learning about now is that singing is about saving. If you don't hit the note right, you either slide into it, you make it sound like something else, you pretend you were crying, or you find a way to save it. If you can't hit the note, you hit the next note, the one that harmonizes with it. Singing is all about saving because that's what makes it okay in the end. And acting is about saving. You can't stop. The ability to know that you can save yourself is what separates the men from the boys.

Lea Thompson. *Cabaret* (Sally Bowles)

I was in *Jesus Christ Superstar* on Broadway, understudying the role of Simon. I felt like I hadn't had enough rehearsal. I didn't feel a hundred percent prepared. One day, I arrived at the theater a half hour before the show, and they announced that the guy playing Simon was out. I was going to be on for the first time.

I panicked. Simon had to sustain a high A note. "I'm with you Jesuuuus." I was in the dressing room warming up, thinking, "Oh, my God, I don't have an A! But I will. I have to sing a few songs before I sing my solo."

While I was singing "Hosanna," I thought, "Oh, my God. I don't have it. In just a few seconds I have to climb up that bridge and sing the solo." As I was climbing up the bridge, things were going well. However, I was not acting well because I knew the note was coming up.

When the note came, my voice basically blew up. I sang, "I'm with you Jesaaauu!" Like a dog. Instead of just dropping off, I did the whole phrase over again. You'd think you would just crack and end. Nope. Not me.

I kept going back to it.

"I'm with you Jesaaauu." Crack.

"I'm with you Jesaaauu." Crack.

I just kept trying it over and over and over. The orchestra, however, didn't stop and go back. I just kept trying until I got it right.

And I did get it right.

My agent was in the audience that night. She said she didn't notice. She was lying.

Daniel C. Levine. *Jesus Christ Superstar* (Disciple) [O], *The Rocky Horror Show*, *Chicago** (Mary Sunshine), *Les Misérables** (Marius u/s), *Mamma Mia!**

In the beginning of the second act of *Carousel*, there was an intense moment at a clambake where all of the townspeople were upset. Fisher Stevens, who was playing Jigger, would come in and calm everyone down. He would sing, "Stonecutters cut it on stone, woodpeckers peck it on wood . . ." It was his great moment. Everything went to him.

However, one night, rather than singing, "Stonecutters cut in on stone," he sang, "Stonecutters cut it on wood."

We all froze, thinking, "What did he just say? What will he say next?" And then he continued with, "Woodpeppers perk it on porn."

I had never heard anything funnier. He was off-track, and was trying to get back on. We went from playing angry townsfolk to a bunch of people with our backs to the audience, shoulders shrugging up and down.

Brian d'Arcy James. *Sweet Smell of Success* (Sidney) [O][t], *Titanic* (Frederick Barrett) [O], *Carousel* (Captain) [O], *Blood Brothers*

At the end of *The King and I*, the King, played by Yul Brenner, was dying. I played the schoolteacher's son who had come to say goodbye. The King wanted my mom to stay, but she wanted to go back to England. They were at odds and they hadn't spoken much.

In the final scene, a boat whistle blew and I would say, "Mother, it's the boat!"

After a long dramatic pause, my mother would tell him that we were not going. Everybody would cheer, and then the King would die. It was a bittersweet scene, and a sad ending to the play.

During the run of the national tour, we played two-thousand-seat theaters. When it was time for me to deliver my all-important line, I would be all the way at the back of the stage. I didn't have a body microphone, so I had to really project. I did my best.

One night, in a two-thousand-seat theater in Nashville, I went to the back of the stage and delivered my line. "Mother, it's the boat."

Out of nowhere, Yul Brenner, while on his deathbed, yelled, "Louder!"

I took a deep breath, and said it again. "MOTHER, IT'S THE BOAT!" I ran off stage and cried.

Anthony Rapp. *Rent* (Mark Cohen) [O], *You're a Good Man, Charlie Brown* (Charlie Brown) [O], *Precious Sons* (Freddy) [O], *Six Degrees of Separation* (Ben) [O], *The King and I** (Louis)

Stop the Show

For some reason, one night during a particular song in *She Loves Me*, I thought the introduction went around and around for four musical bars. It didn't. In reality, I only had two musical bars to come in. I came in after four. The song was already off and running. It was a big patter song—a fast song. I was two bars behind the music, and there was no way on Earth that the audience didn't know that something was seriously wrong.

About halfway through, I just sat down on stage and thought, "I've got to stop. I don't know where I am." I called to the orchestra. "Can you stop? Can you stop?" They didn't hear me. So I had to shout to the wings, "Stop. Stop." I walked to the front of the stage. I thought I was going to die. "Sorry. Sorry."

I had to pick up all the props because it was a prop number. I had to put all the props back in the right place again, and start over. I was on stage for another fifteen minutes. When I got off stage, I remember literally falling to my knees and sobbing. An old guy who had been in the theater for years said, "Darling, we are walking the highest tightrope in the world—live theater!"

I did the same thing in the first preview for *Putting it Together* on Broadway. We had our first audience, and I had a brain fart. I went completely blank. I didn't know where I was. I had to stop. I said, "I am talking a load of rubbish and you know it." The audience just hooted with laughter. They thought it was hilarious. They were extremely forgiving, and I got a huge round of applause.

After the show, Stephen Sondheim came out and said, "That was wonderful. Marvelous. You really handled that well. But don't you ever do that again." He told me a story about a woman who had forgotten her words one night, and received an enormous round of applause, so she started working it into the show. She did it again. Stephen Sondheim said, "I hope you are not going to do this every night."

I said, "No, thank you. Once is enough. I don't need to humiliate myself every night."

Things happen on stage. You do your show. You are as professional as you can be. Sometimes things come along that are just out of your hands.

Ruthie Henshall. *Putting It Together* (The Younger Woman) [O], *Miss Saigon* (Ellen), *Chicago* (Velma)

We had to wear about eleven or twelve different wigs each night in *Side Show*. The wig changes were choreographed down to the millisecond. At one point in the show, we had to change into Egyptian costumes. We would back up on stage, doors would close around us, and our dressers would quickly rip off our clothes and put on new wigs and clothes. We would then get into a sarcophagus and do the Egyptian number.

One night, our dressers started taking off our clothes as usual. However, when they tried to put on my next costume, I thought, "I haven't gained that much weight. Christ, why won't this fit?"

They were trying to put me into my understudy's costume. She was a size two. I was a size twelve. By the time we realized it simply was not going to happen, the other performers were already on stage, doing the prequel to the number. The sarcophagus was supposed to open and we were supposed to be inside. When it opened, nobody was there.

Ultimately, they had to stop the show. My dresser ran down and got me into my costume. However, when we finally got into the sarcophagus, we got in the wrong way. They had to stop the show for another five minutes.

Emily Skinner. *Side Show* (Daisy Hilton) [O][t], *The Full Monty* (Vicki Nichols) [O], *James Joyce's The Dead* (Mary Jane Morkan) [O], *Jekyll & Hyde* (Emma u/s) [O], *Dinner at Eight* (Kitty Packard) [O]

Dressed for Disaster

I was in *Carrie*, the biggest flop in musical theater history. The show opened in London and we received the worst reviews ever. Everything got slammed. When we came to New York, very little in the show had changed. In fact, they didn't really change anything except for replacing Barbara Cook with Betty Buckley. We just knew that we were going to get slaughtered.

The musical took place in Grecian times, and we wore Grecian gym wear. I can't even explain what it was—just odd, white cotton clothing. To make matters worse, the director was adamant about us not wearing stockings. Worse yet, when the costumes were sent over from London, they were washed—apparently using very hot water. They shrunk to tiny little things. I mean, literally, when we kicked our legs, the audience saw everything. We were naked and kicking.

I remember going home and saying, "Mommy, we were booed on stage." The show opened and closed in a weekend.

Charlotte d'Amboise. *Jerome Robbins' Broadway* (Anita/Peter Pan) [O][t], *Carrie* (Chris) [O], *Company* (Cathy) [O], *Song and Dance* [O], *Contact* (Wife), *Damn Yankees* (Lola), *Chicago* (Roxie Hart), *Cats* (Cassandra)

In *Aspects of Love*, I had twenty-three costume changes. I think it might have been a record. Things were always moving. I played a temperamental actress. For my very first change, I had to rip off all of the period clothes that I was wearing in the play-within-the-play and throw them onto the stage. Then, I would sit down in a tiny little teddy. A young man, played by Michael Ball, would enter and I would indicate to him to get my dress, which was hanging on a rack. Next, I would slip on the dress and turn around for him to zip me up. It started our big love affair.

One performance, he went to get the dress, and there was no dress. Nothing was on the rack. Suddenly, everything on the stage started moving. The scene was changing and we suddenly found ourselves sitting in a café. I was in my underwear. Michael was trying so hard not to laugh. There were people eating at the tables around us and I was sitting in my underwear with high heels. We were singing the whole time and the orchestra kept playing.

Everyone, both on stage and off, was laughing. Next, our characters would decide to catch a train. I went off stage and someone handed me a suitcase. I was on the run. I went downstairs and came up through the cellar onto a train platform. I thought, "Surely, they put a dress in the suitcase." Nope. The train conductor was on his way, and I was still in my underwear. Michael came over and we got on the train. The conductor was hysterical. He handed me some flowers.

On the train, we began singing the ballad "Seeing is Believing." I was still in my underwear. We could barely get through the song because we were both hysterical.

Next, we had to climb some mountains. I was still in my underwear. The conductor was not visible any more because he had fallen onto the floor of the pit, laughing.

Next, we had to break into an estate in France. This was the big seduction scene. Fifteen minutes had gone by since I was last wearing any clothes. Michael mimed unzipping my dress. The audience was screaming. They were absolutely going wild. He got on top of me and leaned down to kiss me. The lights went down. That was the first real chance I had to put on clothes.

Ann Crumb. *Anna Karenina* (Anna) [O][t], *Aspects of Love* (Rose) [O], *Chess* (Svetlana u/s) [O], *Les Misérables* (Fantine u/s) [O], *Swing** (Lead), *Music of the Night** (Headliner), *Man of La Mancha** (Aldonza), *Evita** (Eva Peron)

I have always had bunions on my feet. The costume designer for *Pippin* designed these horrible little shoes. They were custom made, but they killed my feet. There was just something about the design I couldn't stand. Before the show came to New York, I had a slight temper tantrum at the Kennedy Center in Washington, D.C. For maybe the fifth time, they said, "Okay, John, your new shoes are in."

"Ah, great," I thought. When I put them on, I thought, "Oh, no!"

I took off the shoes and I threw them at my dresser.

"Burn them," I thought. I was going to protest, and do the show barefoot—they could all go to hell.

In the show, I had to dance. I had to jump. I had to do all kinds of ridiculous physical stuff. Also, Bob Fosse and Tony Walton had designed a subway grating, through which huge headlights would shine on our white gloves for the song "Magic to Do." We were always stepping on the subway grates, catching our feet. There were all kinds of holes and cracks. Regardless of the danger, I did the show barefoot, thinking, "Well, I've shown them. They are going to come with five shoemakers and beg my forgiveness."

Nope. After the show, Fosse ran in and said, "John, great touch. Barefoot! Gives you that innocence." After that, two years with no shoes—and whenever you see *Pippin* anywhere, even in high school, no shoes, because of that.

> **John Rubinstein.** *Children of a Lesser God* (James Leeds) [O][T], *Pippin* (Pippin) [O], *Fools* (Leon) [O], *Getting Away with Murder* (Martin Chisholm) [O], *The Caine Mutiny Court-Martial* (Lt. Barney Greenwald) [O], *Ragtime* (Tateh), *Hurlyburly* (Eddie), *Love Letters* (Andrew), *M. Butterfly* (Rene)

Set for Disaster

At the end of *Beauty and the Beast*, the big surprise was when the Beast would transform into the Prince. The effect was amazing. The Beast would float up from the stage, twirl around in midair, and poof, turn into a prince. I don't think there was ever a glitch when the original company performed the show. When I arrived, I guess the warranty had run out on the equipment.

I signed a piece of paper swearing I would never reveal how any of this worked. What I can say is that, one performance, I was sitting on stage with this huge six-foot three-inch man lying in my lap who was supposed to start floating over the stage and twirl around. Nothing was happening. The orchestra was playing, and things were supposed to be happening—fireworks were going off and the whole cast was coming on stage. He was still the Beast. The trick was not working. He was just lying on the floor, as the Beast.

They said, "Do something!"

What could I do? Somehow, I had to make over two thousand people believe that he had magically turned into a prince. I took off my cape and laid it on top of his head. Next, I pulled off some of the pieces of his costume which made him look like the Beast. I hid the pieces under my cape. Then, I stood up and announced, "You're a prince!" And he stood up.

Usually there was huge applause. This time, everyone just looked at me like I was insane.

> **Sarah Uriarte Berry.** *Taboo* (Nicola) [O], *Les Misérables* (Eponine), *Beauty and the Beast* (Belle), *Sunset Boulevard** (Betty Schaeffer), *Carousel** (Julie Jordan)

I was in Minneapolis playing Cosette in *Les Misérables*. During my entrance for "In My Life," I would walk onto a huge spinning turntable. Once it stopped spinning, I would begin singing the ballad.

One night, the turntable didn't stop. During a normal performance, I was supposed to run to a fence, look forlorn, and turn around. That night, the turntable kept spinning. There was no way off it. I needed to think of something, and fast. I decided that instead of being pensive, I would skip joyfully through the song. I sang my entire solo that way. I didn't know what else to do. There was no other way to stay in one place.

Halfway through the song, Jean Valjean came out on stage and sang, "Cosette, you're such a lonely child. How pensive, how sad you seem to be." Meanwhile, I was skipping on this damn turntable that wouldn't quit.

Jodie Langel. *Les Misérables* (Cosette/Eponine), *Martin Guerre** (Bertrande Alternate), *Cats** (Grizabella), *Joseph and the Amazing Technicolor® Dreamcoat** (Narrator)

I was the understudy to Eva in *Evita*. When I went on for the lead for the first time, I had yet to rehearse the show on the full set. My problems began as a result of no one telling me that there was a giant cable bundle on the floor behind the Casa Rosada balcony.

Wearing a big white dress, with a giant spotlight on me, I completely tripped over the cable bundle and went flying. Suddenly, I was lying on my face in the middle of the Broadway stage. I said, "Oh, this is bad." Mandy Patinkin was singing "High Flying Adored." He was not coming to help. The actress who played the maid was in the wings. She flashed me a look of horror, her hands on her face. I tried to get up, but my heels were hooked into my skirt. I rocked back and forth like a turtle upside down on its shell.

The actress who played the maid was in shock. She came running over to help. I thought, "I've got to use this. I've got to incorporate this into the show. It's foreshadowing." As she picked me up, I began weaving a bit, holding my stomach.

Then, I said, "Oh, that uterine cancer is kicking in again." I was such an idiot.

Nancy Opel. *Urinetown* (Penelope Pennywise) [O][t], *Evita* (Eva u/s) [O], *Triumph of Love* (Corine) [O], *Sunday in the Park with George* (Frieda) [O], *Teddy & Alice* (Eleanor Roosevelt) [O], *Ring Round the Moon* (Capulat u/s) [O], *Getting Away with Murder* (Dossie Lustig u/s) [O], *Anything Goes* (Hope Harcourt)

Broadway Carnage

I was playing Jean Valjean in *Les Misérables*. There was a scene in the show where Jean Valjean visited a Bishop's house. I would run in and the

Bishop would be standing with a woman. On a table, there would be a loaf of bread on a wooden platter. I would grab the bread and slam it down on the table. Next, I would put my face right in the bread and start eating. There would always be an old antique fork on the table as well.

One night, as I slammed the bread on the table, I hit the prongs of the fork into the air. Right as I was supposed to dive my face into the bread, the fork happened to be wedged perfectly upright on the table. I didn't notice, and all four prongs of the fork pierced my cheek.

I knew I had done something bad, but I was just stunned. Everyone was panicking. I just kept singing. I didn't realize that I was bleeding profusely. I sang for the next ten minutes, passing everyone on stage. When I came off stage, my face was covered with blood. As I wiped it off, I saw four little prong holes in my cheek where the fork had once been.

Dave Clemmons. *The Scarlet Pimpernel* (Ben) [O], *The Civil War* (Sergeant Virgil Frank/Auctioneer's Assistant) [O], *Les Misérables* (Jean Valjean), *Whistle Down the Wind**, *Jekyll & Hyde** (Bishop)

In *Grease!*, I swallowed hydrogen peroxide in the middle of a quick change, thinking it was water in a cup. I couldn't go on for the second act. I threw up all night.

Brooke Shields. *Cabaret* (Sally), *Grease!* (Rizzo)

In *Beauty and the Beast* I played Lumiere, the candlestick. Terrence Mann was playing the Beast. He had just saved Belle's life, who was played by Susan Egan.

In one scene, I would stand with my candles lit, looking in. One night, all of a sudden, Susan looked at me with terror in her eyes. I looked over and quickly noticed that both of my candles—my hands— were on fire. I turned the gas off, but they stayed lit. These things, which were totally guaranteed to not catch on fire, were completely ablaze. Two big rings of fire!

I tried to blow my hands out in front of the huge audience. The audience was in hysterics. After much effort, it finally worked. It created the foulest smelling smoke that you could ever imagine.

Gary Beach. *The Producers* (Roger DeBris) [O][T], *Beauty and the Beast* (Lumiere) [O][t], *The Moony Shapiro Songbook* [O], *Doonesbury* (Duke) [O], *Something's Afoot* (Nigel) [O], *Sweet Adeline* (Dan Ward) [O], *Annie* (Rooster Hannigan), *1776* (Edward Rutledge), *Les Misérables** (Thénardier), *Of Thee I Sing**

In *The Phantom of the Opera*, there was a scene where Christine pulls the famous Phantom mask off the Phantom's face and runs away. It was an exciting moment. But the smoke from earlier in the show had left an oily residue on the terrible steel stage. One night, when I pulled the mask off, my feet slipped out from under me.

As I started to run away from the Phantom, I slipped and slid from the downstage area onto a pointy spike on a gate. It impaled my calf, my dress was caught, and I couldn't get away from the Phantom, who was rapidly approaching. Blood was going everywhere, and the Phantom was trying desperately to rip my dress off the spike. I think some people in the audience thought it was part of the show. I was truly scared.

Rebecca Luker. *The Music Man* (Marian) [O][t], *Showboat* (Magnolia) [O][t], *The Sound of Music* (Maria) [O], *The Secret Garden* (Lily) [O], *The Phantom of the Opera* (Princess/Christine) [O], *Nine* (Claudia)

Unplugged

It was a matinee of *Guys and Dolls*, and Peter Gallagher was singing a ballad to Josie de Guzman. All of a sudden, the power flickered out for a second or two, and then came back on. When the power went out, the computers started back at the beginning. Before the show, the computers would do an entire sound check. The computer immediately went to the disc from the sound check. The disc was Steely Dan.

So, in the middle of the show, Steely Dan started playing full blast. The crew couldn't get it off for a while. The audience was screaming and yelling. Peter and Josie started dancing. Live theater!

Scott Wise. *Jerome Robbins' Broadway* [O][T], *Fosse* [O][t], *State Fair* (Pat Gilbert) [O][t], *Movin' Out* (Sergeant O'Leary) [O], *Goodbye Girl* (Billy) [O], *Damn Yankees* (Rocky) [O], *Carrie* (Scott) [O], *Guys and Dolls* (Guy) [O], *Song and Dance* (Man) [O], *A Chorus Line* (Mike), *Cats* (Plato/Macavity), *Victor Victoria* (Jazz Hot Ensemble)

CHAPTER 10

Please Remain Seated

In order for theater to be effective, there must be a strong relationship between those on stage and those in the audience. As Jason Alexander explains in the Foreword, the audience needs to approach theater "as a partner" and as a "soul mate." It is true that the more intimate the relationship between actors and patrons, the more theater will flourish. However, there are limits to any relationship, and one's relationship with the theater is no exception.

The following are a few basic rules that any audience member should keep in mind. First, during the production, please remain in your seat. If you need to get up, do not charge the stage, but exit through the lobby. Second, as a sign of respect, dress appropriately when going to the theater. Third, turn off your cell phone. Fourth, no matter how much you need to express yourself, do not yell at the actors during the performance. Fifth, announce yourself before coming backstage. Sixth, if you feel compelled to write a letter, please be respectful. And seventh, stalking is completely unacceptable. This list is by no means meant to be exclusive, and please be aware that other rules of etiquette not mentioned here remain in full effect.

Once these rules are complied with, a meaningful relationship can be established which can deeply touch the lives of all who are involved.

Breaking into Show Biz

We were doing *Cats* in Indiana. As a part of the show, Rum Tug Tugger would go into the audience. During one performance, there was a guy in the fourth row clad in a homemade *Cats* costume. It was just like ours, complete with leg warmers, a crazy wig, and make-up. Rum Tum Tugger leaned over and quietly asked him, jokingly, "What are you doing here? Shouldn't you be on stage?"

With a big Southern drawl, he replied, "I wish."

Cats. Photo credit: Photofest

When Tugger got back on stage, he warned the cast that there was a guy in the audience who was really strange. "If you see a glimpse of steel, hit the deck!"

The next day we got a note from the guy. It said something like, *"By the grace of God, if I ever get the chance to join the cast of* Cats *again, I will take you up on the opportunity."* Along with the letter, he included several drawings of superhero cats, including a drawing of a "Cat-Man" with rather large genitalia.

We began to see him at the performances almost every night, in costume. One Sunday, as we were singing, "Oh well, I never, was there ever a cat so clever," the Cat-Man started running from the back of the theater in the direction of the stage. The security guards started chasing him. It was the climactic moment of the show, and this guy made it all the way onto the stage.

Bryan Batt. *Seussical* (The Cat in the Hat s/b) [O], *Saturday Night Fever* (Monty) [O], *Sunset Boulevard* (Joe Gillis u/s) [O], *Cats* (Munkustrap), *Beauty and the Beast* (Lumiere), *Starlight Express* (Rocky One), *The Scarlet Pimpernel* (Percy s/b), *Joseph and the Amazing Technicolor® Dreamcoat* (Reuben)

Quiet Please!

I did *Grease!* with Rosie O'Donnell. She had been in the show for a while and was ready to leave. One night, a man in the audience was on a cell phone. Rosie literally stopped the show and said, "Hey, who are you talking to?" She was really mad. She wasn't trying to get a laugh. She asked, "Do you think you could take the conversation in the hallway?"

Ray Walker. *Jesus Christ Superstar* (Annas) [O], *Grease!* (Doody), *Les Misérables* (Marius), *Whistle Down the Wind* (Preacher), *Music of the Night* (Principal Soloist), *Joseph and the Amazing Technicolor® Dreamcoat* (Joseph u/s), *Falsettos* (Whizzer)

You're not supposed to bring children to the theater unless they are five years old or older. But since we were doing Disney's *Beauty and the Beast*, people would bring two-, three-, and four-year-olds. Even fifteen-month-old children. During the show, they would run down the aisle to the front of the stage and yell, "Belle, Belle, don't go in the castle!" This was during a Broadway show. The music would be playing, and kids would be yelling, "Belle, Belle, Belle!" They simply wouldn't shut up. God only knew where their parents were.

One performance, I had to break character and say, "It's okay. Go sit down with your mommy and daddy." Then I had to flip right back into character and say, "Oh, Beast, please don't throw me in the dungeon."

Sarah Uriarte Berry. *Taboo* (Nicola) [O], *Les Misérables* (Eponine), *Beauty and the Beast* (Belle), *Sunset Boulevard* (Betty Schaeffer), *Carousel* (Julie Jordan)

I went to see *The Lion King* during its first year. It was wonderful to see children in the theater, but if their parents are not going to educate them, they should be left at home. During the performance, I sat between rows and rows of children who were talking, eating, and responding out loud to what was going on. Their parents did nothing. The parents should have said, "This is the theater. At the theater, you are quiet. You are not in front of a television."

Also, I hate that we sell concessions during the show. In *Urinetown*, you were allowed to bring food back to your seat. There is a sanctity that has been lost in the theater. When you go to the movies, you bring your popcorn, you crunch it around, and you do whatever the hell you want. People are doing that at the theater now and it is horrendous. In the past, people didn't talk during a Broadway production. Now, even after the announcements are made, people still don't turn off their cell phones. Should we say it in different languages?

When I saw *Tommy* on the road, people were eating, drinking, slurping, talking, and walking up and down the aisles during the show. It's not the rodeo roundup at Disneyland, with the bears dancing on stage. It's a real craft.

Anastasia Barzee. *Henry IV* (Lady Mortimer) [O], *Urinetown* (Hope Caldwell), *Miss Saigon* (Ellen), *Jekyll & Hyde* (Emma), *Sunset Boulevard* (Betty), *City of Angels* (Mallory)

In *Martin Guerre*, I played an idiot who had a scarecrow as a girlfriend. In one scene, the villagers would torture me and then rip the scarecrow apart. During one performance, it was too much for a woman in the audience to take.

She stood up and screamed, "This is fucking terrible! How can you do this?"

Then, someone else stood up and said, "This is too much!"

They both stormed out of the theater.

Meanwhile, I was all alone on stage with this doll. Everything seemed to happen in slow motion. I had this heightened sense of reality. I wasn't sure if someone else was going to run up on stage. I can't remember ever being that naked and that terrified.

Michael Arnold. *42nd Street* (Andy Lee) [O], *The Who's Tommy* [O], *A Funny Thing Happened on the Way to the Forum* (Swing) [O], *Little Me* (Belle's Boy/Newsboy) [O], *Cats* (Mr. Mistoffelees), *Cabaret*, *Chicago*, *Martin Guerre** (Benoit), *Busker Alley**, *Durante**

Stage Door Drama

Broadway is weird. You walk a few feet out of the stage door and everyone wants your autograph. You walk a hundred feet or more and nobody knows who you are. I get uncomfortable sometimes when I am asked for my autograph. I know deep down that in five minutes I am going to be on the subway and nobody could care less.

Idina Menzel. *Rent* (Maureen Johnson) [O][t], *Wicked* (Elphaba) [O], *Aida* (Amneris)

During *The Civil War*, there was a group of fans called "Civies." They were an offshoot of "Jeckies," fans of *Jekyll and Hyde*, and "Pimpies," fans of *The Scarlet Pimpernel*. They were fanatics. They would come to every show and want autographs with the exact day written on their *Playbill*. I had my picture taken every night with the same people. I thought, "Don't you have something to do? Don't you have lives?" This went on just about every night for two months.

It was so strange. One moment, I would have fifty people flocking for my autograph. Then I would walk a few blocks to a restaurant and become invisible again.

Michael Lanning. *The Civil War* (Captain Emmett Lochran) [O]

I was followed once. Close to my home. At one point, I had to stop taking the subway that was next to the theater. Instead, I would walk all the way to the East Side just to make sure that people wouldn't follow me home. Often, fans stop thinking that actors are human. They forget that I am a person who needs to go to sleep because I just had three hours of singing and dancing. They want a piece of me—if I fart, and they can catch the stench, they can get a piece of me. Sure, that's a part of being a celebrity, but celebrities have bodyguards. Most Broadway actors don't, and I didn't.

Wilson Heredia. *Rent* (Angel) [O][**T**]

I was in *George White's Scandals* in 1939. I was sixteen years old. I remember that there was a man who came every night and sat in the front row. He brought a diamond bracelet. All he wanted was to give me the bracelet and take me to dinner. I was only sixteen, so of course my mother couldn't allow that to happen. The man still came to see me perform anyway. I don't think he ever missed a show. It was just a different world back then.

Ann Miller. *Sugar Babies* (Ann) [O][t], *George White's Scandals* [O], *Mame* (Mame Dennis)

Backstage Tours

I've always wanted to write a book called *I Met Mel Brooks in My Underwear.* Here is why.

I was doing *Crazy For You* at the Paper Mill Playhouse. Just as I had taken off everything except my underwear, I heard a knocking on my dressing room door.

"Jim, there's someone here that I would like you to meet."

The door swung open, and in walked Mel Brooks.

"You were terrific. Great show. You're funny." He was just full of praise. I just stood there in my underwear, and said, "Thank you, Mr. Brooks. I'm a big fan of yours."

Another time, I was on as Marcellus in *The Music Man.* I shared the floor with Rebecca Luker and Paul Benedict. Since they would never pass by my dressing room, I would leave the door open. One night, when I was wearing nothing else but my underwear, I saw two young kids standing at my door. They were just staring at me with their eyes wide open.

I said, "Hi, kids, looking for somebody?"

They just stared at me. Then I saw Kevin Kline. I was in my underwear! I said, "Hi, Kevin. I'm a big fan of yours!" I shook his hand.

Then Phoebe Cates came in. Meanwhile, I was still looking for my pants.

Jim Walton. *The Music Man* (Harold Hill s/b) [O], *Merrily We Roll Along* (Franklin Shepard) [O], *Sweeney Todd* (Anthony Hope) [O], *Perfectly Frank* [O], *Stardust* [O], *42nd Street* (Billy Lawlor)

One of my nightmares, and unfortunately it happens with great regularity, is having someone show up at the stage door and not know who the hell they are.

"Hello, Geoff. It's so good to see you!"

Meanwhile, I'm thinking, "Who is this person?"

It's embarrassing. Sometimes, I'll just act and say, "Oh, yes! It's so good to see you. How are you? Come on, let me give you a tour." I'll give them a tour, they will leave, and I'll think, "Who the hell was that?"

Geoffrey Blaisdell. *Jekyll & Hyde* (Lord Glossop) [O], *Cyrano—The Musical* (Captain De Castel Jaloux) [O], *Amadeus* (Servant), *Les Misérables** (Javert), *The Phantom of the Opera** (The Auctioneer)

Love Letters

I've been stalked. I've had my garbage gone through. I've had murder confessions on tape sent to me. It's quite disconcerting. All kinds of things have happened. Most people who come to see me are good people, but once in a while, somebody wants something more.

Sam Harris. *The Life* (Jojo) [O] [t], *Grease!* (Doody) [O], *The Producers* (Carmen Ghia), *Joseph and the Amazing Technicolor® Dreamcoat** (Joseph)

During *Sweeney Todd*, I received some very suspicious cards at the theater. Sympathy cards in weird writing with cut-out pasted words saying, *"For whom the bell tolls, it tolls for thee."* And then the letters started coming to my home.

When I went to the police, they told me to make a report. When I asked what good that would do, they said that basically, if he killed me, they would have a file. Nothing ever happened, but for a couple of months, I had a stagehand walk me out of the stage door.

Betsy Joslyn. *High Society* (Patsy) [O], *Sweeney Todd* (Johanna) [O], *The Goodbye Girl* (Paula s/b) [O], *A Doll's Life* (Nora) [O], *A Few Good Men* (Lt. Galloway s/b), *Into the Woods* (The Witch), *Sunday in the Park with George* (Dot), *Les Misérables* (Madame Thénardier), *Beauty and the Beast** (Mrs. Potts), *City of Angels** (Oolie/Donna), *Camelot** (Guenevere), *Of Thee I Sing**, *Let 'em Eat Cake**

When I was in *Smokey Joe's Cafe,* I was being stalked. It scared me to pieces. I was ready to quit the business and leave New York. I wore hats and coats to the theater so no one could recognize me. Policemen had to escort me to a cab because the theater couldn't afford to take me home.

Someone said, "Well, Madonna is being stalked."

I said, "Yeah, on the set of her movie where she has ten security guards and you need proper identification to get anywhere near her."

So there I was, a star on Broadway, all my dreams were coming true, and my biggest fear was happening. I thought, "I can't do this anymore. I have to quit." I went into therapy in order to figure out how to overcome this man who was ruling my life.

It all started with him sending me a fan letter with my picture attached. It was a nice little fan letter from a man who said he was a country-western singer in New Jersey. He wanted me to send a picture. I never did. I simply didn't have time because of the Tony Awards. Then I started getting threatening letters at home. He cursed at me in the letters and told me what he was going to do to me when he got ahold of me.

I had a security system put in my home. It was really expensive. I had to carry my own mace. That was all I could do. Finally, my husband found out who he was. The cops took care of it from there. After several months, it finally stopped.

As a Broadway performer, you are so vulnerable. The minute you step on stage, if someone wants to get you, they can get you. It is not the same as in television and film. A New York paper did an article entitled, "When the Broadway Lights Go Down the Stalkers Come Out." They quoted me in the article saying, "Every night when I come out to shimmy, I wonder if he's there."

My mother called from Houston the next day and said my dad was coming to New York with a gun. It was major. I hadn't told my family because I didn't want them to be afraid.

DeLee Lively. *Smokey Joe's Cafe* [O][t], *A Chorus Line* (Val)

Annie attracted some strange fans. I remember one fan in particular—he was deaf. I found it strange that a deaf man was so taken with a singer. He would send me bicycles, rings, and even fur jackets.

I didn't think anything of it until one night when I was singing at the St. Regis Hotel. He snuck into the hotel with a rifle. The police arrested him, and I had to go to the district attorney and identify him in a lineup.

Several years later, when I was doing *Starlight Express*, I saw him again. He was sitting near the very front of the stage. I remember falling down because I was so shocked to see him. I had to get bodyguards because it got so bad.

Later, he started sending me troll babies from Germany and letters soaked in blood.

Andrea McArdle. *Annie* (Annie) [O][t], *Starlight Express* (Ashley) [O], *State Fair* (Margy Frake) [O], *Les Misérables* (Fantine), *Beauty and the Beast* (Belle), *Cabaret** (Sally Bowles), *Jerry's Girls**

I always have been really friendly with the fans. Sometimes, all people want is to make a connection. When you take the time to say hello, it can make them feel special.

One night, I was playing Jean Valjean on the national tour of *Les Misérables*. We were in San Francisco. When I came out of the stage door, tons of fans were waiting.

One woman approached me and said, "You were so wonderful. Can I give you a hug?"

I said, "Sure." That was the end of that. Or so I thought.

The next day, I received a letter which thanked me for saying hello.

A few days later, I received another letter, which read, "*Les Misérables* is my favorite story and Jean Valjean is my favorite character."

The next night, I received two roses with two cards. One card was addressed to Dave Clemmons; the other card was addressed to Jean Valjean.

The following day, I received two more letters—a letter to me, and a letter to Jean Valjean, this time written in French. And I don't even speak French.

Then, she called backstage at the theater. She said, "I belong to a group that believes the world is going to end. There are too many cataclysmic events going on right now. We are moving to a place near Little Rock, Arkansas. There, we can find the best crystal deposits. The crystals are going to protect us. Once I move there, I'll be cut off from society. I'll never have a chance to see the show again. I'm coming to the show one last time. I have a final request. After the show, before you take your wig and makeup off, could you please come outside and give me a hug as Jean Valjean?"

I said, "No, no, no."

She kept calling. It drove me crazy.

Finally, I said, "Fine. Before I take my wig off, I will run out of the stage door and give you a hug." Why I consented to this request, I will never know.

So, on the appointed night, I ran out of the stage door to say a final goodbye to this woman. Once I arrived in her arms, she just kept hugging me, almost chanting, "Goodbye, Jean Valjean. Goodbye, Jean Valjean." I thought she was going to pull out a gun and shoot me on the spot, or take me with her.

Finally, it was over. Or so I thought.

Once again, I was wrong. Somehow, she proceeded to get the backstage numbers to theaters across the country. All of a sudden, in a random town, I received a call backstage. A crew guy picked up the phone. Not knowing anything about "the situation," he said, "Oh, Dave, he's right here."

I picked up the phone.

"Can we have lunch?"

"This week I have to do all eight shows. Sorry."

Then, a stagehand told her where I was staying. She called my hotel.

"How did you get this number?"

"Oh, I talked to a stagehand and he told me. Can we go have breakfast?"

"No."

The next stop on the tour was Little Rock. We were staying at a hotel outside the city limits. I registered under a different name. I told everyone, "If you see anybody who wants anything to do with me, you don't know who I am."

She showed up at the stage door, pleading, "Let me follow the bus and go to your room with you."

I said, "No. I can't do that. Bye!"

She literally ran down the street chasing the bus. That was the last I ever saw of her.

Dave Clemmons. *The Scarlet Pimpernel* (Ben) [O], *The Civil War* (Sergeant Virgil Frank/Auctioneer's Assistant) [O], *Les Misérables* (Jean Valjean), *Whistle Down the Wind**, *Jekyll & Hyde** (Bishop)

I had just taken over the role of Javert in *Les Misérables* on the Broadway national tour. We were in Boston. I was twenty-nine years old and I didn't have an agent.

One day, a fruit basket was sent to my dressing room. The note read, *"Fine performance in Les Misérables, Robert. I am doing some PBS television now. Best regards."* It was an enormous fruit basket, apparently from a famous, Oscar-winning actress. It was unbelievable.

I wrote back saying, *"If you are the famous actress, I am incredibly flattered. If not, thank you so much."*

A few days later, I received another note. It read, *"I was with the actress. I am her niece. I freelance with William Morris, ICM, and a few other talent agencies in Boston. Would you like to get together and talk?"* I was hitting it big.

She took me to a great restaurant in Boston. She was a thin, bird-like woman in her fifties. She was very well dressed. One of the first things she said was, "You don't look like him." She was referring to Javert.

"Well, those wigs do wonders," I said. I thought she was funny.

"I think you are incredible and I want to represent you. I think you have a big future ahead of you." She dropped names of people at ICM and William Morris. She said that she was also a lawyer. Next, she asked me if I would be interested in doing a Dewar's Profile. At the time, Dewar's was running an advertising campaign for up-and-coming people.

Les Misérables. Photo credit: Joan Marcus/Photofest

"Yeah, that would be great!" She said it would pay $5,000.

We went out to dinner a few more times, and I did the Dewar's Profile. She gave me a check. It cleared.

The *Les Misérables* tour left for Washington. The woman told me the Dewar's Profile was debuting in Los Angeles. She told me exactly where I could find it. For some reason, I was starting to grow suspicious. I called a friend, who called several agencies that were supposedly running the ad. They had never heard of me.

I remember feeling like I had been raped. This woman was not the person she said she was. It was unbelievable. I didn't know anything about her besides what she had told me. Meanwhile, I had told everyone that I was doing a Dewar's Profile. I was embarrassed. And then I got a little scared. I had signed a contract with this woman.

Finally, she called.

"Listen," I said. "I know the ad is not coming out."

In a very threatening tone, she said, "Don't you know what I've done for you? How can you be so ungrateful?" I remember being very grateful that I was in Washington and she was in Boston.

I said, "I have another agent now. I don't think this relationship is going to work. Thank you so much for all of your help."

A week later, just after I finished the Javert suicide scene in *Les Misérables*, I went to check my mail backstage in the National Theater. I was shirtless, and my hair was a mess. When I turned around, she was standing there, right in front of me, deep inside the theater.

She started speaking nonsense. "You should be wearing glasses. Why aren't you wearing glasses? You are much more intelligent than that." Crazy stuff. It absolutely freaked me out. She then said, "We have to have dinner."

I said, "My niece is in town. I can't. Sorry."

Somehow, I managed to get her out of the theater.

During our stay in Washington, I received many fan letters. One day, I opened one from the Washington Hilton. It quoted *Macbeth* and said, *"You are going to be covered in blood tonight."* No one signed it.

I simply didn't know what to do. I was a thirty-year-old man and there was a fifty-year-old woman scaring the hell out of me. I kept it a secret for a while. But then I received more letters—crazy, gibberish, five-page, single-spaced letters of psychological babble. In many of the letters, certain words appeared, such as *"blood," "bloodshed,"* or *"Make sure you don't harm her . . . I'll have to take action if you harm her."*

The letters soon turned into faxes and telegrams.

And then she started calling me at two, three, and four in the morning. She would try to disguise her voice. It was incredibly threatening.

There was a scene in *Les Misérables* where Javert was tied up at a barricade. My hands were behind my back, and Jean Valjean would fire a shot into the air. I thought that's when she would try to kill me. She would even write in her letters, *"I am going to have to do it tonight."* I couldn't even avoid reading her letters because she sent them from different places with different names and with different postmarks.

When I made my Broadway debut, she sent letters to Cameron Mackintosh and Alan Wasser, the general manager. *"I saw the show and I want my money back because of Robert."*

People began asking me, "What have you done to this lady?" I remember feeling helpless.

Finally, I retained a lawyer. The situation was messing up my life and my career. I went to Boston and I served her with papers for a temporary restraining order. I had to go to court. It cost me thousands of dollars. The management of *Les Misérables* did very little to help.

In the courtroom, I was white as a ghost. I remember shaking and being terrified that she would try to kill me.

She approached the judge.

"My gosh, I went to university with your daughter."

I thought that was it. She duped me for months. She pretended to be somebody she wasn't, and she was brilliant at it. She announced that she was representing herself. She said that she had a law degree.

My lawyer began by showing some of the letters that contained her threats. She was submitting stuff into evidence as well. She had a big stack of stuff.

And then, she stood up in front of the judge and announced, "Robert raped me. I have several affidavits from people who saw him pull me out into the alley and rape me."

I wanted to jump out of my skin. For a second, I thought I would be arrested.

Then I remembered, "I'm gay. For God's sake, I am gay! I can prove I have a boyfriend. I can dispute this. I can fight this. This is insane."

Then she said that she went to a doctor. She submitted more papers to the court. I couldn't believe it. She went on and on until it reached a point that, once again, I thought I would be arrested. There was nothing I could do.

Finally, she said, "I have a picture I want to show the court. It's me. It's me. It was taken a few years ago. I was very forlorn. I was very sad in the picture, but I would like to submit it." She proceeded to pull out the *Les Misérables* logo with the young Cosette illustration.

The judge granted me the order of protection right then and there.

Robert DuSold. *Les Misérables* (Javert), *Jekyll & Hyde* (Archbishop of
Basingstoke), *Kiss of the Spider Woman* (Marcos), *Cats** (Deuteronomy),
*The Phantom of the Opera** (André), *Chicago** (Little Mary Sunshine s/b),
*Showboat** (Pete)

The Ultimate Payoff

I was with the national tour of *Les Misérables* and we were performing in Salt Lake City. At the time, we were doing the poster sales for Broadway Cares/Equity Fights AIDS. If someone donated $50, they would receive a poster signed by the entire cast.

After one performance, I was in costume selling posters in the lobby. I noticed a little girl who was looking at me like I was the Messiah. I heard her say, "Please, Mom, please, please, can I have a poster? Please, oh, please, please, please?" Her mom said no, and they walked away. It was a moment I will never forget. In my left ear, quite distinctly, I heard a little whisper. It said, "Go, Doug, go."

Suddenly, without giving it any more thought, I took off in full costume outside the theater. After walking through the crowds, I saw the girl and her mother down the block. They had already crossed the street. As I was running down the street in my *Les Misérables* costume, I thought that I was so busted. But I didn't really care.

As I approached the girl, I said, "Excuse me." She turned around, and just stared.

"You forgot your poster." I handed her a poster, and I was gone.

I turned around and ran back to the theater before anyone could say anything. I went to the company manager's office and I said, "I gave one of the posters away. Here is fifty dollars, my contribution to Broadway Cares."

A few days later, there was a letter that showed up on the callboard. It read:

"*Dear cast of* Les Misérables, *you moved me so much. Thank you. I also want to thank you for giving my daughter this poster. I don't know who you were, but it was a nice young man, and he was gone before anyone could say thank you. Let me tell you a little about my daughter. She is sick. She was not expected to live past a very young age. She always wanted to see* Les Misérables. *They even snuck her out of the hospital that night so she could see the show. The tickets were a gift from a family friend. I am a single mom. Money is very tight. It broke my heart to not be able to buy the poster for my daughter. Thank you so much, whoever you are. Thank you, thank you, thank you.*"

The whole cast was standing around weeping. I didn't say a word.

Four years later, the night before *The Scarlet Pimpernel* closed, I remember being bitter and jaded. Soon, I would be unemployed again. Out of nowhere, at the stage door, I heard a little voice.

"Mr. Storm?"

I thought, "Oh, God, who's calling me 'Mr. Storm,' for crying out loud?" I looked down. I froze. It was that same little girl.

"Hi. I knew you were in the show because I've been following it on the Internet. I brought you a little package. Here's a card."

"Oh, my gosh, how are you doing? Do you want to come in? Are you seeing the show tonight?"

"No," she said. "I'm not seeing the show tonight. I'm seeing it tomorrow. I'm seeing the last one."

I said, "Why don't you come around tomorrow before the show? I'll take you backstage."

I went upstairs and started putting on my makeup. I stopped for a second to read her card. "*I just want to let you know that I've just been accepted to NYU Tisch School of the Arts for Drama, and I'm going to enroll because someday I want to give a kid a poster. Thank you for helping shape my life.*"

I lost it. In a moment of my own despair and selfish jaded bitterness, there was that kid. Everything came full circle. That alone is why I got into this business.

Doug Storm. *Dance of the Vampires* [O], *The Scarlet Pimpernel* (Leggett), *Les Misérables* (Feuilly)

PART FIVE

THE SECRET LIFE

CHAPTER 11

The Broadway Lifestyle

Once the curtain comes up on a Broadway stage, the audience is transported into a world of glamour and extravagance, where every detail is attended to and actors perform to full houses and receive standing ovations. For many, excluding those mentioned in the previous chapter, this may be their only contact with a Broadway performer. Many assume that the glamour of the performance itself extends beyond the stage, into the dressing rooms, and into the homes of Broadway's stars.

However, the sights and sounds of a Broadway stage can be deceiving. While the stars of Hollywood perform in immaculate studios and live in million-dollar mansions, the stars of Broadway live a much more humble existence. The glamour that many expect to find backstage is nowhere to be found. Often, dressing rooms are not dotted with gold stars but with rat droppings. Even the air can be difficult to breathe.

And unless you are a Hollywood celebrity, don't expect to find million-dollar deals on Broadway. Even when starring in a new show, performers remain in cramped and claustrophobic apartments. Shows can suddenly close, and performers need to be prepared for the worst. Some continue working as waiters. Others take on jobs as secretaries or salesmen. Many continue to audition for other Broadway shows. The harsh reality is that, once Broadway dreams come true, there is often just enough money to get by.

Furthermore, since performers only "work" three hours a day, many assume that a life on Broadway is a life of leisure, consisting of relaxing in lavish apartments and socializing with the rich and famous. A life on Broadway, however, can be very demanding. The pressure of putting on a new show can be intense, and many personal sacrifices must be made. For many, just staying healthy in a long-running show can become a twenty-four-hour job. Welcome to Broadway.

Take the Elevator to the Third Floor

I was raised in the San Fernando Valley and had never been to New York. After I was cast in my first Broadway show, *Starlight Express*, I remember the first time I got out of the subway and saw the Gershwin Theater. I found the address, looked up, and saw that the theater was at the bottom of an office building. I had a romantic idea of seeing a big, magnificent, beautiful theater. While there were some signs on the side of the building reading *Starlight Express*, they were dwarfed by the signs of the office building. That threw me for a loop.

When I found the stage door, there were trashcans all over. It looked like the entrance where they took out the trash. It looked like an old tenement. As you walked in the stage door, there was the freight elevator for the building.

I introduced myself to the old man at the door, who was older than time and as sweet as can be. He welcomed me and said, "Take the elevator to the theater." I thought, "I have to take the elevator to the theater? Don't you just walk in?"

I took the elevator, and suddenly I was backstage. It was dark, with ropes and pulleys. It was not how I had pictured it. My dressing room was a cement block inside a fifty-story building on the third level of what they call a theater. It was a huge letdown. It was very industrial. It wasn't magical.

Robert Torti. *Starlight Express* (Greaseball) [O][t], *Joseph and the Amazing Technicolor° Dreamcoat* (Pharaoh) [O]

Call the Cleaning Lady

Barnum was my first big Broadway show. I played Tom Thumb. For my grand entrance, I was magically revealed from behind a chair in the center of the stage. To get there without the audience noticing, I literally had to crawl behind the lighting. It was dirty and dusty. The only way to get there was to crawl on my hands and knees.

That was when I realized that Broadway isn't a glamorous business. It appears glamorous from the seats, but when you get down to it, it is just work. It is great work, but it is hard work, and it isn't so glamorous when you are doing it.

Ray Roderick. *Grind* (Knockabout) [O], *A Funny Thing Happened on the Way to the Forum* (Protean) [O], *Crazy For You* (Billy) [O], *Wind in the Willows* [O], *Cats* (Carbucketty), *Barnum** (Tom Thumb)

The state of the theaters shocked me. It is amazing that the theaters are in such bad condition. I don't understand it. If you go to the National

Theater in Spain, you can literally eat off the floor. Here, the theaters are falling apart. They need serious improvement. I think anybody on Broadway would agree with me. It is like the star on a Christmas tree. It shines very much in front, but if you look in back, it is just paper. It is the nature of our business.

Antonio Banderas. *Nine* (Guido Contini) [O][t]

I remember the first day I walked into the Imperial Theater, where *Les Misérables* was performed. I was so excited. And then I walked into the basement where everyone got ready; it was a slate floor basement with lockers. It looked like a junior high school that was about to be condemned. It was a horror. It was like walking into a sweatshop where people made clothing.

There were cages. Everything was layered in about half an inch of dust. All of the dust from the stage would come through the cracks of the orchestra pit and pour into the basement area. People would stand under fluorescent lights, covered in dust, and apply their makeup using a little piece of mirror on the side of a junior high school locker. When I saw that, I realized that Broadway was not going to be what I had imagined.

Craig Rubano. *The Scarlet Pimpernel* (Armand St. Just s/b) [O], *Les Misérables* (Marius)

People think the life of a Broadway performer is glamorous. It is anything but. The dressing rooms are awful. They are hideous. The pipes bang when the water runs. Nobody has redone or rethought the bathroom situation. Everyone uses the bathrooms like they are in a dorm. The windows are nailed shut and are filthy. The air conditioners are just grimy. God knows what they have in the ducts of the air conditioning, which have been there for something like fifty years. We all catch these weird diseases in our lungs that nobody else seems to get.

The curtains themselves need to be taken outside, beaten to death, and then put back up because of the dust which comes down every time they drop. You have to go to your ENT doctor about ten times a year to get something just to keep you going—whether it's for allergies, mold, or some kind of weird infection.

Faith Prince. *Guys and Dolls* (Miss Adelaide) [O][T], *Bells are Ringing* (Elle Peterson) [O][t], *Jerome Robbins' Broadway* (Ma/Tessie) [O], *Noises Off* (Belinda Blair) [O], *Nick and Nora* (Lorraine Bixby) [O], *What's Wrong with This Picture?* (Shirley) [O], *Little Me* (Belle) [O], *The King and I* (Anna), *James Joyce's The Dead* (Gretta Conroy)

The Gershwin Theater is not well kept. Backstage, layers of soot cover the place. You can even see it clinging to the walls. It looks as if the theater is never cleaned. There were times when the bathrooms weren't even cleaned. It smelled gross and it looked gross. They didn't care about our health. Once, I even had to fight the stage manager to get more toilet paper for the bathroom so I could swab around the toilet. It is nasty.

Joseph Cassidy. *1776* (Leather Apron) [O], *Showboat* (Ravenal u/s) [O], *Les Misérables* (Courfeyrac)

In so many of the Broadway theaters I have been in, there are mice. When I was in *Les Misérables,* we would come into our tiny dressing room and the mice would have gotten into any food that we had hidden in boxes. Their droppings were all over. There were dropping in our make-up. There were droppings in our costumes. There were droppings in everything.

Kerry Butler. *Little Shop of Horrors* (Audrey) [O], *Hairspray* (Penny Pingleton) [O], *Blood Brothers* (Donna Marie u/s) [O], *Beauty and the Beast* (Belle), *Les Misérables* (Eponine)

The porters used to kill rats during *Grease!.* The rats would get caught in glue traps. Sometimes, in the middle of the show, the porters would put a box on top of a rat and stomp on the box. This happened during a Broadway show! One time, I was downstairs and I heard this squealing. It was awful.

Hunter Foster. *Little Shop of Horrors* (Seymour) [O], *Urinetown* (Bobby Strong) [O], *Footloose* (Bickle) [O], *King David* [O], *Grease!* (Roger) [O], *Les Misérables* (Marius u/s), *Martin Guerre** (Martin u/s), *Cats** (Rum Tum Tugger)

Misconceptions

People outside the theater community don't understand what it means to be a working Broadway actor. Nor should they. Often, after I tell people I am a dancer, they ask, "Oh, a go-go dancer?" I've gotten that my whole career. People look at the life of a Broadway performer in a sleazy, judgmental way.

People still ask me, "What do you do during the day?"

"You only have to work a couple of hours a night, right?"

"You have the days off, right?"

Michael Arnold. *42nd Street* (Andy Lee) [O], *The Who's Tommy* [O], *A Funny Thing Happened on the Way to the Forum* (Swing) [O], *Little Me* (Belle's Boy/Newsboy) [O], *Cats* (Mr. Mistoffelees), *Cabaret, Chicago, Martin Guerre** (Benoit), *Busker Alley*, Durante**

Since I was fifteen years old, it has been my passion to perform in front of people. It was a big dream for me to come here and be in a Broadway musical, but you never suspect how hard it is once you get inside. You have to become very disciplined in order to enjoy the experience. If you are not disciplined, then you can start to have problems with your voice, and you can start having problems physically. You have to carry a cross on your shoulders all the time when you go into the theater. It is the sacrifice one must make. It is a big challenge. It is not an easy thing.

I feel a great deal of respect for every performer on Broadway. If I commit to something, I commit fully. Tonight is the 184th performance of *Nine*, and I haven't missed a show yet. I wanted to really live this business fully, without trying to cheat or anything like that. I want to make a statement because Hollywood actors come here and go away. I like to live like everybody on Broadway—sometimes suffering physically, having low energy, but knowing you have to go on stage and play.

Antonio Banderas. *Nine* (Guido Contini) [O][t]

My first voice teacher said, "Because people go to the theater in their downtime and they are relaxed, they equate performing with leisure." My teacher was right. No matter how much people look at the stage and logically know that performers are working, they still equate theater with recreation. Also, it is our job to make people feel like it is easy. The easier we make it look, the harder we are working.

The biggest misconception is that we only work three hours a day. People don't realize that, as singers, we are working from the moment we get up in the morning. Our whole day is geared towards that performance.

I didn't know any other way to do a great job in *Les Misérables* other than to live in a bubble. I stayed in a hotel near the theater. All I did was eat, sleep, and vocalize. When I would arrive at the theater, people would ask me what I had done that day. I would wonder what they meant. There was nothing else but *Les Misérables* in my world.

Deborah Gibson. *Cabaret* (Sally Bowles), *Les Misérables* (Eponine), *Beauty and the Beast* (Belle), *Grease!* (Rizzo), *Joseph and the Amazing Technicolor® Dreamcoat** (Narrator)

A Twenty-Four-Hour Job

I can do almost anything on very little sleep, except for sing. Performing on Broadway is the first thing I have ever done where my sleep is mandatory—eight hours every night. Before Broadway, I existed on four to six hours my whole life.

When I am performing on Broadway, my day is all about making sure my voice is okay. I get up, monitor it, and make sure I am eating the right things. I go to the gym, steam, and see if I need to check in with the doctor. You become strangely panicked. You can't get a cold. Your day becomes about trying to rejuvenate yourself enough to be able to give 100 percent come 8:00 P.M. I stopped having lunch with people. I was talking too much. I stopped calling people on the phone.

Brooke Shields. *Cabaret* (Sally), *Grease!* (Rizzo)

It is not an easy life. When I was on Broadway, I was exhausted by the time Monday rolled around, and I had no personal life. After Sunday matinees, I was so tired that I'd have an early dinner and go to bed. I'd stay in bed all day Monday, only to roll out of bed and have dinner again. Then, on Tuesday, I was back on stage.

I had no real beau or personal life of any kind. I knew the folks in the show. I just knew them. That was my life. It was like being a nun. I couldn't talk or laugh too much because it would strain my voice. It was like being in a monastery.

Ann Miller. *Sugar Babies* (Ann) [O][t], *George White's Scandals* [O], *Mame* (Mame Dennis)

When I was starring in *Hairspray*, I lived like a nun. I lived in a bubble. I rarely went to any of the parties. The parties I attended were opening night things that I would go to for ten minutes, and leave.

Also, I couldn't go outside. I took a cab if I had to travel more than two blocks because I was so scared of getting sick. I was constantly living in fear. I would even wake up in the middle of the night and sing a couple of lines just to see if my voice was still there—and then try to fall back asleep.

I thought, "If I get a cold, I am screwed. I could be out for a week. If I develop nodes, I could be out for even longer."

Basically, it was a year of complete panic.

We were in Seattle with the show before we came to Broadway. Although it was June, I remember wearing a thick winter trench coat. I couldn't drink. I couldn't smoke. I missed the whole "bonding thing" with the cast because I wasn't going out. I wasn't doing anything. I had no life.

Worse yet, I couldn't call anybody back for a year. The greeting on my answering machine literally said, "Here's my e-mail address. E-mail me. I cannot talk on the phone. Sorry." It even got to the point where I didn't talk to my parents for three months. The only time I talked was during the show and for the press. There was just so much pressure.

Marissa Jaret Winokur. *Hairspray* (Tracy Turnblad) [O][T], *Grease!* (Jan)

When I am performing on Broadway, I don't speak the entire morning. I just stay home. I may go to the park and run to keep myself in shape. I might come back to the hotel and take a sauna and eat light before the play. I read, go on my computer, call Spain and speak to my family. I get to the theater almost two hours before the show starts. I put on my make-up and get ready for the play. After the play, I go straight home. I don't go to clubs or dinners because I am very afraid of losing my voice and I want to be in shape all the time. That is a normal day.

I have had no normal days lately. I have been promoting movies at the same time that I am starring on Broadway. One morning, I was at NBC at 9:00 A.M. talking like hell, and then I had to do fifteen interviews until 3:00 in the afternoon and eat something very fast. I do some vocal exercises and eat candy in order to keep my voice the way it has to be. I come to the theater, perform, and the next day, do the same thing. That is how I have been living for the past couple of weeks because I have a couple of movies coming that I had to promote. There is no way I could escape from that. It has been a little bit tough these days, but I really think it is all a matter of will.

I complain sometimes. "Oh, my God, what am I going to do?" I don't want to be a fraud for the audience. They deserve exactly the same treatment every night. I'm going to give them that. Sometimes I get upset with myself that I didn't go 100 percent, because I couldn't. I just didn't have the energy. I have this kind of continuous fight with myself to give them exactly what I think they paid for.

Antonio Banderas. *Nine* (Guido Contini) [O][t]

When I see pictures of myself during the time I was in *Les Misérables*, I look like one of the peasants from the show. Literally. I had dark circles under my eyes because I was so exhausted. The show was three hours and ten minutes long, and I had to die on stage every night. I was tired all the time.

Randy Graff. *City of Angels* (Oolie) [O][T], *A Class Act* (Sophie) [O][t], *Les Misérables* (Fantine) [O], *Moon over Buffalo* (Rosalind) [O], *High Society* (Liz Imbrie) [O], *Laughter on the 23rd Floor* (Carol), *Saravà* (Rosalia) [O], *Fiddler on the Roof* (Golde) [O], *Grease!* (Rizzo u/s), *Falsettos* (Trina)

I auditioned for the tenth-anniversary production of *Les Misérables*. I was doing *A Christmas Carol* at the time. I was in the middle of a three-show day when I went in for the audition. We had an 11:00 A.M., a 2:00 P.M., and a 5:00 P.M. show. I was trying to make it to the audition, do some Christmas shopping, and perform all three shows in the same day.

During the audition, as I sang, "Now life has killed the dream I dreamed," I passed out on the floor. I had a panic or anxiety attack. At the end of the song, I felt my chest tense up and my heart beat really hard. I couldn't get air. I sort of lost consciousness. Cameron Mackintosh, Trevor Nunn, and John Caird just sat there and looked at me. They thought it was part of my act. They thought I was being dramatic.

Finally, someone said, "Oh, my God, she's not moving. Go get her a glass of water." They all jumped up and ran over.

Emily Skinner. *Side Show* (Daisy Hilton) [O][t], *The Full Monty* (Vicki Nichols) [O], *James Joyce's The Dead* (Mary Jane Morkan) [O], *Jekyll & Hyde* (Emma u/s) [O], *Dinner at Eight* (Kitty Packard) [O]

Only Human

I had been down to Ground Zero, and I had been doing all the press for *Cabaret,* and finally it took its toll. I went to sing a note in the song "Maybe this Time," and my voice just cut off. I pretended like I was crying.

I spoke the rest of the song, navigated through it, pretending that it was simply too much for Sally to handle in this vulnerable moment of her life. When I made it backstage, I started crying for real. The next day, when I went to the doctor, she told me not to do the show that night. I was in a panic, and no one in my life accepted it. They thought I was being "dramatic."

Brooke Shields. *Cabaret* (Sally), *Grease!* (Rizzo)

We did a lot of press during *Side Show*. They had us on just about every early-morning television show. We didn't have any days off. There was simply no vocal recovery time. I remember the day when we sang on the *Rosie O'Donnell Show*. We had finished our performance the night before at 11:15 P.M. I had to get up at 6:00 A.M. to make it to the television studio by 7:00 A.M. During the sound check, I felt something happen.

I went home and took a nap. When I woke up, I had nothing—just air. I went to the doctor in the afternoon. She said, "You can't do the show. You burst a blood vessel. I'm putting you on steroids and you have to be on vocal rest for the next few weeks."

She called the company manager. The company manager said, "What are you talking about? She can't be out of the show. We don't have understudy costumes. She has to be here!" Nothing was coming out, except for air.

They had to close the show for a night. They lost a lot of money. It was mortifying. No matter how terrific your technique, some roles you can't do eight times a week. You just can't.

Emily Skinner. *Side Show* (Daisy Hilton) [O][t], *The Full Monty* (Vicki Nichols) [O], *James Joyce's The Dead* (Mary Jane Morkan) [O], *Jekyll & Hyde* (Emma u/s) [O], *Dinner at Eight* (Kitty Packard) [O]

I've seen people in my company go on stage sick, in pain, or with a knee or hip injury. They come to work every night pretending that they are all right in front of the audience. They are very special people. They know self-sacrifice. They know that in order to entertain, you have to actually go into a kind of suffering experience. It doesn't matter if I feel like hell. When I come to the stage, even if I have a fever, I forget about it.

Antonio Banderas. *Nine* (Guido Contini) [O][t]

When I was performing on Broadway, my skin was breaking out from the smoke or from the lack of sunlight in the building, or who knows what. My knees were shot and I was wearing an orthopedic brace to keep my patellae in place. I took an expectorant every day to clear the phlegm from my throat, which was likely caused by something in the theater. I was in physical therapy and had an MRI. I frequently went to the dermatologist and the throat and nose doctor. I was on steroids.

Craig Rubano. *The Scarlet Pimpernel* (Armand St. Just s/b) [O], *Les Misérables* (Marius)

Not for the Money

My first Broadway show was *They're Playing our Song*. Six months into the run, I realized that I wasn't making enough money to cover my bills. I wasn't even spending a lot of money. I wasn't buying clothes or anything. I was just barely making enough to get by. Once, when I was thinking about getting a job as a late-night singing waitress to cover my bills, Robert Klein said, "That's crazy. You're on Broadway." There I was, on Broadway, and I was barely making enough to live.

Donna Murphy. *Passion* (Fosca) [O][T], *The King and I* (Anna) [O][T], *Wonderful Town* (Ruth) [O], *The Mystery of Edwin Drood* [O], *The Human Comedy* (Bess Macauley u/s) [O], *Privates on Parade* [O], *They're Playing our Song* (Swing)

I know people on Broadway who have sales jobs during the day and are in a Broadway show at night. They work as notaries and legal secretaries. The only glamour of Broadway is what you see on the stage. There is little glitter and tinsel to the life of a Broadway performer. There's probably not a ton of it for a Broadway star.

Go back sixty years, and there was probably a lot more glitter. I'm sure Carol Channing was the belle of the town. Now, you can be "the belle of the town" on the west side of New York from 38th Street to 57th Street. If you are the lead in a new hit show, you can be treated very well in any restaurant. But that's about it.

Jason Alexander. *Jerome Robbins' Broadway* (Emcee) [O][T], *Merrily We Roll Along* (Joe) [O], *The Rink* (Lino/Lenny/Punk/Uncle Fausto) [O], *Broadway Bound* (Stanley) [O], *Accomplice* [O], *The Producers** (Max Bialystock)

I did a Broadway show where the producers bounced so many checks that I didn't have enough money to get home. I remember standing on the stage in a beautiful expensive dress, singing a beautiful song in front of a full house, thinking, "These people will never know that I don't have enough money to get home." It was one of those moments where the glamour and the reality came face-to-face.

> **Jessica Molaskey.** *Dream* (Performer) [O], *Parade* (Mrs. Phagan) [O], *Crazy For You* (Irene Roth u/s) [O], *Oklahoma!* [O], *Chess*, *The Who's Tommy* (Mrs. Walker), *Les Misérables* (Madame Thénardier u/s), *Cats* (Jellylorum u/s), *Falsettos**, *City of Angels**, *Joseph and the Amazing Technicolor® Dreamcoat**

I was hired to replace the lead in *Carnival!* They took pictures of me and put my name over the title at the Imperial Theater.

About two months later, I got a bill from a sign company in Paramus, New Jersey.

I asked, "What is this?"

They said, "That is for putting your name over the title."

The company manager had billed me for the cost of putting that sign up because it was not in my contract. They just asked me if I had wanted my name up there and I said, "Of course." I took it to the union and lost.

> **Anita Gillette.** *Chapter Two* (Jennie Malone) [O][t], *Guys and Dolls* (Sarah Brown) [O], *Kelly* (Angela Crane) [O], *Carnival!* (Gypsy) [O], *All American* (Susan) [O], *Mr. President* (Leslie Henderson) [O], *Jimmy* (Betty Compton) [O], *Don't Drink the Water* (Susan Hollander) [O], *Gypsy* (Thelma), *Brighton Beach Memoirs* (Blanche), *They're Playing Our Song* (Sonia Walsk), *Cabaret* (Sally)

Moonlighting

I was working evenings at the Hyatt when I was cast in *Gypsy*, my first Broadway show. I was only hired to replace a guy who was injured. I was only going to have the Broadway gig for two weeks. I thought that I had better not leave the job at the Hyatt. I told the hotel manager, "Look, I am going to run over, do a Broadway show, and then come back to the hotel and close up." That is exactly what I did.

> **Cory English.** *A Funny Thing Happened on the Way to the Forum* (Protean) [O], *Guys and Dolls* (Brandy Bottle Bates) [O], *Hello, Dolly!* (Barnaby Tucker) [O], *Damn Yankees* (Bubba) [O], *Gypsy* (St. Paul)

I was the "summer vacation swing" in *Les Misérables*. They would call me a day before they needed me and I would do the show. One Friday, the stage manager could not reach me. On Saturday, when I was serving eggs benedict at Marlowe, a restaurant in the theater district, the stage manager suddenly came in and said, "Someone is missing. You have to perform this afternoon."

I finished working brunch, and at 1:20 P.M. ran over to the theater. I did the afternoon show. After the performance, I ran back to Marlowe and worked for another two and a half hours. Then, I ran back to *Les Misérables* and did the night show, only to return to Marlowe and finish up.

David Josefsberg. *Les Misérables* (Marius u/s), *Grease!* (Doody)

Homes of the Stars

I am working with fantastically talented ladies on Broadway, and yet they have to do unbelievable exercises with their money in order to pay for their apartments. I know the realities. There is not so much money going out to the Broadway performer. The reason is because musical theater is so expensive. There is the orchestra, the technicians, the performers, and the theater itself, so there are an incredible amount of things to pay for. There's not so much money at the end of the month to share with everybody. It's a different world than in the movies. In the movies, people live in mansions because they can make a living. They make a big amount of money. It is not so glamorous on Broadway.

Yet it is good for the audience to think that we are glamorous. It is good for them to think that the actors live in mansions. It would be horrendous if people came to Broadway thinking that we are a bunch of people searching to pay our rent and barely making it at the end of the month. People would be sitting in the seats thinking, "Poor guys." We don't want that. We want to entertain and pretend to be a certain way.

Antonio Banderas. *Nine* (Guido Contini) [O][t]

I always had the same apartment while I was performing on Broadway. My whole career was in that apartment. The bathroom was so small that there wasn't even a sink. If I bent over too far, I would burn my rear end on the heater.

I used to have so many mice, but I didn't want to kill them in the traps. I couldn't bear hearing them squeal in the middle of the night. So instead, I would catch them in baggies, stick them in the freezer, and hypothermia them to death. I figured that was the best way to go about it.

Jessica Molaskey. *Dream* (Performer) [O], *Parade* (Mrs. Phagan) [O], *Crazy For You* (Irene Roth u/s) [O], *Oklahoma!* [O], *Chess*, *The Who's Tommy* (Mrs. Walker), *Les Misérables* (Madame Thénardier u/s), *Cats* (Jellylorum u/s), *Falsettos**, *City of Angels**, *Joseph and the Amazing Technicolor* Dreamcoat**

In my old New York apartment, as you walked in the front door, on the right were two doors that looked like a hall closet, and yet, it was a kitchen. There was a half-refrigerator shoved under the counter. In this refrigerator I could fit a head of lettuce, a jug of milk, a carton of orange juice, and maybe an egg. Then it would be full.

The entire kitchen sink was basically the size of a tiny bathroom sink. It had a little slice of countertop where you could put a dish rack and another slice of countertop where you could put a coffee pot. That was it. It was completely claustrophobic.

There was only one window in the place, and it looked onto a brick wall. There was absolutely no light. There was one closet, and since it was a sublet, someone else's stuff was hanging in it. There was probably two feet of space on the hanging bar for all of our clothes.

We slept on a loft. I remember torturing my husband during the time I was on the *Les Misérables* tour and he was living in the apartment alone. I would call him at 3:00 A.M., knowing that he would have to hurl himself off the loft to answer the phone. It was a cruel joke. It sucked if you had to use the bathroom. Forget it. If you missed the ladder, you were dead.

I couldn't believe that we were Broadway stars. I had a leading role on Broadway and we were living in this apartment.

Sarah Uriarte Berry. *Taboo* (Nicola) [O], *Les Misérables* (Eponine), *Beauty and the Beast* (Belle), *Sunset Boulevard** (Betty Schaeffer), *Carousel** (Julie Jordan)

When I was in *Dance of the Vampires*, it marked my ten-year anniversary of when I moved to New York to become a superstar. There I was, ten years later, having already been in *Les Misérables*, coming home to a tiny shoebox apartment. I would walk into the apartment and, literally right above my head, where there was supposed to be a ceiling, there was the loft. That was my bed.

The apartment was in the theater district across from my favorite bar, Marlowe. So, I would suck down my hooch, roll myself across the street, and lock up in my shoebox. The place was almost no bigger than a box that most people keep their jewelry in and shove under their bed at night.

And the worst part was, I had a roommate. We were living like we were in the Navy. I had my bunk and he had his. We had the television suspended from the ceiling because there was no room to put it anywhere else. We had a tiny little computer and a stove that looked like it was manufactured by Betty Crocker. It was electric. It was terrible. It plugged into an outlet. It was one step above a hot plate. We couldn't even really cook on it. Basically, I would have to cook my soup in a thimble.

There I was, living in this apartment with my buddy who was nominated for a Drama Desk Award opposite Nathan Lane, wondering, "God damn, how many pennies do I have? Do I have enough for a beer? Can I bum a smoke?"

Doug Storm. *Dance of the Vampires* [O], *The Scarlet Pimpernel* (Leggett), *Les Misérables* (Feuilly)

When I was starring in *The Civil War* on Broadway, I lived in four different apartments. I was moving my stuff around constantly. It was a nightmare. One of the places I lived was on 50th Street and Eleventh Avenue. Basically, it was a shack. And, as a part of the deal when I rented the place, I had to take care of a dirty sick cat for a few months.

It was a tiny studio apartment which had a kitchenette in the bedroom. That was it. Not counting a small bathroom, that was the whole apartment.

And then there was this sick cat throwing up hairballs everywhere. I felt sorry for the poor thing. Although I gave it medicine every day, it was barely staying alive. Even worse, it shat everywhere. Not just a little bit. There was diarrhea, everywhere. It was awful. After each Broadway show, on my way home from the theater, I would wonder how many hairballs and piles of diarrhea I would soon be cleaning up.

Michael Lanning. *The Civil War* (Captain Emmett Lochran) [O]

When I first started out on Broadway, I was living at home with my parents. One day, a friend of mine said, "You have to get your own apartment. You must get out." I was extremely embarrassed. I needed to get my own place.

I got an apartment on Milligan Place. The entire apartment was fifteen by fifteen feet. That included a kitchen, a living room, a dining room, and a bedroom. I stayed there until I was twenty-eight years old. I did many Broadway shows during that time. I couldn't leave because I was scared that I wouldn't get another job and wouldn't be able to afford a bigger place. I was always acutely aware of the precariousness of show business.

Lonny Price. *A Class Act* (Ed) [O][t], *Merrily We Roll Along* (Charley Kringas) [O], *"MASTER HAROLD" . . . and the boys* (Hally) [O], *Broadway* (Roy Lane) [O], *Rags* (Ben) [O], *The Survivor* (Rudy) [O], *Burn This* (Larry), *Durante** (Durante), *Apprenticeship of Duddy Kravitz**

The Glamour of It All

In *Les Misérables*, the show was structured so that the members of the ensemble made all of their costume changes in the basement. So, after every scene, we had to run downstairs and change. Most of the women in the show wore three layers of socks—brown, green, and pink. Some of the costume changes consisted of taking off one pair of socks and running back on stage. Other times, we would finish a scene, run downstairs, put on an apron and run back upstairs, then run back downstairs again, wipe the dirt off and smudge red circles on our face to look like hookers, and run back on stage again. The costume changes were never-ending. There must have been over fifteen of them.

When I was moved up from the ensemble to play the role of Cosette, I still had to perform with the ensemble and make most of these costume changes. But rather than run downstairs, I had to run upstairs to the third floor, where Cosette shared her dressing room with Eponine. We had to run down three flights of stairs, do a scene, and then run back up three flights of stairs, change costumes, and run back down again. Each show, we would have to do this over and over again.

We would sometimes laugh at how ridiculous it was. We were starring in a Broadway show, yet we were running up and down stairs like we were waiting tables.

Jodie Langel. *Les Misérables* (Cosette/Eponine), *Martin Guerre** (Bertrande Alternate), *Cats** (Grizabella), *Joseph and the Amazing Technicolor® Dreamcoat** (Narrator)

I remember my opening night of *Grease!*. In the show, there was a scene where the whole cast had to stick their faces through holes. There was a drop that showed all these students in caps and gowns at graduation. We had to stand behind the drop and stick our faces through the holes so just our faces showed and our bodies were part of the drop. Like a carnival.

They miscalculated the distance. It was too tall for us. To solve the problem, they went out and got twenty New York City phone books.

There I was. Opening night on Broadway. I'm thinking, "Wow, my first Broadway show!" I looked over and we were all standing on these giant New York City phone books. This was Broadway, where there was supposed to be all the glitz and the glamour. They didn't build something to fix the problem. No. They just got phone books. That sums it up right there.

Hunter Foster. *Little Shop of Horrors* (Seymour) [O], *Urinetown* (Bobby Strong) [O], *Footloose* (Bickle) [O], *King David* [O], *Grease!* (Roger) [O], *Les Misérables* (Marius u/s), *Martin Guerre** (Martin u/s), *Cats** (Rum Tum Tugger)

Terrence Mann likened the whole experience of playing the Beast in *Beauty and the Beast* to taking twenty cats and taping them to your body and running around the stage for two and a half hours, not being able to breathe, and just sweating profusely. It was like gaffer-taping a bunch of dead animals to your body. He also had to wear plastic hands, and his face was covered with hair.

There was a point in the second act of the show where Terry and I were facing upstage, supposedly reading a book. We had some alone time, and Terry and I would catch up.

"How's your wife Charlotte?"

"Oh, she's great!"

I would hold up a fan and try to cool him off. Every so often, he would have fuzz on his tongue from the mask. He couldn't get it off because he couldn't feel anything with his plastic hands. Furthermore, his hands were so hairy that it would just make things worse. He would turn to me, stick out his tongue, and I would pick off the fuzz.

One night, I remember saying, "So, this is it. This is the glamorous part, right?" It is a job that you go to every day, and it's picking hair off someone's tongue.

Susan Egan. *Beauty and the Beast* (Belle) [O][t], *Triumph of Love* (Princess) [O], *Cabaret* (Sally), *State Fair*, *Thoroughly Modern Millie* (Millie), *Bye Bye Birdie** (Kim)

CHAPTER 12

Sex in the Workplace

Theater, by nature, can lead to a type of sexual intimacy not common in other professions. Actors thrust into romantic roles can quickly lose track of reality. Boundaries are blurred, and lines are often crossed, resulting in the kind of touching that could keep a sexual harassment lawyer busy for a lifetime.

Many in the theater community disagree that there is a problem, claiming that different rules of conduct should apply to the world of theater. Not everyone is of the same opinion. For some, it is a matter of respect. For others, it is a matter of decency. Regardless, issues of sexuality and gender play a large role in many actors' experiences on Broadway.

The Showmance

I think it was Patti LuPone who said, "It's a long walk from the dressing room to the stage." And it's true. The experience of being on stage is about 10 percent of your experience as an actor. The rest is interpersonal bullshit. It's like being in summer camp. You are sequestered in a building with no light and a whole bunch of needy people. We are all in a business that makes us feel insecure and unstable.

If you have an office job, you don't take off all your clothes each day in front of your coworkers and smear dirt all over your body. In theater, you are really exposed. It's scary. You get dressed and undressed twenty times a night. I once figured out that I changed clothes in front of other people about eighty times in one week, maybe more. You are always walking around in the dark in your underwear.

Craig Rubano. *The Scarlet Pimpernel* (Armand St. Just s/b) [O], *Les Misérables* (Marius)

I've developed a theory about musical theater. You get a musical theater cast together and there is instant bonding. There is the feeling of, "I don't know you today, but tomorrow I will be touching your breasts." It always amazes me.

When you are in rehearsal, you sit really close, and sing in each other's ear. That afternoon, you are dancing. You are partnering. You've got your hands all over each other. The familiarity happens that fast.

You should have seen the rehearsal process for *Urban Cowboy*. It was out of control. People were naked within a week, running around in front of each other. To me, that's the beauty of musical theater.

Jeff Blumenkrantz. *Urban Cowboy* [O][t], *A Class Act* (Charlie/Marvin) [O], *Into the Woods* (Jack/Rapunzel's Prince u/s) [O], *How to Succeed in Business Without Really Trying!* (Bud Frump) [O], *Damn Yankees* (Smokey) [O], *3 Penny Opera* (Filch) [O], *Joseph and the Amazing Technicolor® Dreamcoat** (Brother)

I notoriously fell for my leading man. I really did. By the third or fourth leading man, I said, "No, Mom, it's real. I love him. I know it is sort of like a pattern, but I love him." There is legitimacy to a showmance. In theater, you are asked to tell stories, to be vulnerable, and to fall in love with somebody every night. You have to open your heart and connect. Unless you are a robot—and some people become robots—there is residual stuff that is in you when you walk out the stage door. There is fondness.

Erin Dilly. *Follies* (Young Phyllis) [O], *The Boys from Syracuse* (Luciana) [O], *Into the Woods* (Cinderella), *Martin Guerre** (Bertrande), *Beauty and the Beast** (Belle), *South Pacific** (Nellie)

The lines get blurred. When you have to kiss, hug, and be in love with somebody on stage, people easily come to believe that it's really happening. I don't fall for that, but I know a lot of people who do. I shouldn't judge them. But I do.

I want to say, "Grow up! You are acting. It's not real." Maybe they don't want to make that distinction. Maybe they are not happy in their personal lives and want to lose themselves on stage.

I was working with somebody who I knew was unfaithful to his wife. I had a huge problem with that. It got in the way of my relationship with him on stage. I just couldn't relax.

Sarah Uriarte Berry. *Taboo* (Nicola) [O], *Les Misérables* (Eponine), *Beauty and the Beast* (Belle), *Sunset Boulevard** (Betty Schaeffer), *Carousel** (Julie Jordan)

I had an awfully good time being a straight man in musical theater. The original Broadway company of *Les Misérables* was the most heavily testosterone-laden company with which I have ever been involved. It was wild. We were all sniffing around. There was an unusual texture backstage—very much a locker room environment. There was a good deal of sexuality.

Paul Harman. *Les Misérables* (Foreman) [O], *Chess* (Arbiter) [O], *Triumph of Love* (Dimas u/s) [O], *Candide* (2nd Bulgarian Soldier) [O], *What's Wrong with This Picture?* (Mort u/s) [O], *It's So Nice to Be Civilized* [O], *Joseph and the Amazing Technicolor® Dreamcoat* (Simeon), *Ragtime* (Doctor), *Cats* (Asparagus), *Evita** (Peron u/s), *Zorba** (Niko)

Testing Boundaries

There's a thing that happens when you are in the theater. In any other job, after you get hired, you have time to develop relationships with people. That process is accelerated in theater to a large degree. You walk into rehearsal and immediately you are kissing a total stranger. Your hands are all over their body. The intimacy borders disappear because you are living in a surreal world. It's your job to project a relationship that doesn't necessarily exist. Part of you wants it to exist. There are times when actors lose sense of what is appropriate behavior. I have been guilty of that.

I remember my first job. I was scared and I wanted to fit in. I was shocked at how open people were. While it was very nice and liberating, some people ran with the ball a bit too far. They felt like they had permission to do whatever they wanted.

Once, a man reached over, grabbed my crotch, and made a crack about it. It was shocking. There are boundaries, and you need to be very careful about what those boundaries are.

Michael Berresse. *Kiss Me, Kate* (Bill Calhoun/Luciento) [O][t], *The Gershwin's Fascinating Rhythm* [O], *Chicago* (Fred Casely) [O], *Damn Yankees* (Bomber) [O], *Fiddler on the Roof* [O], *Guys and Dolls* (Crapshooter), *Joseph and the Amazing Technicolor® Dreamcoat** (Pharaoh), *Busker Alley**

Musical theater is selling sex. Half of the time you are running around on stage with scantily clad men and women. That is what we do. Many people who are young in the business don't know how to channel that energy. I used to think that because I was standing in the back row, I could get away with anything. I would slap girls on the ass whenever I wanted. I would screw around. I didn't think it mattered because I was just a dancer in the back row. I would push flirting to the furthest extreme. I would make overtly disgusting and crude comments to women all the time. In any other job, if I was standing by a water cooler, it would be sexual harassment. In musical theater, nine times out of ten, people don't take it that way.

James Sassar. *Riverdance* [O]

Actors know where the line is. We know when to cross it and when not to cross it. We are not supposed to steal focus. Period. If I want to pull down my pants and masturbate on stage, and if I can do so without stealing focus, go right ahead. That's kind of it. That's all a part of professional acting.

Lea DeLaria. *The Rocky Horror Show* (Eddie/Dr. Scott) [O], *On the Town* (Hildy) [O], *Chicago** (Mama Morton)

Crossing the Line

People get loose backstage. I've seen people take it across the line. I've seen gay men get really inappropriate with straight women. The environment is close and loose, and some gay men feel like they can't be threatening to a woman because they are gay. I've heard some really serious groping horror stories, both on and off stage. People who just got too familiar. Some women are completely cool with it. Others think, "I don't care who you are, or what your sexual preference is. Don't touch me like that." It can become extremely ugly.

Dave Clemmons. *The Scarlet Pimpernel* (Ben) [O], *The Civil War* (Sergeant Virgil Frank/Auctioneer's Assistant) [O], *Les Misérables* (Jean Valjean), *Whistle Down the Wind**, *Jekyll & Hyde** (Bishop)

Once, while on a national tour, a cast member grabbed my ass while I was getting off a bus and pretended like he was riding me like a male prostitute. Everyone started laughing.

I turned around angrily and said, "Get your hands off me!"

He looked surprised, and said defensively, "What? I was just joking around."

I said, "No. It's not okay. It's disrespectful."

Everyone looked at me like I was overreacting. He became the victim and I was seen as the bad guy. I was furious. I couldn't believe no one understood where I was coming from.

Jodie Langel. *Les Misérables* (Cosette/Eponine), *Martin Guerre** (Bertrande Alternate), *Cats** (Grizabella), *Joseph and the Amazing Technicolor® Dreamcoat** (Narrator)

There was someone in a cast who would touch my butt all the time. He would tease and massage me.

After the first time he did it, I politely said, "Hey, stop that, okay?"

After the second time, I looked him in the eye and I said, "I mean what I am saying. Stop it."

During *Les Misérables*, a problem arose. Someone had brought in

Miss Saigon. Photo credit: Joan Marcus/Photofest

pornography and it was being passed around. It was inappropriate for a work environment. After that episode, they brought in an expert to speak about "sexual harassment issues." They only asked the Equity deputies to attend. I wish they had asked everyone.

Joan Almedilla. *Miss Saigon* (Kim), *Les Misérables** (Fantine), *Jesus Christ Superstar** (Soul Girl)

In my last contract, I had to sign a sexual harassment clause. It said that sexual harassment was not tolerated. We all found it very amusing. In theater, what is sexual harassment? Everyone is so touchy-feely. The clause apparently included talking in dressing rooms and making people feel threatened in a sexual way.

Michael Arnold. *42nd Street* (Andy Lee) [O], *The Who's Tommy* [O], *A Funny Thing Happened on the Way to the Forum* (Swing) [O], *Little Me* (Belle's Boy/Newsboy) [O], *Cats* (Mr. Mistoffelees), *Cabaret, Chicago, Martin Guerre** (Benoit), *Busker Alley**, *Durante**

There is a lot of pressure from gay men. There are a lot of things that are done to you that really shouldn't be acceptable. I have had my ass grabbed by more old queens than I can count, telling me, "You don't know what you're missing." It is always there.

You always assume that you are going to get hit on and that people are going to say inappropriate things. You learn to let it roll off your back. I have been in situations where somebody just wouldn't take no for an answer. Once, I was taking a shower, and a guy walked into the bathroom just to talk to me. I knew that he was attracted to me. He knew that I was straight and engaged. He knew all kinds of things.

If I had raised a stink about it, I would have felt uncomfortable. People would say, "You have to take it like a joke." I can't imagine that behavior would have been acceptable if it had happened to a woman. But I couldn't take exception to it because I would look homophobic.

Andrew Varela. *King David* [O], *Les Misérables* (Jean Valjean u/s)

Straight guys in musical theater—no matter how cute, ugly, creepy, or weird—get laid. I have seen the dorkiest straight men with the hottest girl-friends. The straight guy in musical theater is very, very lucky. He proba-bly crosses the line the most because he is interested in crossing the line.

Almost every straight man in musical theater has a bad reputation. They are like the kid who goes into the candy store and takes all the candy. I have found them mostly to be dogs and players.

Marissa Jaret Winokur. *Hairspray* (Tracy Turnblad) [O][T], *Grease!* (Jan)

I have Midwestern values. When I do a job, I am very aware of myself both physically and mentally. Other people are not. If I have to kiss a woman on stage, I will talk to the woman about it before it happens. I feel it's appropriate to do so. Although we do it all the time, it doesn't make it any less personal.

Backstage life can be fun, but I've never felt as vulnerable as when I am in that environment. There have been times when I have felt person-ally harassed. I would never treat someone the same way that I have been treated. Both men and women do it. One person may feel fine walking around the theater naked. Someone else may not. We all share the same dream, the same love, but that does not warrant a complete freedom with each other.

Frank Baiocchi. *Miss Saigon* (Chris u/s), *South Pacific** (Cable u/s)

They Don't Do This on Wall Street

It seems like we are always talking about sex and making inappropriate comments. Recently, a woman who does hair told me that a man in her show said to her, "You know, you have really beautiful breasts."

She said, "Well, thank you!"

In no other business would you say, "I admire your breasts!" I guess that is crossing a line, but the lines are so blurry because you always see everyone in the cast naked.

The day I left *Urinetown*, almost every woman in the show flashed me. They flashed their boobs. They didn't think anything of it. It was like, "Okay, now you've seen them." I just can't think of any other job where that happens. Just imagine someone saying, "Hey, Bob, I hear you are leaving Merrill Lynch. Let me show you my breasts!"

Hunter Foster. *Little Shop of Horrors* (Seymour) [O], *Urinetown* (Bobby Strong) [O], *Footloose* (Bickle) [O], *King David* [O], *Grease* (Roger) [O], *Les Misérables* (Marius u/s), *Martin Guerre** (Martin u/s), *Cats** (Rum Tum Tugger)

Broadway is one of the few professions where the touchy, huggy, feely thing is accepted. In any other workplace, you go to your office, say hello, and do your work. If someone touches you inappropriately, you sue them for sexual harassment. I personally don't like touchy, feely, huggy. I'm not into that shit. When I go to the theater, I say hello. I'm friendly, but I want to do my job.

There are always a lot of people walking up to me, saying, "Hi, baby," and squeezing up against me. I don't think it's appropriate. Most people don't mind. We are artists, we're out there, we're free, and we're in touch with our inner child, so it's all good. We are a family, a club. We're all in this together. I think it's a lot of bullshit.

Sarah Uriarte Berry. *Taboo* (Nicola) [O], *Les Misérables* (Eponine), *Beauty and the Beast* (Belle), *Sunset Boulevard** (Betty Schaeffer), *Carousel** (Julie Jordan)

It's amazing what is accepted in theater—the flirting, the sexual comments, the fact that we all get undressed in front of each other. Furthermore, there seems to be this sort of unwritten expectation that if you're gay, you can walk into the opposite sex's dressing room without knocking. Married men make comments to married women. People think it's funny when they grab your ass on stage or slip you the tongue during a stage kiss. In corporate America, for any of that you would be fired in a second. You would be sued. Your company would be sued. I'm just waiting for the first person to file a lawsuit. I'm waiting for it to happen.

Erin Leigh Peck. *Dance of the Vampires* (Zsa-Zsa) [O], *Grease!* (Swing), *Brighton Beach Memoirs**

I did a show where we had to preset ourselves in the dark before the lights came up. There was an actor who would come up from behind a friend of mine and put his hands on her breasts. I begged her to go to stage management. She wouldn't. She was afraid, embarrassed, and humiliated. I couldn't believe it. It was a clear case of severe sexual harassment.

In another show, I also had a problem with a person who I had to kiss. Instead of a stage kiss, he would stick his tongue down my throat. It was completely inappropriate. I remember going to management and saying, "Can you help me with this?"

They told me to talk to him myself. If he didn't stop, they would say something. That was wrong. I should never have had to confront him. That would never have happened in corporate America.

Lucy Vance. *Miss Saigon* (Ellen u/s), *Les Misérables** (Eponine/Cosette u/s)

We had a guy in our show who sent a formal complaint to Equity that he was being sexually harassed. Our company was baffled. It was very hard to deal with.

He complained that people were saying stuff about his ass.

"Oh, your ass looks great in those pants."

We don't know if it was a ploy, if he needed attention, or what. Everyone walked around on pins and needles for a month.

I have seen shows where guys would grope each other's asses and everyone would laugh. In the corporate world, you don't see two guys groping each other by the water cooler. It doesn't happen, unless it's some bad porno movie. If anyone in corporate America were to come backstage to any Broadway show for an hour, they would walk away and say, "Oh, my God!" They would freak out.

Jerry Tellier. *Saturday Night Fever* (Frank Junior) [O], *42nd Street* [O], *Smokey Joe's Cafe*

Straight Man Out

I have to be honest. I feel that because so much of the industry is gay, if you are a straight man, you feel a bit like an outsider. Almost everybody's attitude is about being gay—gay culture and going to gay bars. None of which I have any problem with. I get along with gay people well. We have a good time together and go out to bars.

However, sometimes it's a little strange. If you go into a show, no one knows you, and they know you are straight, there is just a slight anti-straight attitude amongst the gay management and predominately gay companies. I think it's more in management than in the performers. You're kind of the odd man out.

Dave Clemmons. *The Scarlet Pimpernel* (Ben) [O], *The Civil War* (Sergeant Virgil Frank/Auctioneer's Assistant) [O], *Les Misérables* (Jean Valjean), *Whistle Down the Wind**, *Jekyll & Hyde** (Bishop)

There are difficulties to being a straight man in musical theater. It is so hard to get past the casting directors who obviously can smell you a mile away and couldn't be less interested. What's up with that?

Craig Bennet. *Miss Saigon* (Marine/Reeves), *Les Misérables** (Thénardier u/s), *Mamma Mia!** (Bill), *Ragtime** (Willie Conklin)

There is a gay mafia in the New York theater community. It exists. There are a lot of gay men who love Broadway and who are deeply involved in the business, both on the entertainment and the business side of things. They want to be close to other gay men. If you are a man in a Broadway show, people automatically assume you are gay. It is one of the first things I heard.

There is a certain amount of reverse discrimination that exists because I am straight. I am looked upon in a different light than a gay man who is up for the same part when we are both in front of a gay casting director. There is just an underlying aspect of "the club." It isn't organized like the mafia. They aren't going to "off" somebody with a shot to the head or anything, but there's a sense of subtle discrimination.

And it's underlying. It's not overt, so you can't really put your finger on it. You can't say, "Hey, you're being discriminatory." It's very subtle, but there is a sense of "I might not get this part because I'm not gay." I've seen incidences of it. It exists. I will defy any gay man who tells me it doesn't.

Michael Lanning. *The Civil War* (Captain Emmett Lochran) [O]

There's nothing organized about "the gay mafia." It just boils down to the fact that most of the powerbrokers in theater are gay, and so it is the "gay experience" that they relate to. It's not a whole lot different than in the days of drugs. Those who were involved in the drug culture just didn't associate with those who weren't—they spoke a different language. Today, straight men are discriminated against because they are not a part of the language. I don't think it is intentional. It's just a result of people flocking to their own group. Sometimes, the straight man gets left out.

John Leslie Wolfe. *Parade* (Tom Watson) [O], *Passion* (Fosca's Father) [O], *Evita* [O], *Saravà* [O], *Martin Guerre** (Pierre Guerre), *Cabaret** (Ernst Ludwig)

The majority of men in theater tend to be homosexual, so there is an element that the straight man is the odd man out. However, sometimes I feel discriminated against in this business because I am gay.

With respect to the "gay mafia," I have felt pressure when someone in casting fancies me. Throughout the years, I have run into casting directors on the street and in bars. They could have a large impact on my career. What kind of line are you going to draw? Falling for the casting couch trap could actually have harmful consequences. Unless you are going to be their baby and live with them for the rest of your life, it could create a very uncomfortable situation. You might not even get into future auditions with that person because he wants to protect his reputation. So, the perceived advantage of being a gay performer might actually be a double-edged sword.

Sean Jeremy Palmer. *Carousel** (Mr. Snow), *Martin Guerre** (Guillaume u/s)

CHAPTER 13

Forget the Picket Fence

One of the advantages of being on Broadway is that you never need to worry about what you will be doing on Friday or Saturday nights, or during the day on weekends. You will be in the theater, working. The disadvantages, however, are clear—say goodbye to nice romantic dinners, weekends in the country, and a normal social life, or any social life whatsoever outside the theater.

Since childhood, many actors dream of becoming a star on Broadway. However, at the same time, many also dream of having a family. Once one dream is realized, however, the other becomes more difficult to grasp. Few challenges are more formidable to a Broadway actor than sustaining a meaningful personal relationship, whether it be with a fellow actor or with a "civilian." As a result, many have no choice but to travel down the Great White Way alone. Those who do manage to get married and wish to have a family often must rethink their place within the Broadway community.

Courting Civilians

I have dated a few "civilians," or non-actors. I tried a couple of times. One of them referred to us as "you people." How do "you people" do it? I was offended. He didn't know how we did it. He didn't understand how we could work six days a week, without any weekends.

One of my former boyfriends had a summer house in the Hamptons. I could never go. During the week, I would always be the one who would show up at 11:00 P.M. when the party was pretty much over. Everyone would already be three sheets to the wind, and I would be pulling mascara glue off my eyes.

When I'd arrive late, I would often find myself the center of attention. It was really the last thing I wanted after a show. I felt out of it. It cut away, little by little, at any kind of positive growth in the relationship. And, of course, the last person I wanted to date was a fellow actor.

Paige Price. *Saturday Night Fever* (Stephanie) [O], *Beauty and the Beast* (Silly Girl) [O], *Smokey Joe's Cafe*

The problem with being a straight man in the theater is social. It is difficult to meet women who are not in show business. Society being structured the way it is, if you are busy on Friday nights, Saturday nights, Saturday afternoons, and Sunday afternoons, it's difficult to meet regular girls. Also, as a Broadway actor, I don't offer a particularly stable financial stream. I hope it gets easier sometime soon.

Jeff Gardner. *The Wild Party* (Burrs u/s) [O], *The Scarlet Pimpernel* (Mercier) [O], *Cyrano—The Musical* (Sylvian) [O], *The Queen and the Rebels* (Traveler) [O], *Jerome Robbins' Broadway* (The Setter u/s), *Les Misérables** (Foreman)

A common misconception that people have about a single person on Broadway is that they go out on dates with anybody and everybody every night. When I was nominated for a Tony Award for *Smokey Joe's Cafe*, two other women in my show were also nominated. None of us could get a date. We even wrote a song called "Tony Nominated and Can't Get a Date." Our plan was to send it to Oprah and ask for her help. We were just over ourselves. We had functions to go to and dresses to wear, but who was going to be on our arm?

People assumed that I went out on dates all the time. No one realized that every night after the show, I would put on my tennis shoes and walk home alone.

DeLee Lively. *Smokey Joe's Cafe* [O][t], *A Chorus Line* (Val)

Marrying Civilians

I'm divorced. I was married to a man who was not in the business and who didn't understand what it was truly going to be like when he married an actress. There is something very glamorous to someone not in the business about his girlfriend or his wife working on Broadway. However, when she has to go work in St. Louis for six weeks, or when she gets offered a job in London for a year, somehow it's not so convenient anymore.

There's also something about seeing your wife kiss a man on stage every night. No matter how secure he is with the relationship, it's hard. There's something so intimate about theater, and casts can get very close. Backstage, everyone is always running around in their panties. Other people don't understand that.

In *Miss Saigon*, I had a big dressing room. One day, when my costar, Matt Bogart, was sitting in my dressing room in his boxer shorts, my husband walked in. Trying to explain that to my husband was futile. It took a toll on my marriage.

Anastasia Barzee. *Henry IV* (Lady Mortimer) [O], *Urinetown* (Hope Caldwell), *Miss Saigon* (Ellen), *Jekyll & Hyde* (Emma), *Sunset Boulevard** (Betty), *City of Angels** (Mallory)

I married a man who was not in the business. When I went on tour for six months, my husband would come visit me on the road. It was hard for him to be a "theater husband."

He would say, "I'm going out to the movies with all the other theater wives."

That was how he felt. When he would visit me during a five-show weekend, I could barely spend time with him. He wanted to do things and I was tired. I had to rest for the show. My marriage just couldn't survive.

Heather MacRae. *Falsettos* (Charlotte) [O], *Coastal Disturbances* (Faith Bigelow) [O], *Here's Where I Belong* (Abra) [O], *Hair* (Sheila)

The entire time I was performing with the national tour of *Cats*, I was married. It was extremely difficult. I would work extremely long hours and I would get home really late. My husband would fly out just to see me. We had to chart out the weeks and the days when we could see each other. Ultimately, he became an e-mail and a voice, not a body and a face. I ended up coming home to a divorce that was unexpected.

Christie McCall. *Cats** (Sillabub)

Keeping It in the Family

Dating someone who is also in the business is difficult. An actor's job is to be self-aware, which can easily translate into being self-absorbed. A fellow actor can understand what you are going through, but that doesn't necessarily mean that he or she is able to put up with it any better. Every time you audition, it could change your life and your status in the business. The highs are high and the lows are low.

And then, if someone is more successful than the other, it can get really complicated. It's not that you don't want the other person to do well. You do. You just want a slice of the pie as well. That's the reality of it all. And when one person has more pie than the other, it gets hard. It's hard on the person who is doing well, too, because you want to be happy for what you have, but you also don't want to be oblivious to the other person's feelings. It's a juggling game. I feel like it's the hardship of a relationship, with a twist.

Michael Berry. *Les Misérables* (Enjolras u/s), *Sunset Boulevard** (Artie)

If you are in a relationship with another working actor, you always wonder if he has his eye out for something better. By nature, our business is based on what we look like and how good we are. It's intoxicating.

The business is so romantic. Your cast is always good-looking. There will almost always be a couple of straight guys in the cast. In almost every show, there is someone that you will have your eye out for. It alleviates the boredom of doing the show night after night, and fulfills that newness and excitement that drew you to the business to begin with.

Amanda Watkins. *Cabaret* (Sally u/s), *Cats* (Demeter), *Urinetown, Beauty and the Beast* (Silly Girl), *Grease!* (Marty)

Flying Solo

When I was younger, I only existed because I was an actor. I suppose I exaggerate, but there is some truth in that. I have some emotional catching up to do. I missed out on some basic social skills, some intimacy things. I am shy. Being on the stage allows for a kind of unconditional love without intimacy. You can get that warm, fuzzy feeling without having to do the intimate work that it takes to have a meaningful relationship. I was busy moving around. It helped me keep away from people.

Tom Hewitt. *The Rocky Horror Show* (Dr. Frank N. Furter) [O][t], *The Boys from Syracuse* (Antipholus of Ephesus) [O], *Art* (Serge u/s) [O], *The Lion King* (Scar), *School for Scandal* (Charles Surface), *Sisters Rosensweig* (Geoffrey), *Urinetown** (Officer Lockstock)

Anybody who comes to New York and tries to be an actor lightly is very soon gone. It is too terrible. You have to give up too much. You have to sacrifice everything that your family or your friends would consider normal. You have to sacrifice your hopes for an early marriage, beautiful children, and a nice car. Forget about that stuff.

You are just grinding. You have to make enough money to take the next class. You have to get your new headshots. All of your needs are completely foreign to everybody else in the world, and those needs are all you have.

Steve Pudenz. *Hello, Dolly!* (Rudolph) [O], *Joseph and the Amazing Technicolor® Dreamcoat** (Jacob), *The Sound of Music**

I miss being able to do family things. I don't know my cousins. Now there is a whole new generation in my family, and I barely know them. They are not even far away. After years of not seeing me, they will come and see me in a show. We have an uncomfortable perfunctory visit. It's hard. I feel like a crazy aunt who lives in New York and does that show biz thing.

I have made huge sacrifices. I want babies. I want a house in the suburbs. I want a garden. I can't even have a garden on my terrace. I call it a terrace, but it is actually a ledge, two feet wide and four stories up. One day, I decided I would start growing herbs, tomatoes, cucumbers, and peppers. And then I developed a squirrel problem. While I would be standing on the ledge, putting in masonry nails to hang baskets, those fuckers would jump into the baskets and decimate everything. It was horrible, and the guys working on the building across from me would just laugh.

I had a solution.

I put down glue traps.

I killed a bird.

I couldn't do that anymore, so I just gave up on the garden. I got bitter. I can't even have a plant.

Paige Price. *Saturday Night Fever* (Stephanie) [O], *Beauty and the Beast* (Silly Girl) [O], *Smokey Joe's Cafe*

Planned Parenthood

In this business, if someone stops to have a baby, people say they have given up. Isn't that terrible? They're not working, so they've given up. They can't hack it. Anytime that you do something that has nothing to do with the business, you've given up. It's a terrible thing.

Christiane Noll. *Jekyll & Hyde* (Emma) [O], *It Ain't Nothin' but the Blues*, *Miss Saigon** (Ellen), *Grease!** (Sandy), *City of Angels** (Mallory), *Urinetown** (Hope Cladwell)

I had a baby and I left the business for two years. I literally had to move away. I knew that if I didn't, I would stay in the business. The lure is too strong. I was warned by some people, "If you stay away too long, they will forget who you are."

Damn it, that's right. They do forget, and I don't care. I did the right thing for my family. Do I have regrets about the things I may have missed? Not really. A scrapbook isn't the same as a healthy well-adjusted child.

Nancy Opel. *Urinetown* (Penelope Pennywise) [O] [t], *Evita* (Eva u/s) [O], *Triumph of Love* (Corine) [O], *Sunday in the Park with George* (Frieda) [O], *Teddy & Alice* (Eleanor Roosevelt) [O], *Ring Round the Moon* (Capulat u/s) [O], *Getting Away with Murder* (Dossie Lustig u/s) [O], *Anything Goes* (Hope Harcourt)

Momentum and continuity are extremely important unless you are a big established star. If you are a big established star, you can disappear off the face of the Earth for five years, maybe ten years, and then reappear. When you do, it's a comeback, or it's a rediscovery. But if you haven't achieved big star status and you disappear, you are gone. And when you come back, people won't necessarily remember you. And it's hard.

This makes some women decide not to have families and not to have children. So, they find themselves in their late thirties or forties with no families, and suddenly, they don't want the business anymore. They don't want to be pounding the road and touring in Ohio. They want to have a family.

And then there are those who have a family when they are young. They cart their kids around on the road and make it work somehow, but they also feel that they lost something—maybe they had to turn down a part for which they were perfect, or maybe they were too pregnant when a show they wanted came into town.

> **John Rubinstein.** *Children of a Lesser God* (James Leeds) [O][**T**], *Pippin* (Pippin)
> [O], *Fools* (Leon) [O], *Getting Away with Murder* (Martin Chisholm) [O], *The
> Caine Mutiny Court-Martial* (Lt. Barney Greenwald) [O], *Ragtime* (Tateh),
> *Hurlyburly* (Eddie), *Love Letters* (Andrew), *M. Butterfly* (Rene)

After the first reading of *Jane Eyre,* I was certain it was on its way to Broadway. I knew it was going to be huge. I did the reading. Then I did a small production in Kansas. Half a year later, I did a production in Toronto. After Canada, it was supposed to go directly to Broadway. It didn't. I was playing the role of a schoolgirl. At the time, I could pass for that.

Time passed, and I became pregnant. My schoolgirl look was gone forever. When I got a call that they were doing the show again at the La Jolla Playhouse, I was breast-feeding. It passed me by. Three years after having my daughter, the show came to Broadway. I was happy for my friends, but it was bittersweet.

> **Angela Lockett.** *Parade* (Angela) [O], *Les Misérables* (Fantine u/s), *Martin
> Guerre** (Catherine), *Once on This Island**, *Ain't Misbehavin**

Working Parents

When I was in *Miss Saigon*, I had just given birth. That I was able to have a child and immediately work was one of my greatest accomplishments. I would have to interrupt nursing and run on stage. I had nursing pads in my bra so I wouldn't leak. It was hysterical. I didn't sleep. I was exhausted. It was crazy.

> **Liz Callaway.** *Baby* (Lizzie) [O][**t**], *Miss Saigon* (Ellen) [O], *Merrily We Roll Along*
> (Nightclub Waitress) [O], *The Three Musketeers* (Lady Constance Bonacieux) [O],
> *The Look of Love* [O], *Cats* (Grizabella)

I'm from Huntington, West Virginia. It's a small town, maybe fifteen thousand people. Some of the guys I went to school with are doctors now. They think that I am excessively wealthy. "You make what, two, three million a year? What are you worried about?" Then I tell them what I go through to make the pittance that I get. They can't believe I make such a nominal amount of money.

I have a new fifteen-month-old daughter. I have tried to save as much money as possible. I'm not starving, but when I finish Jean Valjean in *Les Misérables,* I will be unemployed. Broadway doesn't make stars. It's an everyday grind. I am constantly aware that my job is going to end. It's always on my mind. How am I going to support my fifteen-month-old child?

J. Mark McVey. *The Best Little Whorehouse Goes Public* (Sam Dallas s/b) [O], *Les Misérables* (Jean Valjean), *The Who's Tommy* (Captain Walker), *Carousel**

When I was on Broadway, here is an example of a typical day, after I had kids. I would wake up at 7:00 A.M. to the sounds of my three kids. I would try to put off dealing with them for another thirty minutes or so. Mommy was nursing one baby, another kid had to be at preschool at 9:00 A.M, and the other child had to be at daycare right after that. Daddy would drop them off. Then I would come home, go on the computer, and take care of business. I would be on the phone the whole time, dealing with my agent, trying to juggle auditions and find out my schedule for that given day.

For instance, take last Tuesday. I had a noon appointment to meet with an agency. I came running in and had to make up some crazy excuse for being late. I had only an hour to spare before a 1:00 P.M. rehearsal for a corporate gig. At 1:15 P.M., I was still talking to the agent. By the time I made it to the rehearsal, I was already thirty minutes late. The corporate rehearsal was over at 4:00 P.M., and at exactly 4:00 P.M. I had to be downtown for a television audition. I left the rehearsal at 3:00 P.M. I changed clothes for the television thing, fought traffic, and made it to the audition. The television audition lasted a while. I then had to rush uptown and sign in for the Broadway show. After the show, I drove home and relieved Mom of the youngest so she could take a shower. I would then check my e-mail. I made it to the gym maybe once a week. I need so badly to go. It's important for a leading man, and I was competing with people much younger.

However, before I had my first kid, my daily routine was quite different. I lived in Greenwich Village. I rolled out of bed at around 11:00 or 12:00 P.M. I had a little morning sex, and wondered where I was going to have brunch. I would drop my clothes off at the Chinese laundry. Maybe I'd do it myself. When I looked at the clock for the first time, it was already the afternoon, so it was time to hit the New York Sports Club. I'd go over to the club, do my thing, and feel good about myself.

If it was Monday, there was no show. Time to pick up a bottle of wine. It was wine and cheese time. I would break out the nachos and the salsa, listen to a little music, get a little groovy, and then go out to a club or something. Life was very different.

Robert Evan. *Jekyll & Hyde* (Dr. Jekyll) [O], *Dance of the Vampires* (Count von Krolock s/b) [O], *Les Misérables* (Jean Valjean)

I've had people tell me that I need to be more selfish in order to pursue my career. However, along with dreaming about having a career in the arts, I also dreamed about having a family and raising kids. It's not only important for me to provide for my kids, but it's important for me to watch them grow up. I've seen many marriages split up because one person focuses too much on his or her career. Let's be frank: it's a choice people make. Sometimes, to be incredibly successful, that's what it takes.

Yet there will come a time when you no longer have a career, and then what do you do? As you go along, it becomes more difficult to find work. You need to have something else. A career in theater can be very frustrating, and is full of drudgery and hard work. When I come home at the end of the day and hear three little kids say, "Daddy's home, Daddy's home," nothing else really matters. But it's a sacrifice.

Craig Schulman. *Les Misérables* (Jean Valjean), *Jekyll & Hyde* (Dr. Jekyll), *The Phantom of the Opera** (Phantom)

The theater is still great, but things change. Questions pop into my head. How am I going to pay for a child? How am I going to live in the future? How am I going to go out of town on tour if I have a family? Am I going to miss my child's recital or baseball game? How am I going to live without my wife? If you want a family, you have to make a commitment to another person. You can't have that commitment while doing theater.

Currently, I am struggling with that. My fiancée left the business. She wants to have a steady job so that she can support my theater career for a while. How can I allow her to do that while I go out on tour and drink? All that sacrifice just to be in the chorus?

I know I am doing something with no future. Am I going to be a father who's on unemployment all the time? I want to have a relationship the way my parents did. I saw them every day. They took me to baseball. If I am an actor, I can't do that. That is one major reason why performers in their late twenties or early thirties get out of the business. People who have done two or three Broadway shows begin to question if they are even good enough. Good enough to do what? Good enough to be out of work every six months? That's not a life.

David Josefsberg. *Les Misérables* (Marius u/s), *Grease!* (Doody)

CHAPTER 14

Road Trip

Even after making it to Broadway, few actors can sustain a successful career by only working in New York City. Life on the road has become an unavoidable necessity for many Broadway performers, placing additional strain on an actor's personal life and romantic relationships. For some, however, performing on a Broadway national tour is preferable to performing on Broadway. There is more money to be made, in every town you are treated like a rock star, you get to see the country, and you are free from the everyday responsibilities and challenges that come with living in New York City. However, many performers simply lose their grip on reality.

Fantasyland

Tour life is fantasyland. You have nothing to do all day. Life is fun. You see sights. You golf. You party. You've got all this money, because you aren't paying rent and because you are earning a per diem.

You think, "Oh, look at that really cool leather coat. I'm going to buy that. Give me that three-hundred-dollar pair of sunglasses." A three-hundred-dollar pair of sunglasses? You buy it because you're in fantasyland.

We'd smoke and then go to an underground club. We would drink our asses off. That is what life is like on the road. It's like being a rock star. All you have to do is walk into a bar with your show jacket, and you get attention. You stay at beautiful hotels, and then you do the show at night.

Jeff Gurner. *The Lion King* (Ed the Hyena)

One Friday night, when I was on the national tour of *Jekyll & Hyde* in New Orleans, I forgot to set my alarm clock to wake me up for the 2:00 P.M. Saturday matinee. At 1:35 P.M., I received a call in my hotel room from a frantic stage manager.

"Where are you? Where are you?"

I quickly rushed out of bed. I arrived at the theater wearing only boxer shorts—no T-shirt, no socks, and no shoes. In the cab ride over, I washed my hair by sticking my head outside the window and pouring a bottle of Evian water on my head.

William Thomas Evans. *Camelot* (Sir Dinadan u/s) [O], *The Scarlet Pimpernel* (Hastings) [O], *Jekyll & Hyde** (Proops/Utterson u/s), *A Funny Thing Happened on the Way to the Forum** (Miles Gloriosus)

On tour, you get up very late because you go to bed at two or three in the morning. The show gets out at 11:30 P.M. and you are so energized that you can't go to sleep unless you take sleeping pills, which is what I later learned to do.

So you stay up late, watch television, or drink at the hotel bar. The next day, you may or may not have a matinee performance or a rehearsal. If it is a free day, you probably go to the mall and spend money out of sheer boredom. You might see a movie.

That's where a lot of your money goes, especially if you are young and immature and don't realize that money doesn't come so easily. I would buy full-length leather coats. Christmas was extremely good for my family that year. I had money for the first time. It wasn't that much, but it was $1500 per week instead of the $100 that I was used to. I'd go to The Body Shop and drop $100 without even thinking about it. It was absurd.

Then back to the theater. You do the show at night, and then repeat the same goddamn thing.

After performing a five-show weekend, you come home on Sunday night and pack. Monday, you travel to a new town. Now, for the first time, you realize that nothing fits in your three large suitcases because you bought so much stuff at the mall. Packing becomes a three-hour ordeal.

The next day, you get on a plane at 7:00 A.M.

Marsh Hanson. *Les Misérables* (Marius), *Joseph and the Amazing Technicolor® Dreamcoat** (Brother)

On the *Les Misérables* tour, I bought six hundred dollars' worth of Christmas presents for the girl I was messing around with behind my girlfriend's back. Also, I remember buying a three-hundred-dollar leather jacket for a girl I was "hanging out" with.

David Josefsberg. *Les Misérables* (Marius u/s), *Grease!* (Doody)

I hate tour life. It's like being in high school. Life isn't real. I mean, it's great in some ways and horrible in others. You're making a lot of money, and you have no responsibilities. It's a breeding ground for trouble.

If you are smart, you will save your money. If you're not, you will spend it all.

I was on the road at twenty-four years old. I went from having no money to making thousands a week. I only saved a little bit. I mean, a *little* bit.

I had bought more crap than you can possibly imagine. I had to buy an extra duffel bag for all of my boots. I had fourteen pairs of boots. When we were in Boston, I brought my boot bag home. I had to choose just a couple pairs to travel with because they were getting too heavy and clunky. I put them in the basement of my old apartment. They were stolen.

My point—fourteen pairs of boots. That's about $4,000, and it was stolen. You know what? Good. It taught me a lesson. Don't spend your money on shit. That was just stupid.

> **Marc Kudisch.** *Thoroughly Modern Millie* (Trevor Graydon) [O][t], *Bells Are Ringing* (Jeff Moss) [O], *The Wild Party* (Jackie) [O], *Joseph and the Amazing Technicolor® Dreamcoat* (Reuben) [O], *High Society* (George Kittredge) [O], *Assassins* (Proprietor) [O], *The Scarlet Pimpernel* (Chauvelin), *Beauty and the Beast* (Gaston), *Bye Bye Birdie** (Conrad)

Because I had to work so hard to get through college, I knew I needed to save because I wanted to be free to audition when I was not performing. So, when I went on the road, I sent my entire paycheck every week to a savings account and made investments. I never touched my paycheck. I lived only off the per diem. That allowed me, later on, to make choices which helped me move into new roles. I am a child of immigrants. My parents are both from Cuba, and they have always drummed into my head the importance of saving. I had a great time on tour, but I chose to put my money away. I had something else in mind.

> **Ana Maria Andricain.** *Marie Christine* (Dakota/Emma Parker) [O], *Les Misérables* (Fantine u/s), *Beauty and the Beast* (Belle), *By Jeeves* (Stiffy Byng), *Evita** (Eva Alternate), *Annie Get Your Gun** (Annie u/s)

Love on the Road

As an actor, you have to always be aware that you could go on tour at any moment. I have seen so many relationships fall apart. In this business, we work so intimately with people—everyone is always falling in love with his or her costar. It is ridiculous. You work with someone for nine hours a day and then you go out with him at night. It is so easy to fall in love with someone that way—you are thrown into intimacy within twenty-four hours of meeting. On tour, you just get swept away into a fantasy life.

> **Jessica Snow Wilson.** *Little Shop of Horrors* (Audrey u/s) [O], *Les Misérables* (Eponine), *A Funny Thing Happened on the Way to the Forum* (Philia)

Your world becomes an encapsulated microcosm that bounces from city to city. You all have a similar goal, so obviously, you have a lot in common. I have had my share of road flings. They were very important to me at the time. But they were all doomed because they were born out of this fantasy world. They weren't real. It's easy and safe. On my first show, I saw a lot of roadkill. It was really sad and eye-opening.

Christiane Noll. *Jekyll & Hyde* (Emma) [O], *It Ain't Nothin' but the Blues*, *Miss Saigon** (Ellen), *Grease!** (Sandy), *City of Angels** (Mallory), *Urinetown** (Hope Cladwell)

The first rehearsal of a show is a lot like the first day of school. You start looking around the room and checking everyone out. The older you get, the more you start looking for wedding rings. It's really fun, especially when you are on the road.

It is such a playful place. Inevitably, when two people find each other attractive, one of them is always involved with someone else back at home. I have been in that situation. We had to sneak around and hide it from the rest of the cast.

People saw it coming from a mile away. There is always some cast member who is up at 3:00 A.M. and sees you walking down the hall, thinking, "He doesn't live on this floor." I had a great affair that didn't require any kind of dating and very little attention, other than sexual. I just wanted to have great sex after the show.

John Antony. *Passion* (Augenti/Count Ludovic), *Titanic** (John Jacob Astor), *Sunset Boulevard** (Joe Gillis u/s), *Annie Get Your Gun** (Frank Butler)

Being a straight man in musical theater is an incredible thing. You are surrounded by beautiful women with terrific bodies. You have no competition because everyone else is gay. This is especially true on the road, because people get really lonely and you're the local rooster.

If you are married, like I was, it can cause a lot of problems and frustrations. It was painful at times. I was lonely on the road and wanted companionship. I am a saint, so I didn't do anything, but it was really difficult.

After a while, the women in the show got very ornery and things got difficult. They weren't with their boyfriends or husbands, and there weren't enough straight guys in the show to satisfy their sexual desires.

They had to try to take care of themselves in other ways. I did my best to make sure that just about every girl had a state-of-the-art custom vibrator, which I specifically picked out for them. I'm not kidding. Ask anyone on tour. I became the "vibrator master."

Adrian Zmed. *Grease!* (Danny), *Blood Brothers* (Narrator), *Falsettos* (Marvin), *Chicago* (Billy Flynn), *Same Time, Next Year**

Seeing the Country

We were in Topeka, Kansas. *Cats* had never been there before. One day, somebody came into my dressing room and said, "People are picketing the show!"

I wondered, "They are picketing *Cats*?" I didn't get it. Did they think it was cruelty to animals? They couldn't be that stupid. What the hell was going on?

When I heard the news, I had my *Cats* make-up on and my hair was in pin-curlers. I must have looked like a kabuki weirdo. When I went outside to see what was going on, there were about fifteen people with signs, marching. The signs read: "New York Fags Go Home" and "Fags Die of AIDS."

I was flabbergasted. I immediately asked to speak with the owner of the theater. The owner said the guy outside was a fundamentalist preacher who pickets everything that comes into town. This was the same guy who picketed Matthew Shephard's funeral and the wakes and funerals of people who die of AIDS. I was worried about safety.

A woman came up to us and said, "This happens all the time. We just ignore it."

I said, "You can't ignore this kind of stuff. It doesn't go away unless you say something." I wrote to the city council.

The mayor's name was Butch. He responded by saying, "You New Yorkers think you know about the First Amendment, but you don't. We can say whatever we want here in Topeka."

Three weeks later, we were in Raleigh. One day, when I checked my mailbox, I noticed that everybody had been sent a five-page note. It read, in part: "*I am trying to explain these peoples' position. This is why God doesn't condone homosexuality.*" It was signed by five people on the *Cats* tour. It had Biblical references. "*God loves you, he just doesn't love you being a homosexual.*" Needless to say, it caused a huge rift in the cast.

Robert DuSold. *Les Misérables* (Javert), *Jekyll & Hyde* (Archbishop of Basingstoke), *Kiss of the Spider Woman* (Marcos), *Cats** (Deuteronomy), *The Phantom of the Opera** (André), *Chicago** (Little Mary Sunshine s/b), *Showboat** (Pete)

I was on tour with *Into the Woods*. Because I was one of the stars, I had to do a lot of press. We did split weeks and one-nighters. Sometimes, we performed in three different cities in one week.

I remember one day in particular. I don't know where the hell we were. When we arrived at the hotel, I had only five minutes before a phone interview. I literally had five minutes before the phone was going to ring.

When I got to the room, it was disgusting. Someone had been smoking. The room hadn't been cleaned. Nevertheless, I had to stay in the room because of the call. So there I was, sitting off a parking lot in a flea-pit motel in Podunk, Iowa, with the doors open to get some air, when this woman calls and starts talking about how glamorous my life must be. And, while I was thinking, "If you could only see the cigarette butts," a stray cat wandered in. That's the reality.

Betsy Joslyn. *High Society* (Patsy) [O], *Sweeney Todd* (Johanna) [O], *The Goodbye Girl* (Paula s/b) [O], *A Doll's Life* (Nora) [O], *A Few Good Men* (Lt. Galloway s/b) [O], *Into the Woods* (The Witch), *Sunday in the Park with George* (Dot), *Les Misérables* (Madame Thénardier), *Beauty and the Beast** (Mrs. Potts), *City of Angels** (Oolie/Donna), *Camelot** (Guenevere), *Of Thee I Sing**, *Let 'em Eat Cake**

Guns and Drugs

I was on the road with *Les Misérables,* and we were playing West Point. For a couple of months, I had been performing the lead role of Jean Valjean, the convict who broke parole and was running from the law.

We had a couple of days off before we were to perform in West Point. I got sick. I went to the doctor in New York City and he prescribed antibiotics. On the way back to West Point, I rented a car with three other guys from the cast. We left at 4:00 P.M. to beat the traffic.

I was driving the car down the Palisades Parkway and we were about forty-five minutes from West Point. I was in the left lane. The next thing I noticed was a cop car. It came up from behind and zoomed out in front of us. I saw him pull over in the distance. I slowed down as I passed. Suddenly, I heard a siren.

The cop pulled us over and began asking us a lot of strange questions. He kept mentioning drugs. Suddenly, I looked around the car and I realized that we were four long-haired and bearded guys in a brand-new rental car. The cop individually pulled everyone out of the car. He asked my friends how long they had known me and what we were doing. He searched the trunk, and said something about trafficking weapons.

I had gotten a ticket a year earlier, but the state of Tennessee, my home state, never received record that the ticket had been paid. Once the cop saw the outstanding ticket on my record, he put me in the back of the squad car and took me to jail.

It was now 5:30 P.M. and we had a sound check at 6:30 P.M. In jail, he told me that there was a warrant out for my arrest. He said that unless I could come up with $500 in cash, immediately, I was going to sit in the jail cell all night. Meanwhile, we were in the middle of rural New Jersey. This was before there were cash machines on every street corner. It was now 6:00 P.M.

My fellow cast members said, "We have to go."

I said, "You are not leaving me here!"

Luckily, one of the guys in the car had cashed his paycheck before we left New York City. He gave $500 to the cop, and they released me from jail.

Dave Clemmons. *The Scarlet Pimpernel* (Ben) [O], *The Civil War* (Sergeant Virgil Frank/Auctioneer's Assistant) [O], *Les Misérables* (Jean Valjean), *Whistle Down the Wind**, *Jekyll & Hyde** (Bishop)

When I was on the road with *Cats*, I was surrounded by dancers who would take eight Advil at a time. Pain pills were everywhere. Even though my character, Grizabella, could be fat and ugly, I felt pressure to be skinny like everyone else. At the same time, I wanted to have fun and be social each night after the show. I couldn't smoke—it was bad for my voice. I couldn't drink—it would make me fat. The pills would have to do.

I started taking Percocet with the dancers after the show. I needed it for an escape. Like so many people in the show, I quickly became addicted. In every new city, I scouted for pills. I would go backstage and ask the stagehands. It got to the point where I needed to have two Ambien and a glass of wine each night before going to bed. As wonderful as road life can be, you sometimes turn into the worst version of yourself.

Jodie Langel. *Les Misérables* (Cosette/Eponine), *Martin Guerre** (Bertrande Alternate), *Cats** (Grizabella), *Joseph and the Amazing Technicolor® Dreamcoat** (Narrator)

In the *Cats* national tour, many people in the cast relied on pills. One of the actors would take four to six Ripped Fuel, a drug with ephedrine, just to get through the show. I knew his body hurt, but I wondered why he did the show if he was so injured and he needed drugs just to get through. It was pathetic, and he had major mood swings. He was really high or really low, always complaining, and never happy.

There were so many people on tour who were unhappy. One of the main reasons they stayed in the show was out of fear of not finding another job. They also knew that tons of people would die to have their jobs. So they just continued to do the show, unhappy and in pain.

Kevin Loreque. *Cats** (Rum Tum Tugger), *Hot Shoe Shuffle**

The dynamics were hard. I had never experienced anything like that in my life, where you are working, eating, sleeping, and spending all of your time with the same group of actors. I lost my mind for a while. I thought I would have to go on Xanax because the thought of going to work made me physically ill. I started to get stomach problems. I had irritable bowel syndrome. I had acid reflux. I made myself sick from overexposure to these people.

What I missed the most on tour were refrigerator magnets. Of all things, I missed having magnets on the fridge that I would see every day.

One day, I walked out of a stage door and broke down because I didn't know where I was. I didn't know what city I was in. I didn't know what day of the week it was. All of the stage doors looked the same. I absolutely started to lose my mind.

And then I started to go to synagogue in each city. I needed something that was familiar. I hadn't gone to synagogue since I was thirteen. I wasn't a religious person at all. In each city, the Jewish community took me in. They thought I was this amazing person on the national tour of *Les Misérables*.

"Come into our synagogue."

"Marry our grandsons."

"Eat our gefilte fish."

So every week, in every city, I started going to synagogue, and it saved my life.

Rena Strober. *Les Misérables* (Cosette u/s)

A Big Star in Toledo, Ohio

Tour life is not reality. When I played Jean Valjean in *Les Misérables*, I was a huge star. In every city, my face was on the front page of the newspapers. Life-size posters of me were in the front of the theaters. I received great reviews. Everyone wanted to know me.

When I moved back to New York, no one knew who the hell I was. What I did on the road didn't mean jack to anyone in New York. I had to start all over again. I had to put my face in front of these same people and play the game once again.

Dave Clemmons. *The Scarlet Pimpernel* (Ben) [O], *The Civil War* (Sergeant Virgil Frank/Auctioneer's Assistant) [O], *Les Misérables* (Jean Valjean), *Whistle Down the Wind**, *Jekyll & Hyde** (Bishop)

CHAPTER 15

What Am I Doing Here?

In order to make it to Broadway, there are countless obstacles to overcome. In order to stay there, difficult sacrifices have to be made. Some of those obstacles and sacrifices have been addressed in the previous chapters. Many believe that the feeling of performing on a Broadway stage, night after night, will justify it all. It will make them feel whole, and fulfill them as a person. And, as an artist.

However, once the dream is realized, it is often not quite as grand. When so many Broadway actors find themselves uninspired and unhappy, it is time to start asking the question, "Why?"

Careful What You Wish For

When I was a swing in *Cats*, my opening night was everything I wanted it to be. At the end of the show, when I did my final tumbling pass, I couldn't even hear the audience because the cast was screaming so loud. It was beautiful. When I went up to the dressing room after the show, the actor who played Skimbleshanks asked, "What is it like to blow an entire Broadway company out of the water on your opening night?"

The next night, all the other swings were on except for me. The show started. I sat in this old, dusty, dirty dressing room, on a sweaty, stained, thirty-year-old sofa. As I was sitting by myself, hearing the music from the show, I thought, "This can't be it. This can't be my whole life's dream—sitting on this sweaty sofa in a dressing room all by myself."

That's when everything started to change. I had always thought that being on Broadway was going to fill this hole inside of me. It didn't.

Mark Moreau. *Cats* (Swing), *The Music Man* (Traveling Salesman), *The Will Rogers Follies*, *Grease!*

I had been performing with the German company of *Cats* when I was cast in the Broadway national tour. I was so excited. They gave me one week to learn the entire show—they normally give people three. I guess they figured that since I did the show in Germany, in German, there would be no problem. I had to learn the English in a week, along with very different choreography.

There was a number in the show where I had to dress up in a cockroach shell with wings, a hat with wires for antennas, and a huge pair of sunglasses. I had to hold knives and forks in my hands while tapping in the background. I was one of about twenty cockroaches in tap shoes. No one could tell who I was.

On my opening night, I was so nervous because I had so little rehearsal time with my new cast. Some opening nights go smoothly. Mine did not. During the cockroach number, my fork went flying and ended up on someone's head. Without hesitation, I scrambled over in my huge cockroach costume, desperately trying to recover my fork.

Then, at that very moment, for the first time, it hit me.

"What the hell am I doing here?" I thought. "I am an anonymous cockroach, with twenty other cockroaches, tapping on stage. Is this what Broadway is all about?"

Christie McCall. *Cats** (Sillabub)

Before I was cast in *The Lion King,* I was playing guitar at O'Flaherty's, a bar on Restaurant Row. I was doing voice-overs, I had a temp day job, and played with a band. Things were really good. Then I got the brass ring. I was cast in *The Lion King*. The night I was cast, I went to a bar to celebrate with my friends. I thought, "Now I don't have to be the guy in the group who has never been in a Broadway show." It was the worst year of my life.

Jeff Gurner. *The Lion King* (Ed the Hyena)

Les Misérables was my dream show. I'd do anything to be in that show. Before I was cast, I used to think that I would even play a dead person on the barricade just to be a part of the production.

I remember doing *Les Misérables* in Seattle. I was sitting on stage left and I was ready to run on stage. After watching some of the jaded actors mingle around the barricade, I remember breaking down and crying. This had been a dream of mine ever since I was thirteen. Now that I'd done it for a while, it didn't seem grand or amazing anymore. It seemed like work. It was time for me to leave the show.

My dream was just about shattered. In the beginning, I used to think *Les Misérables* was the biggest thing in the world. Now, I thought, "This fucking show, I can't believe I have to do it again."

Daniel C. Levine. *Jesus Christ Superstar* (Disciple) [O], *The Rocky Horror Show*, *Chicago** (Mary Sunshine), *Les Misérables** (Marius u/s), *Mamma Mia!**

Les Misérables. Photo credit: Joan Marcus/Photofest

Why Aren't I Smiling?

I began my first Broadway show with a glamorized view of Broadway. I was in *Miss Saigon*, a hit Broadway show. I was surrounded by talented people. Nevertheless, I was miserable within a year, and I am not a miserable person. It was just a difficult situation. There was a lot of unhappiness in the cast. People had been in the show for years. For whatever reason, they couldn't get another job, or they didn't want to get another job. They liked the security, but didn't like the show. I felt like I was in the middle of a tornado.

Frank Baiocchi. *Miss Saigon* (Chris u/s), *South Pacific** (Cable u/s)

By this point in my career, I thought I would be the next Richard Burton. Now, however, I feel like I am trapped in a pattern. It lowers my self-esteem. I have become bitter and jaded, like so many other people on Broadway.

When I was cast in *Smokey Joe's Cafe*, I was excited and vibrant and enthused. I said to myself, "I finally made it to Broadway. This is what it is all about!" However, the show had been open for three years, and the cast members were jaded. I couldn't talk to them without wondering if what they told me was real. I thought, "We are on Broadway and making a lot of money and you are bitter about it. Is Broadway this hard?"

Now, looking at the past few years of my life, I can understand why they were jaded and bitter. Some were old and just tired of fighting. They wanted to get ahead and something was stopping them. They couldn't accept a new energy. I was the new kid who came in thinking, "Oh, isn't this great. I am on Broadway. I've made it." They said, "Listen, kid, just chill and find your place." I couldn't enjoy the ride.

Jerry Tellier. *Saturday Night Fever* (Frank Junior) [O], *42nd Street* [O], *Smokey Joe's Cafe*

I went through a period where I thought, "What am I doing?" I chose this business when I was a kid. I didn't know what I was doing. Now I'm a grown man and I'm trying to make sense of it and it just doesn't make sense. I wouldn't be living in this city if it wasn't for the theater. I was basically depressed, apathetic, and uninspired.

Jim Walton. *The Music Man* (Harold Hill s/b) [O], *Merrily We Roll Along* (Franklin Shepard) [O], *Sweeney Todd* (Anthony Hope) [O], *Perfectly Frank* [O], *Stardust* [O], *42nd Street* (Billy Lawlor)

I was in *Dream*, a huge Broadway show, with wonderful people, thinking, "I might be okay if this thing closes." It was horrible to say, because there were people kicking and screaming to get in. It's not to say that I didn't appreciate and respect it, but there was a little egg timer in my body which said, "I don't want to do this anymore—maybe this specific show, maybe this profession entirely."

Jonathan Dokuchitz. *Tommy* (Captain Walker) [O], *Into the Woods* (Rapunzel's Prince) [O], *The Boys from Syracuse* (Antipholus of Syracuse) [O], *Company* (Peter) [O], *Dream* [O], *The Look of Love* [O]

I was thirty years old when I got *Les Misérables*. Although it was special, it felt normal. Tens of thousands of actors wanted to be in that show. I became jaded with the Broadway scene. I thought, "Is this all there is?" I started to wonder what it was that I was reaching for. I wondered what I was really trying to do. Initially, I arrived on Broadway and thought, "This is cool." After a few months, I thought, "This is a job."

It's so funny that I talk about being jaded, because here I am, fifteen years later, thinking, "I wish somebody would give me a job so I could feel jaded again." A good question would be, "If I did get another Broadway show, would I become jaded again, or is jaded something you can only become once in your life?"

Alex Santoriello. *Les Misérables* (Montparnasse) [O], *3 Penny Opera* (Jimmy) [O], *Chess* [O], *Jesus Christ Superstar** (Pilate), *Cats** (Asparagus)

I spent almost six years doing *Jekyll and Hyde*. During the fourth year, I thought, "Oh, God, am I ever going to do anything else?" I was not challenged creatively or artistically. I had very little emotional involvement in the show. I often had to remind myself, "You are working on Broadway. You are living your dreams."

Brad Oscar. *The Producers* (Franz Liebkind) [O][t], *Aspects of Love* (Swing) [O], *Jekyll and Hyde* (Archibald Proops) [O]

PART SIX

A NEW
ERA

CHAPTER 16

The Disneyfication of Broadway

The 1980s marked the beginning of a new era on Broadway. Musicals by Sir Andrew Lloyd Webber and Claude-Michel Schönberg took America by storm, broadening the appeal of musical theater to unprecedented levels. The power and elegance of these breathtaking musicals captured the imagination of millions, and served as the inspiration for a new generation of Broadway performer.

These mega-musicals, however, cost millions of dollars to produce. Money needed to be raised by investors, who in turn wanted to maximize the return on each dollar invested. When producers such as Cameron Mackintosh saw an opportunity to market musicals as never before, the world of Broadway changed forever. New marketing efforts combined with the gentrification of Times Square made it possible for shows such as *The Phantom of the Opera* and *Les Misérables* to run indefinitely. *Cats* finally closed in 2000 after 7,485 performances, and *Les Misérables* closed in 2003 after 6,680.

Rather than going to see the show for the individual performers, people went to see *Cats* for the make-up, *Les Misérables* for the barricade, *Miss Saigon* for the helicopter, and *The Phantom of the Opera* for the chandelier. Further, the shows were not marketed by the actors but by the logos, such as the dancing yellow-green eyes of *Cats,* the mask of *Phantom,* and the young Cosette of *Les Misérables,* which made their way onto everything from beach towels to Christmas ornaments.

Disney soon joined in the action and raised the stakes with *Beauty and the Beast* and *The Lion King*, where actors are so hidden in elaborate costumes that some performers on stage are nowhere to be seen. The arrival of Disney further broadened the appeal of Broadway to millions of families who would otherwise never have attended a Broadway musical, and who were suddenly willing to spend hundreds of dollars to be dazzled by multimillion-dollar productions.

In the new era of Broadway, the shows themselves, not the actors who perform in them, have become the stars. The spectacle has taken over. Long gone are the days when shows were built around Broadway personalities such as Ethel Merman and Carol Channing. Furthermore, in an attempt to broaden the appeal of musicals as wide as possible, shows are increasingly the product of test groups and corporate committees. Television and Hollywood celebrities are brought in, sometimes during their summer vacations, just to keep things going.

As a result, not only are there more actors in New York City competing for fewer parts than ever before, but worse, Broadway performers have begun to lose their value to Broadway itself. Ask anyone who has just seen one of these mega-musicals to list the names, or even one name, of any of the actors they just saw perform on stage. Unless the actor is a Hollywood or television celebrity, many will have no idea. The Broadway actor has become virtually anonymous, even to many of those within the Broadway community itself.

Despite fighting all their lives to make it to Broadway, once there, many actors find themselves to be expendable, and easily interchangeable. Paradoxically, this is largely the result of the very shows which inspired them to join the ranks of Broadway in the first place. As shows have become increasingly commercial, and as audiences have grown less sophisticated, the life of a Broadway performer has become more challenging than ever before.

Where Did All the Stars Go?

Broadway doesn't make stars anymore. The shows are the stars—*Cats, Les Misérables, Starlight Express,* and the whole Cameron Mackintosh/ Andrew Lloyd Webber onslaught. There were no stars in those shows.
> **Terrence Mann.** *Les Misérables* (Javert) [O][t], *Beauty and the Beast* (Beast) [O][t], *Cats* (Rum Tum Tugger) [O], *The Scarlet Pimpernel* (Chauvelin) [O], *Barnum* (Chester Lyman) [O], *Rags* (Saul) [O], *Getting Away with Murder* (Gregory Reed) [O], *Jerome Robbins' Broadway* (Emcee), *The Rocky Horror Show* (Dr. Frank N. Furter)

The star of the show is not the performer—it's the show. The star of *The Phantom of the Opera* is the chandelier. The star of *Les Misérables* is the turntable. All of us in the show are just cogs in a wheel. The shows are going to run no matter what.
> **Ray Walker.** *Jesus Christ Superstar* (Annas) [O], *Grease!* (Doody), *Les Misérables* (Marius), *Whistle Down the Wind** (Preacher), *Music of the Night** (Principal Soloist), *Joseph and the Amazing Technicolor® Dreamcoat** (Joseph u/s), *Falsettos** (Whizzer)

Miss Saigon. Photo credit: Joan Marcus/Photofest

Musicals have become so expensive. Usually, it is ten million bucks, minimum, to do a Broadway show. It's an expensive venture. Cameron Mackintosh made a fortune by making the logo of his show the star. That's what he does. There was a sign in New York that read, *Broadway's Best.* It featured the *Miss Saigon, Les Misérables,* and the *Phantom* logos. We know what those things are. It's a business decision. It makes sense. I understand it, but it's very painful for us.

> **Ron Bohmer.** *Fiddler on the Roof* (Fyedka) [O], *The Scarlet Pimpernel* (Percy), *Les Misérables* (Enjolras), *Aspects of Love** (Alex), *Sunset Boulevard** (Joe Gillis), *The Phantom of the Opera** (Phantom)

Nobody knows who we are. I've done tests. When I was on a national tour, I asked people all over the country, "Have you ever heard of Faith Prince?"

"No."

Nobody knows Faith Prince and some of the other biggest "stars" in musical theater. Nobody knows who they are.

"Know who Britney Spears is?"

"Yeah!"

She's been around for just a few years. If you are in this to get famous, forget it.

> **Sarah Uriarte Berry.** *Taboo* (Nicola) [O], *Les Misérables* (Eponine), *Beauty and the Beast* (Belle), *Sunset Boulevard** (Betty Schaeffer), *Carousel** (Julie Jordan)

It was a different era when I was on Broadway. It was a glamorous era. We had these fabulous songwriters, like Oscar Hammerstein and Irving Berlin. All the shows were bigger than movies. It was a most exciting period. When the songwriters died off, Broadway wasn't the same. And then the British shows started coming into town. They were all so strange.

Earl Wilson was a famous newspaper reporter at the time. He had his own column in a big paper. We both attended the opening night of *Cats*. During intermission, I said to Earl, "You know what, I'm going to open a show across the street called *Dogs*." The next day, there was a big headline in the paper that read, *"Ann Miller Wants to Open a Show Called Dogs."* I was so embarrassed.

The new British shows were outstanding in their own way. They took a different approach than the shows that were running at that time. Imagine being a train like in *Starlight Express*, or a pussycat like in *Cats*. It was just weird. They did it. That alone was crazy. I can see why Andrew Lloyd Webber and Cameron Mackintosh were so successful. The audiences wanted to see something different. It was a new thingy-dingy. People wanted to see that. They got it. Those shows ran and ran and ran.

The trick the producers developed was to make the logos the star of the show, not the performers. It was a business decision, because if anyone dropped out of the show, they could insert somebody new into the show and nobody would know the difference. The show could carry on and draw crowds, whether on Broadway or a national tour.

I was starring in *Sugar Babies* at the time the British shows started coming in. Mickey Rooney's name and mine were above the title. If one of us dropped out, it would have been a big deal. If I had dropped out of *Mame*, there would have been a big problem. The audience came to see me.

Ann Miller. *Sugar Babies* (Ann) [O][t], *George White's Scandals* [O], *Mame* (Mame Dennis)

The Death of the Gypsy

When I first started on Broadway, *42nd Street* had just opened. *Barnum* had just opened. These were traditional kinds of musicals that would have a long life. Back then, a long life could mean two or three years. If it ran a year, it was a hit. In the old days, if it ran six months it was a hit. Because shows didn't have to run as long to turn a profit, there were more shows out each year. And thus, you could be a gypsy. You could make a living on Broadway going from show to show. Now the shows can't make their money back in such a short amount of time. The dynamics have changed.

Old theatrical posters. Photo credit: Photofest

In 1982, when *Cats* opened, things began to change. The mega-musicals needed to run for years because they cost millions to mount. *Barnum* was the most expensive musical of its time. I think it was around three million dollars. People thought they were out of their minds by spending three million dollars. When *Cats* came to Broadway, I think it was six million for the actual cost of production, but by the time they paid for the advertising and marketing, posted a bond, and renovated the theater, I think it was close to ten million dollars.

That changed the dynamics of theater. Now, shows had to run a much longer time. If they couldn't, they closed. Suddenly, there was no turnover. If a show was a hit, it would stay in a theater for many years. And so would the actors. If a show wasn't a hit, it would close very quickly and the theater would remain dark. It became feast or famine. Either you were in a show, or you weren't. The costs of things have changed the world and have changed theater.

We have corporate theater now. Corporations decide if a show gets produced, how it gets produced, when it gets produced, and what theater it's in. Consequently, it has changed the way actors get work, how much work they get, and how many opportunities are available.

Ray Roderick. *Grind* (Knockabout) [O], *A Funny Thing Happened on the Way to the Forum* (Protean) [O], *Crazy For You* (Billy) [O], *Wind in the Willows* [O], *Cats* (Carbucketty), *Barnum** (Tom Thumb)

In the fifties, being a Broadway performer was easier because there were so many musicals. If you were an ingénue with a good voice, which I was, there were many shows you could get into. People paid more attention to Broadway music. Now, it seems like we have gone back to being more like circus people, carnival people—big sets and spectacle.

Anita Gillette. *Chapter Two* (Jennie Malone) [O][t], *Guys and Dolls* (Sarah Brown) [O], *Kelly* (Angela Crane) [O], *Carnival!* (Gypsy) [O], *All American* (Susan) [O], *Mr. President* (Leslie Henderson) [O], *Jimmy* (Betty Compton) [O], *Don't Drink the Water* (Susan Hollander) [O], *Gypsy* (Thelma), *Brighton Beach Memoirs* (Blanche), *They're Playing Our Song* (Sonia Walsk), *Cabaret* (Sally)

Recently, I came upon my appointment book from many years ago. There were just auditions after auditions after auditions that I could go to. Sometimes I would have three Broadway auditions in one week. Now, everything is so high-risk. I can't believe that they are still putting on Broadway shows.

Betsy Joslyn. *High Society* (Patsy) [O], *Sweeney Todd* (Johanna) [O], *The Goodbye Girl* (Paula s/b) [O], *A Doll's Life* (Nora) [O], *A Few Good Men* (Lt. Galloway s/b) [O], *Into the Woods* (The Witch), *Sunday in the Park with George* (Dot), *Les Misérables* (Madame Thénardier), *Beauty and the Beast** (Mrs. Potts), *City of Angels** (Oolie/Donna), *Camelot** (Guenevere), *Of Thee I Sing**, *Let 'em Eat Cake**

There is no such thing anymore as a dancing chorus, or a singing chorus, or even a standing chorus. Everyone has to do it all. It's economics. Broadway casts used to have fifty or sixty actors in a show. Now, casts are comprised of maybe twenty-six actors, or less. It's small. There are as many people playing in the orchestra as there are on stage.

Gary Beach. *The Producers* (Roger DeBris) [O][T], *Beauty and the Beast* (Lumiere) [O][t], *The Moony Shapiro Songbook* [O], *Doonesbury* (Duke) [O], *Something's Afoot* (Nigel) [O], *Sweet Adeline* (Dan Ward) [O], *Annie* (Rooster Hannigan), *1776* (Edward Rutledge), *Les Misérables** (Thénardier), *Of Thee I Sing**

Broadway has changed. Because of the expense, you can't mount a show for two million, three million, or even four or five million. It now costs over ten million. They are so expensive. The stakes are so high right now and nobody is willing to risk it. Today, actors do readings and workshops.

Over and over again. It's a whole new world. It is no longer the case that you audition for a show, six weeks later you go into rehearsal, six weeks later you open in Boston, and then you come to New York. The economics simply don't allow for it anymore.

Debbie Gravitte. *Jerome Robbins' Broadway* [O][**T**], *They're Playing Our Song* (Sonia Walsk) [O], *Blues in the Nigh*t (Woman #2) [O], *Ain't Broadway Grand* (Gypsy Rose Lee) [O], *Zorba* (The Woman) [O], *Perfectly Frank*, *Les Misérables* (Fantine) [O], *Chicago* (Mama Morton)

The Good Old Days

There is so much to say. There is so much to tell about a theater that almost doesn't exist anymore. It's a different can of beans. We are a disposable country. Everything is made to be thrown away. We discard our traditions so quickly. It must be very baffling for a new person in theater. There was a time that I came from where, when you appeared in your first show, you were the kid. The person you performed with had been in the theater for forty years. There was a wonderful exchange. It was a nourishing environment. I don't know whether it exists today. There was an awe of the person who had been in the theater for so many years, and was still in it.

Sondra Lee. *Peter Pan* (Tiger Lilly) [O], *High Button Shoes* (Playmate of the Boy at the Picnic) [O], *Hotel Paradiso* (Victoire) [O], *Hello, Dolly!* (Minnie Fay) [O], *Sunday in New York* (Woman) [O]

I came to New York in 1955. The atmosphere was more innocent. It was a lot easier to "make it." The Broadway community was competitive but not as cutthroat. I never experienced waiting in line or sitting in front of the Equity building at five in the morning. We didn't have numbers. You just went to the audition. If the big choreographers and directors liked you, they would just keep you working. Shows didn't run for ten years.

I was the first Jet replacement in *West Side Story*. Why I got picked, I will never know. I wasn't really a very technical dancer and this was Jerome Robbins. It was hard dancing. When we filmed the movie *West Side Story*, Jerome Robbins taught ballet class every morning. I was mainly a "hoofer," or tap dancer, from Cincinnati, so I learned what a ballet step was from one of the greatest choreographers of all time. First I did shows with Bob Fosse, then Jerome Robbins. They were my mentors. I was blessed. That couldn't happen now.

Today, shows are produced by somebody in Iowa or something. There is no loyalty. There wasn't the desperation then that there is now. Today, you can be talented and be overlooked. When I came to New York in 1955, I'm not sure that it was possible to be overlooked. It was simpler. Not as frantic. Not as big. If you were good, you would be seen. There weren't as many people trying to "make it" either. I came from a period where I loved what I was doing more than how much money I was going to make at the end of the year. I never thought of the future.

Harvey Evans. *Oklahoma!* (Andrew Carnes u/s) [O], *Barnum* (Phineas Taylor Barnum u/s) [O], *Our Town* (George Gibbs) [O], *Follies* (Young Buddy) [O], *The Boy Friend* (Bobby Van Husen) [O], *George M!* (Sam Harris) [O], *Anyone Can Whistle* (John) [O], *Redhead* (Dancer) [O], *New Girl in Town* (Dancer) [O], *Sunset Boulevard* [O], *Sextet* [O], *West Side Story* (Gee-Tar), *Gypsy* (Farm Boy), *The Scarlet Pimpernel* (Ozzy), *Hello, Dolly!* (Barnaby Tucker), *Damn Yankees**, *Nash at Nine**, *La Cage Aux Folles**

When I was cast in the tour of *Call Me Madam*, I was in the chorus. There was simply nothing like being a chorus dancer in those days. The unity was amazing. The respect we had for each other was incredible. Nobody thought that they were any better than anyone else. We were all thinking as one.

Today, I think people get bored. I think it is a sign of the times. Back then, we didn't get bored. We became closer to the cast and we learned from each other more and more as the play went on. We learned more about ourselves. It was like going to class. Everything was a lesson to me. The theater is an amazing place to learn about life.

Nowadays, many people think that the title "chorus dancer" is beneath them. We never felt that way. I got so much energy from the other dancers. I became so much stronger by really relating to my partners. So, when I first came to New York, that was what I knew. I knew the chorus. Eventually, out of chorus would come amazing choreographers and soloists.

I don't see the camaraderie as much anymore. Everyone wants to be a soloist before really learning how to relate. When you can relate to the person next to you without words and be alive, when you can keep the energy and interest going, it is magical.

Chita Rivera. *Kiss of the Spider Woman* (Spider Woman) [O][**T**], *The Rink* (Anna) [O][**T**], *Nine* (Liliane La Fleur) [O][**t**], *Jerry's Girls* [O][**t**], *Merlin* (The Queen) [O][**t**], *Bring Back Birdie* (Rose) [O][**t**], *Chicago* (Velma) [O][**t**], *Bye Bye Birdie* (Rose) [O][**t**], *Bajour* (Anyanka) [O], *West Side Story* (Anita) [O], *Shinbone Alley* (Mehitabel s/b) [O], *Mr. Wonderful* (Rita Romano) [O], *Seventh Heaven* (Fifi) [O], *Born Yesterday** (Billie Dawn), *3 Penny Opera** (Jenny), *Zorba** (The Leader), *The Rose Tattoo**, *Call Me Madam**, *Sweet Charity**, *Can-Can**, *Kiss Me, Kate**

Years ago, when I was in *How to Succeed in Business*, I think I made $150 a week. I started studying acting and voice. It was intense. It was like going to university. Then I would do the show at night. Frank Loesser was my vocal coach. I didn't know who he was. While I was really right off the bus, it didn't take me long to appreciate these people. I learned all that I could.

Now, it's much colder. There is no longer one independent producer for a show, but there are like fourteen producers, plus two corporations, and all of their people that work for them. Everyone is fearful of being creative. Compromises are made far too often. Because of the economic compromises that are made, everybody suffers in many different ways. There was a protocol, a behavior backstage, a respect, a love, and a joy of performing that's no longer here.

> **Donna McKechnie.** *A Chorus Line* (Cassie) [O][**T**], *Company* (Kathy) [O], *State Fair* (Emily Arden) [O], *On the Town* (Ivy Smith) [O], *Promises, Promises* (Vivien Della Hoya) [O], *The Education of Hyman Kaplan* (Kathy McKenna) [O], *How to Succeed in Business without Really Trying!* (Dancer) [O], *A Funny Thing Happened on the Way to the Forum** (Philia), *Call Me Madam** (The Princess), *Sweet Charity**, *Annie Get Your Gun**

Britney Spears on Broadway?

All of those movie and television people are the ones who are taking the roles on Broadway. They are the ones that people want to see. They want to see someone famous. Nobody knows who I am. They know who I am within the Broadway community, but the next job I go up for is going to be between me, Lea Thompson, and maybe a few other big television people. And the producers want the movie actress because she is going to bring in more money. In most cases, the Broadway talent gets booted out. They don't get famous. You can't be a Broadway star anymore. And in Los Angeles, they don't even care if you won a Tony. It doesn't mean anything.

To make a living in this business, you almost have to do both Broadway and television or film. Furthermore, Broadway shows just don't come around. I was making great money doing *Chicago*, but now I am not making a cent. Nothing is coming in. How long can I last with that? And when will another Broadway show even come around that I am right for? In another three years? Four years? What am I going to do in the meantime? Regional theater pays nothing. It is a tough life. A really tough life.

> **Charlotte d'Amboise.** *Jerome Robbins' Broadway* (Anita/Peter Pan) [O][t], *Carrie* (Chris) [O], *Company* (Cathy) [O], *Song and Dance* [O], *Contact* (Wife), *Damn Yankees* (Lola), *Chicago* (Roxie Hart), *Cats* (Cassandra)

I was in a show called *The Rink*. The show was largely and unfairly panned because of the presence of Liza Minnelli, who was actually quite spectacular in the show. However, without her, we might very well have closed right after opening night. With Liza, we ran nine months. As soon as she left, we died. Stockard Channing came in. Although she was wonderful, we closed in a few weeks.

Jason Alexander. *Jerome Robbins' Broadway* (Emcee) [O][T], *Merrily We Roll Along* (Joe) [O], *The Rink* (Lino/Lenny/Punk/Uncle Fausto) [O], *Broadway Bound* (Stanley) [O], *Accomplice* [O], *The Producers** (Max Bialystock)

I played a principal part in my first Broadway show. I went right from that role to Jean Valjean in *Les Misérables*. I thought, "Great. Now I'll start to be seen." But it just didn't happen. It was as if those jobs had never existed.

Later on, I realized that I was on a treadmill. You can only make so much money on Broadway as a working actor. You can be a working actor, or you can have a career. The way to have a career is by doing something outside Broadway—by leaving the nest. Or if you happen to get lucky and you land a role in a new musical, maybe that bumps you up.

When I realized this, it was horribly depressing. I had spent ten years working on Broadway, and seven years before that working regionally and learning my craft, and all of a sudden I didn't have the means to accomplish my goals. You can't do it in this marketplace. It's not possible unless you go to Los Angeles and get a television show, or start working in films.

Philip Hernández. *The Capeman* (Reverend Gonzalez) [O], *Kiss of the Spider Woman* (Esteban) [O], *Les Misérables* (Jean Valjean/Javert), *Copacabana** (Rico)

Twelve years ago, I came from Hollywood back to Broadway, where I began my career. Back then, when a Hollywood celebrity would come back to Broadway, they were pooh-poohed. It didn't matter what they had done on Broadway before.

When I tried to come back, they said, "Who is this guy? He was the Dance Fever man? He was the T.J. Hooker guy? No. He can't do this. We need real actors."

My agent said, "But he can sing and act. That's how he started."

They responded, "Well, he's been away a long time."

So, I paid my dues. I did Off-Broadway. That still wasn't enough. I ended up doing a production of *Godspell* at the Candlewood Playhouse in Connecticut. I had producers see the production. That started the ball rolling again. I had to bust my ass to show that Adrian Zmed could stand on a Broadway stage again and perform with the best of them.

Now, twelve years later, if you are a movie star, it doesn't matter if you have ever sung or danced before in your entire life. You can still star in a Broadway show. All your agent has to do is make a phone call.

Usually, most of the celebrities today suck. It is embarrassing, especially when they are wrapped around quality Broadway performers. They are like high school kids on a Broadway stage. That is what Broadway has become. This is not true for all Hollywood celebrities, such as Antonio Banderas. He is phenomenal. He belongs on Broadway. However, 90 percent of the celebrities they bring in have no business being here.

Today, everything is reversed. Despite having paid my dues for the past ten years on Broadway, I'm still having trouble getting a job. The producers say, "Who cares if he has done Broadway! What was his last blockbuster movie?"

Adrian Zmed. *Grease!* (Danny), *Blood Brothers* (Narrator), *Falsettos* (Marvin), *Chicago* (Billy Flynn), *Same Time, Next Year**

I did *Grease!* on Broadway. The producers brought in a cavalcade of seventies television stars—people who had no business being on stage. Some people couldn't sing, act, or move. It was so unfair.

Sure, it's great to say, "I'm in a show with one of the Monkees!" But when they can't do anything, it's just unbelievable. People want to see Micky Dolenz or Marcia Brady. That's disillusioning. You think, "In order for me to gain any ground, I have to go to Los Angeles, get a successful sitcom deal, and then, if I'm lucky, I can come back to New York and go into the show *Chicago.*" That's the only way to get your name above the title and make money.

Ray Walker. *Jesus Christ Superstar* (Annas) [O], *Grease!* (Doody), *Les Misérables* (Marius), *Whistle Down the Wind** (Preacher), *Music of the Night** (Principal Soloist), *Joseph and the Amazing Technicolor® Dreamcoat** (Joseph u/s), *Falsettos** (Whizzer)

At one point during *Grease!*, the show was about to close. Then, Lucy Lawless came in and we sold out for three months. That meant that we had jobs for three months. I was grateful when she came. I'm the bad actress who thinks "Well, if it's going to keep a show open, then do it."

Marissa Jaret Winokur. *Hairspray* (Tracy Turnblad) [O][**T**], *Grease!* (Jan)

I auditioned for *Urinetown* when it was just a little Off-Broadway show. The cast wasn't even sure if the show was funny or not. The subject matter never seemed like it was going to be on Broadway with *Aida* and *The Lion King*, which are big spectacles. The producers were really smart. They did the show in a small Off-Broadway theater and they basically gave tickets away. It created a buzz and we got a great review in the *New York Times*.

One day, one of the producers came to me and said, "We are going to Broadway."

I said "Broadway? People love it, but it is not a Broadway show. This is an Off-Broadway show, and you are going to kill it. Broadway is for *42nd Street* and *The Producers*."

We opened and were nominated for ten Drama Desk Awards. The producers took a huge gamble in bringing the show to Broadway. Fortunately, our theater was intimate and the right space for the show. The producers did not want to turn it into a big show. They wanted to take exactly what they had and put it on Broadway. They thought they could sell it. They did. It was remarkable that this happened during a time when you need a big star and glitz to sell tickets. The show was the anti-Broadway musical. It was the little Broadway musical that could.

However, the irony of it all is, two years into the run, the producers stooped to the level of bringing in a celebrity. When I left the show, they brought in a television star to replace me—Tom Cavanaugh. It went against everything the show stood for. They got caught up in the producing machine. The show turned around and sold out to the very thing it was trying not to be in the first place.

Hunter Foster. *Little Shop of Horrors* (Seymour) [O], *Urinetown* (Bobby Strong) [O], *Footloose* (Bickle) [O], *King David* [O], *Grease!* (Roger) [O], *Les Misérables* (Marius u/s), *Martin Guerre** (Martin u/s), *Cats** (Rum Tum Tugger)

The industry changed after Broadway went corporate. Believe it or not, I'll never get to do *Cabaret* in New York, because I'm not a "star." I waited a long time to play that role and I'll never get to do it on Broadway because I don't have a television or movie name. I find that very sad. John Stamos is starring in *Cabaret*. No offense, but that makes me sick.

Andrea McArdle. *Annie* (Annie) [O][t], *Starlight Express* (Ashley) [O], *State Fair* (Margy Frake) [O], *Les Misérables* (Fantine), *Beauty and the Beast* (Belle), *Cabaret** (Sally Bowles), *Jerry's Girls**

The most disappointing thing that has happened to me was doing the workshops and raising the money for a show and then not being offered the part. I was passed over for a celebrity. That happens a lot. I understand it, but it's really sad. It doesn't necessarily mean the celebrity is going to do a bad job, but this is our life. This is what we excel in. This is our forte, musical theater. It is a very special animal. There are some people who are famous and who are great on the stage—the Glenn Closes and Meryl Streeps of this world. But, hopefully, there is a place for us too.

Karen Ziemba. *Contact* (Wife) [O][**T**], *Steel Pier* (Rita Racine) [O][t], *Never Gonna Dance* (Mabel) [O], *Teddy & Alice* (Alice u/s) [O], *Crazy for You* (Polly Baker), *42nd Street* (Peggy Sawyer), *Chicago* (Roxie Hart), *A Chorus Line* (Bebe)

There is a silly competition between Broadway actors and Hollywood actors in terms of, "We are the real actors because we perform live, and you are not because you perform in front of a camera." Ultimately, I think audiences are smart. No matter what name you are carrying on your shoulders, if your show is no good, or if you are bad, the criticism can be strong.

When I came to Broadway, I thought that the possibility of being crucified was real. What is Antonio Banderas doing here? I heard that before I came. I knew that there were some people who thought, "What the heck is he going to try to demonstrate or do?" They were waiting for me. Waiting for me with weapons out.

I think I did a good job. I don't want to say I was extraordinary, or do an exercise in modesty by saying, "No, no." I think I did a good job, it was appreciated, and I did what I wanted to do. I was pretty satisfied, and I am happy that I came here. In some ways, I feel as if I have come back home, even though I have never worked on Broadway or in New York. I just went back to something that I consider mine.

Antonio Banderas. *Nine* (Guido Contini) [O][t]

Another Standing Ovation

We'd like to believe that our audiences are these theater-savvy people that could tell the difference between a good performance and a bad one, but the reality is that they are the people that kept *Three's Company* on the air for eight years. They are the people who think Al Bundy, sticking his hand down his pants, is funny. Broadway plays to those people.

Regional theater, such as the Guthrie and the Goodman, draws savvy audiences. However, those "savvy audiences" weren't the ones that keep *Les Misérables* going for sixteen years. On Broadway, give them a good burp, a fart, a slap, and that's all they need.

I don't think audiences know the difference between a good performance and a bad one. I've witnessed some horrendous performances on a Broadway stage that got audiences leaping to their feet.

Craig Bennet. *Miss Saigon* (Marine/Reeves), *Les Misérables** (Thénardier u/s), *Mamma Mia!** (Bill), *Ragtime** (Willie Conklin)

The biggest impact that corporate theater is having is on the development of the audience. Based on the projects that Broadway gravitates towards, spectacles that are often based on animation, they are cultivating an audience of people who are expecting spectacle and something that they can sing along to. The new audiences don't want challenging material. They want stuff they already know. As a result, theater has increasingly become a "comfortable experience," rather than something that could surprise and challenge.

Jeff Blumenkrantz. *Urban Cowboy* [O][t], *A Class Act* (Charlie/Marvin) [O], *Into the Woods* (Jack/Rapunzel's Prince u/s) [O], *How to Succeed in Business Without Really Trying!* (Bud Frump) [O], *Damn Yankees* (Smokey) [O], *3 Penny Opera* (Filch) [O], *Joseph and the Amazing Technicolor® Dreamcoat** (Brother)

One of the things that rankles me about Broadway is that the audience has become numb.

When I saw *Hairspray*, I thought, "This is an incredibly talented show. It has a catchy, fun score. It was designed with creativity. It is totally heartfelt and the performance energies are great. It's a terrific show."

However, one day, one of the producers asked me, "What did you think?"

All I could say was, "Um, uh-huh, it's very good."

He said, "You aren't giving it to me."

And I thought, if *Hairspray* was the exception to what is current Broadway fare, it would be glorious. Like when *Grease!* came into Broadway, most Broadway musicals were in the vein of *Man of La Mancha, Les Misérables,* and *Sweeney Todd. Grease!* was the exception, the lark. It was a fun, kitschy, entertaining show.

However, when everything on Broadway is *Grease!*, then *Grease!* can't be special. When everything on Broadway is *Footloose, Mamma Mia!,* and the like, then that flavor becomes uninteresting. *Hairspray* is light years beyond *Footloose* and *Mamma Mia!* But its brilliance, for me, was diminished because of shows like *Footloose* and *Mamma Mia!*

An audience coming into a mid-prairie theater in Tumbleweed Town doesn't expect it's going to have the experience of a lifetime. The Broadway audience, however, is different. They come in thinking, "This is the best there is, at a ticket price I can't afford. This is going to rock my life!" They come in with that expectation. And they're gonna have it, even when they haven't had it.

In the last ten years, I can't remember going to a show and not seeing a standing ovation. Audiences will stand for anything. It is sort of like they are telling themselves they had an amazing time by standing up and applauding.

To me, one of the current problems on Broadway stems from the relatively new corporate nature of Broadway. The current fad is, "Let's take movies and put them on stage," rather than spend five years and create something new and have it close in one night.

That is the corporate mentality.

When I started going to the theater, the relationship between the performers and the audience was a thing of beauty. It was a giant magic trick. The audience went on the illusion-journey with you. The relationship was beautiful. It was incredibly respectful. The actors respected the audience and the audience respected the actors.

But then, when I did *Broadway Bound*, people put coats, umbrellas, and *Playbills* right on the stage. It got to the point where, during the middle of the show, I would grab all the coats and umbrellas and put them in the onstage closet.

In *Jerome Robbins' Broadway*, audience members would also put their *Playbills* on the stage. In dance numbers, any time I had a little kick, I would kick the *Playbills* off, unfortunately often right onto their heads!

Nowadays, they even announce before a show, "Turn off your cell phones and pagers." Do people do it?

No.

And what is this whole "race for the door" mentality after a show now? If you have an experience at a show, would it kill you to stay for the curtain call? Do you know how offensive and humiliating it is to work for an audience who gives you their backs when you have to bow? The bows are the only chance an audience and a performer have to really acknowledge each other—to appreciate each other for their mutual involvement in the shared experience they just had. When the audience-actor relationship breaks down like that, the audience will wind up being the one who suffers more.

If you want to diminish the loftiness of theater, you can. But what you are going to get in return is a much less important experience. That is what Broadway is in danger of becoming.

Jason Alexander. *Jerome Robbins' Broadway* (Emcee) [O][**T**], *Merrily We Roll Along* (Joe) [O], *The Rink* (Lino/Lenny/Punk/Uncle Fausto) [O], *Broadway Bound* (Stanley) [O], *Accomplice* [O], *The Producers** (Max Bialystock)

The New Business Model

Theater is corporate now. Corporations use "test groups" to create a the-ater product—like when they are marketing a car, for example. I don't think a musical can work that way. It is a living thing. It's a relationship of actors to the audience. Somehow it needs to be more spontaneous.

Nick Corley. *She Loves Me* (Keller) [O]

Disney has unlimited resources and they know how to market. They know how to sell their shows. They know how to take a show, good or bad, and convince people that it is a must-see product. That is what Broadway has become. It is a product, like Ajax or Tide.

Debbie Gravitte. *Jerome Robbins' Broadway* [O][**T**], *They're Playing our Song* (Sonia Walsk) [O], *Blues in the Night* (Woman #2) [O], *Ain't Broadway Grand* (Gypsy Rose Lee) [O], *Zorba* (The Woman) [O], *Perfectly Frank* [O], *Les Misérables* (Fantine), *Chicago* (Mama Morton)

When I saw *Ragtime*, I was struck by a Ford commercial stuck right in the middle of the show. They brought the Model T out and sang the song *Wheels of a Dream*. It was supposed to be the inspirational ballad, but it was really just advertising for Ford. Right on stage. It is a reflection of what goes on at large. Product placement—the bottom line being the most important thing.

Jane Sell. *Over Here!* (Mitzi) [O][**T**], *Irene* (Jane Burke) [O], *George M!* [O], *Moon over Buffalo* (Charlotte Hay s/b) [O], *Pal Joey* (Gladys Bumps) [O], *Happy End* (Lieutenant Lillian Holiday), *I Love My Wife* (Monica)

No one is willing to take risks anymore. Producers won't allow directors to do what they want. We are very Disneyfied. Dancers, especially, have taken a back seat on Broadway because the choreography is not developed along with the show. It's not all conceived at the same time. The dancing is kind of stuck in.

Scott Wise. *Jerome Robbins' Broadway* [O][**T**], *Fosse* [O][**t**], *State Fair* (Pat Gilbert) [O][**t**], *Movin' Out* (Sergeant O'Leary) [O], *Goodbye Girl* (Billy) [O], *Damn Yankees* (Rocky) [O], *Carrie* (Scott) [O], *Guys and Dolls* (Guy) [O], *Song and Dance* (Man) [O], *A Chorus Line* (Mike), *Cats* (Plato/Macavity), *Victor Victoria* (Jazz Hot Ensemble)

I was doing the national tour of *Beauty and the Beast*, and we had just opened the show in Minneapolis. At the opening night party, all of a sudden, a man came up to me and started giving me notes. He told me what he liked and didn't like about my performance. I asked him who he was, and he said that he was on the "Board of Disney." He wasn't a director. Nor did he have any real connection with the theater. He was just some guy on "the Board."

Betsy Joslyn. *High Society* (Patsy) [O], *Sweeney Todd* (Johanna) [O], *The Goodbye Girl* (Paula s/b) [O], *A Doll's Life* (Nora) [O], *A Few Good Men* (Lt. Galloway s/b) [O], *Into the Woods* (The Witch), *Sunday in the Park with George* (Dot), *Les Misérables* (Madame Thénardier), *Beauty and the Beast** (Mrs. Potts), *City of Angels** (Oolie/Donna), *Camelot** (Guenevere), *Of Thee I Sing**, *Let 'em Eat Cake**

Corporate theater, in general, hasn't done the art form much justice. It should be about individuals communicating with the audience, yet the powers that be think that shows like *Les Misérables* are actor-proof. These grand productions have become spectacles. We are even outpricing our market with tickets at $100 each. The Shubert Organization used to be a theatrical organization. Now it has become a realtor. They are looking to rent the space. They aren't interested in theater.

J. Mark McVey. *The Best Little Whorehouse Goes Public* (Sam Dallas s/b) [O], *Les Misérables* (Jean Valjean), *The Who's Tommy* (Captain Walker), *Carousel**

Size Does Matter

The Civil War started out as a small, intimate, theatrical experience. It was a staged rock concert. When we played out of town before coming to Broadway, it was a lovely show. The show had something glorious to say about the heart of America, especially now. It was an intimate show, with a healing quality to it.

When we got to Broadway, all of a sudden, the show changed. It became "Disneyfied." The producers had to turn it into a spectacle to compete with the other musicals like *Beauty and the Beast* and *The Lion King*. We were given guns. New fight scenes were staged. It just didn't work. It wasn't conceived as a spectacle.

Michael Lanning. *The Civil War* (Captain Emmett Lochran) [O]

I was performing in the pre-Broadway tour of *Little Shop of Horrors* in Florida. *Little Shop of Horrors* is a very intimate show. I think all shows exist in a certain world. If you try to make the show exist outside that world, it doesn't work. It fails.

When we were doing the show in Florida, the original team was trying to turn it into a Broadway show. They tried to make the dances bigger. They tried to make the plant bigger. They tried to make everything bigger, but it was intended to be an intimate show. That is the reason why it failed. There was this pressure to turn it into a Broadway show. We were told, "You have to fill a big house." We kept trying to play outward, as opposed to allowing it all to come together and draw the audience in. That's what made the show great. It was a sweet little show that started out in a 150-seat theater. Now it was going to play in a 1,200-seat theater. People who saw the show said it looked like it was trying to be something it wasn't.

Hunter Foster. *Little Shop of Horrors* (Seymour) [O], *Urinetown* (Bobby Strong) [O], *Footloose* (Bickle) [O], *King David* [O], *Grease!* (Roger) [O], *Les Misérables* (Marius u/s), *Martin Guerre** (Martin u/s), *Cats** (Rum Tum Tugger)

Shows like *Les Misérables*, *The Phantom of the Opera*, and *Cats* have enormous, elaborate sets which lend credence to the opinion, held by some, that without these spectacular sets the shows will not work. The tenth-anniversary concert of *Les Misérables* at the Royal Albert Hall in London proved not only that the musical worked without sets, but that it was as powerful in concert as it was in its staged version.

Colm Wilkinson. *Les Misérables* (Jean Valjean) [O][t]

There was a big scandal when I was in *The Scarlet Pimpernel*. Midway through the production, we were bought out by Cablevision. They brought in a new director, a new choreographer, a new artistic staff, everything. They rewrote the whole show and fired many people.

The Phantom of the Opera. Photo credit: Joan Marcus/Photofest

While we were performing the "old show" with the "old cast" at night, we were rehearsing the "new show" during the day with all of the "new people." The old show closed and the new contract started two days later with all of the new people. The new producers claimed it was a big triumph. It was the beginning of downsizing.

This is what is going to happen with other long running shows. The show will open and it will create a product that people want to see. It will create an audience, and then it will downsize. Smaller set, smaller theater, smaller cast, but you call it the same thing. It will save a whole bunch of money.

The Scarlet Pimpernel was one of the first shows to be bought out by a huge corporation. The entire budget that Cablevision put into *The Scarlet Pimpernel* was just a part of their advertising budget. It was like buying a billboard. It became a machine. Being on Broadway has become like working in a pre–Industrial Revolution factory or something. Theater is happening elsewhere now.

Craig Rubano. *The Scarlet Pimpernel* (Armand St. Just s/b) [O], *Les Misérables* (Marius)

Six Flags® Times Square

If you look at a Broadway season in the forties or fifties, which was the Golden Era, there were twice as many Broadway musicals as there are now. These days, it just costs too much money to mount a big Broadway musical. Broadway has become like a theme park. Broadway has become less about quality and more about being sure that the show can appeal to a broader audience. Many people don't want to see sophisticated theater.

> **Heather MacRae.** *Falsettos* (Charlotte) [O], *Coastal Disturbances* (Faith Bigelow) [O], *Here's Where I Belong* (Abra) [O], *Hair* (Sheila)

When I first started doing shows on Broadway, there were generally one or two producers for each show. Now, I think there are eight or nine. Part of it is the cost, and part of it is the corporate hand. I don't know what is "the chicken" and what is "the egg" in the current situation on Broadway. The re-imaging of the theater district is obviously a good and bad thing. It no longer has the character of New York City. It looks like a theme park. But, it is safer and cleaner. It certainly generates more revenue.

> **Jason Alexander.** *Jerome Robbins' Broadway* (Emcee) [O][T], *Merrily We Roll Along* (Joe) [O], *The Rink* (Lino/Lenny/Punk/Uncle Fausto) [O], *Broadway Bound* (Stanley) [O], *Accomplice* [O], *The Producers** (Max Bialystock)

Today, Broadway is about the paycheck. It's like a Six Flags® theme show—especially the musicals. It gives people what they want. If you don't educate people about theater and culture, they don't know anything. So, you get an audience of people who are completely ignorant about theater, history, and culture. They come in for a couple of days and just want to go on a ride.

> **Craig Rubano.** *The Scarlet Pimpernel* (Armand St. Just s/b) [O], *Les Misérables* (Marius)

We are seeing the Disneyfication of Broadway. Is that a word? There is nothing wrong with it, but I'm just not sure that I'm a part of it. I think they are appealing to a very broad audience that isn't necessarily looking for a challenge. I think they are looking for a safe, fun, entertaining night in the theater. I'm not sure if it's going to be the most challenging thing for the actor, especially the ones who are interested in individual identity, but there is certainly a place for it.

Witness the box office sales. There are people out there buying those tickets. I saw *The Lion King* and I loved it! But would I want to be in *The Lion King*? No. That's not what I do. I want to feel like my individuality is important to the ultimate production of the piece. I don't want to be a disposable actor. I don't want to be an actor who fits into somebody else's costumes.

> **Alison Fraser.** *The Secret Garden* (Martha) [O][t], *Romance, Romance* [O][t], *The Mystery of Edwin Drood*

CHAPTER 17

Broadway, Inc.

When performing on a Broadway stage begins to resemble working in a factory or in a theme park, it is inevitable that Broadway itself will begin to suffer. Actors will lose their sense of connection with the music, and the performances themselves will be compromised.

Today, without doubt, many performers in Broadway's most celebrated and longest running shows are treated like cogs in a machine. New actors are inserted into long-running shows without any connection to the creative process whatsoever. Actors are not given parts to play, but tracks to follow. Individuality and creativity are lost. And, as there are so few new parts available each year, actors are forced to stay in the same show for years, sometimes playing the same role over a thousand times.

As this chapter shows, the overall result can be apathy and even disdain. Disconnected from the audience, from each other, and from the show itself, many performers fool around on stage. Broadway no longer becomes something to be taken seriously. Those who do take their jobs seriously are sometimes ridiculed, and even scorned. A corporate employee is born.

Job Security

My *Les Misérables* experience was fascinating. Some people had been there for six or seven years. I thought, "Don't you want to do something else? Aren't you tired of doing this?" People were concerned about job security. They wanted children and a country house. There simply isn't any turnover on Broadway anymore.

> **Debbie Gravitte.** *Jerome Robbins' Broadway* [O][**T**], *They're Playing our Song* (Sonia Walsk) [O], *Blues in the Night* (Woman #2) [O], *Ain't Broadway Grand* (Gypsy Rose Lee) [O], *Zorba* (The Woman) [O], *Perfectly Frank* [O], *Les Misérables* (Fantine), *Chicago* (Mama Morton)

The Phantom of the Opera. Photo credit: Joan Marcus/Photofest

I was so excited when I joined the Broadway company of *Grease!* Broadway had always been my Mecca. I had just turned twenty-one, and it was everything I had ever wanted.

So, once I got there, I couldn't understand why some actors in the show were leaving. They didn't even have other jobs waiting for them. They just wanted to get out.

I thought, "How could you ever leave a Broadway show? You work all your life to get here. How could you just leave?"

Two years later, I was still doing the same show, and I finally understood. Yet, I stayed in the show because I didn't have another job to go to. I got into a rhythm of thinking, "Well, this is my life. This is my job."

All of a sudden, Broadway became a job and not a dream. That's when everything got all cloudy. There I was, on stage, and I couldn't care less. I had done the show for three straight years—the same show, the same part. It was monotonous. It was like living in the movie *Groundhog Day.*

Marissa Jaret Winokur. *Hairspray* (Tracy Turnblad) [O][T], *Grease!* (Jan)

I've seen the best performances and the best actors, including me, fall by the wayside during an eight-show week. It's just hard to do. It's hard to maintain a show eight times a week for two, three, or four years. When you do the same thing over and over again, it is going to have an effect.

When I was in *Grease!*, I felt like I was trapped. There I was, doing what I loved and getting paid to do it, while my friends were scrounging around in sublets and working in the Gap. Yet, I was unhappy because I was unfulfilled. I wasn't really trapped. No one was forcing me to be there, but I felt like I was stuck. I was getting paid and I was a part of the Broadway community, so I didn't want to leave. Even though I was working on Broadway, I wondered, "Is this the only show I'm ever going to do? I can't do this anymore! I've done this so many times." I did the show for three and a half years—one thousand performances. You don't want to be ungrateful, but I was unhappy.

Hunter Foster. *Little Shop of Horrors* (Seymour) [O], *Urinetown* (Bobby Strong) [O], *Footloose* (Bickle) [O], *King David* [O], *Grease!* (Roger) [O], *Les Misérables* (Marius u/s), *Martin Guerre** (Martin u/s), *Cats** (Rum Tum Tugger)

I've never been a fan of the pink contract, which is the chorus contract that gives a person an unlimited run. It was initially negotiated because shows used to only run for a short period of time and they wanted to make sure that people weren't going to get canned.

Now shows run for fifteen years. I believe it's time to do away with those unlimited contracts. People should not be in shows for that long. It is not the nature of what we do. It's not factory work. It was never meant to be factory work.

I'm doing *Mamma Mia!* right now and we are on a Canadian contract. We are putting new people in the show now because people were canned. Every year, we are all up for renewal—ensemble and principals alike. It inspires people to do their jobs well and it weeds out people who have long since passed their prime.

Craig Bennet. *Miss Saigon* (Marine/Reeves), *Les Misérables** (Thénardier u/s), *Mamma Mia!** (Bill), *Ragtime** (Willie Conklin)

Cogs in the Machine

In the original cast of *Les Misérables*, there was a very cohesive unit on stage. We played theater games during rehearsals and then worked on the music. It was amazing. But people left and replacements arrived who were not exposed to the original period of rehearsals. The cohesiveness broke down. Ultimately, we had a company that had never been in an extended rehearsal period together. The audience missed a lot.

Paul Harman. *Les Misérables* (Foreman) [O], *Chess* (Arbiter) [O], *Triumph of Love* (Dimas u/s) [O], *Candide* (2nd Bulgarian Soldier) [O], *What's Wrong with this Picture?* (Mort u/s) [O], *It's So Nice to Be Civilized* [O], *Joseph and the Amazing Technicolor® Dreamcoat* (Simeon), *Ragtime* (Doctor), *Cats* (Asparagus), *Evita** (Peron u/s), *Zorba** (Niko)

I was in *Les Misérables* and *Miss Saigon* for seven years straight. Before starting *Miss Saigon*, I only had rehearsal for about a week. It was so strange because I was the only one rehearsing. I quickly learned that the show runs like a machine.

During rehearsal, they just told me, "Here is where you stand. Here's where you do this and here's where you do that." It didn't feel anything like art. It didn't feel like I was creating. There was little, if any, interaction with the director or other cast members. It was just about hitting my spots, and all of a sudden, I was in a Broadway show.

On my opening night in *Miss Saigon*, I clearly remember performing the song, "Dreamland." I played an American G.I. who was propositioning a prostitute. I felt so out of place. I thought, "Should I touch her knee or shouldn't I?" There was a part of me that wanted to get in character and grab her, but I thought, "I have no clue who this girl is. I just met her a week ago."

When *Miss Saigon* first opened, the original actors rehearsed together. They could get comfortable with each other, and the scene was sexual and explicit in the way it should have been. Over time, the scene became like a high school prom. People were not comfortable with one another and had different ideas about what should be happening.

Unfortunately, the scene really became watered down over the years. It became more about actors talking and chitchatting on stage than about playing an American G.I. or a Vietnamese prostitute. It was not about acting, but more about, "So, did you see the last episode of *Friends*?"

When everyone is on stage and focused, with the same sense of purpose, the show has electricity and energy. When actors are in their corners, doing their own thing, the show suffers.

Only the original cast members knew what the director intended. A year later, five more people came in as replacements. They got a watered-down version of what the director intended, through the eyes of the stage manager. Then the stage manager got replaced, and there was yet another version of the show. This is one of the biggest hazards of the corporate machine.

Roger Seyer. *Les Misérables* (Jean Valjean u/s), *Miss Saigon* (Gibbons)

A Company of Clones

I replaced Gary Beach in *Beauty and the Beast* on Broadway. The only people I had contact with were the stage managers and the company manager, who handed me my paycheck. I never worked with the original director. I never got to work with the choreographer. I never got to know anyone from the Disney office, but they all came to my second performance and couldn't understand why I wasn't exactly like Gary Beach.

It was frightening. They expected everyone to be like an animated gel—just put on the costume and sound and act exactly like the person who played the role before you. They wanted to cookie-cut every person. It was unfortunate.

> **Lee Roy Reams.** *42nd Street* (Billy Lawlor) [O][t], *Lorelei* (Henry Spofford) [O], *Applause* (Duane Fox) [O], *Sweet Charity* (Young Spanish Man) [O], *Hello, Dolly!* (Cornelius Hackl) [O], *An Evening with Jerry Herman* [O], *Beauty and the Beast* (Lumiere), *La Cages Aux Folles* (Albin), *The Producers** (Roger De Bris)

There is a "squeeze the dollar till the eagle screams" mentality on Broadway. I was cast as the Peron understudy in *Evita*, largely because I fit in Peron's—John Leslie Wolfe's—costumes. They wanted someone who fit the costumes.

> **Paul Harman.** *Les Misérables* (Foreman) [O], *Chess* (Arbiter) [O], *Triumph of Love* (Dimas u/s) [O], *Candide* (2nd Bulgarian Soldier) [O], *What's Wrong with This Picture?* (Mort u/s) [O], *It's So Nice to Be Civilized* [O], *Joseph and the Amazing Technicolor® Dreamcoat* (Simeon), *Ragtime* (Doctor), *Cats* (Asparagus), *Evita** (Peron u/s), *Zorba** (Niko)

I did *Les Misérables* for about a year. I left to do some other things. Three years later, I was walking down the street and I saw the stage manager from *Les Misérables*.

Out of nowhere, she said, "Oh, my God, can you come into the show tonight?"

I said, "I haven't done the show in three years, but I will try."

There I was, on a Broadway stage with people I had never met. They all looked one step removed from the people with whom I had done *Les Misérables* a few years before. There was a weird cloning quality to the casting of the show. They were all some bizarre test-tube version of the person who had played the role before.

> **Jessica Molaskey.** *Dream* (Performer) [O], *Parade* (Mrs. Phagan) [O], *Crazy For You* (Irene Roth u/s) [O], *Oklahoma!* [O], *Chess*, *The Who's Tommy* (Mrs. Walker), *Les Misérables* (Mme. Thénardier u/s), *Cats* (Jellylorum u/s), *Falsettos**, *City of Angels**, *Joseph and the Amazing Technicolor® Dreamcoat**

Tracked

It is incredible to be in a show from its inception. In *Les Misérables*, we did improvisations for the entire rehearsal period. The number, "Lovely Ladies," came out of improvisation.

Then I replaced Barbara Walsh in *Falsettos*. I was learning a "track." The stage manager put me into the show and told me where to walk, and where to move the furniture. I didn't get any direction because James

Lapine was busy. I had to do it all on my own. I didn't have a rehearsal period. I had two weeks of moving furniture. It was very difficult.

The director came to see the show and had some problems with my performance. Funny, as I was never directed by him. The week before the show closed, I finally rehearsed with him.

Randy Graff. *City of Angels* (Oolie) [O][**T**], *A Class Act* (Sophie) [O][t], *Les Misérables* (Fantine) [O], *Moon over Buffalo* (Rosalind) [O], *High Society* (Liz Imbrie) [O], *Laughter on the 23rd Floor* (Carol) [O], *Saravà* (Rosalia) [O], *Fiddler on the Roof* (Golde) [O], *Grease!* (Rizzo u/s), *Falsettos* (Trina)

I think it's criminal that directors are not flown in every six months or every year during a long-running show to tighten things up and to work with the cast. It is outrageous to think that producers can't buy plane tickets for directors and put them up in hotels so they can work with the cast at least twice a year.

When I performed in *City Of Angels*, they flew in our director every six months. We rehearsed with him, and the show would get fixed and tightened. So why doesn't that usually happen? How can you do a show on Broadway and never see the director? It's outrageous. They are making their royalties. Why don't they come back? Is it that the producer doesn't want to spend the money to fly them over? What is one day to come in and build the moral of the group and say, "I care. The producers care."

Most of the jobs I've done on Broadway are replacing other actors. I just replaced Jennifer Laura Thompson in *Urinetown*. There is nothing glamorous about replacing. You come into a long-running show where the cast has bonded and you are the "new girl."

I rehearsed in a rehearsal room during the winter. It was freezing, there was no heat, and I was trying to learn the show all by myself with a stage manager on a floor covered with tape markings. The stage manager would say, "Well, in this scene, Little Sally is to your right and Little Becky Two Shoes is to your left. And this guy will swing by your front."

I would try to write it all down.

She'd say, "In the next scene, you are here, here, and here. You're on the third step on this line. Jennifer Laura did this. Jennifer Laura did that."

I thought, "I don't care what she did. I'm different. I can't be her."

When I got to the theater on my opening night, I was trying to figure out, "Who is Little Sally? Who is Little Becky Two Shoes?"

When I first performed the show, it was only my opening night—nobody else's. After the show, I went home with a big bucket of flowers from my agent and a bottle of champagne. I took the subway all by myself.

"Woo-hoo, opening night!"

It was depressing and horrible. You'd think, "Wow, she's starring in a Broadway show. It's so exciting! The successful show *Urinetown!*" Yet the reality was that I was on the subway with my flowers and my bottle of champagne and I was going back to my one-bedroom apartment. Where is the glamour in that?

Anastasia Barzee. *Henry IV* (Lady Mortimer) [O], *Urinetown* (Hope Caldwell), *Miss Saigon* (Ellen), *Jekyll and Hyde* (Emma), *Sunset Boulevard** (Betty), *City of Angels** (Mallory)

I had a brief sojourn at *The Phantom of the Opera* a couple of years ago. Boy, was it weird. I have been in this business for well over twenty-five years. When I come into a show, I am no longer concerned about being the new kid. I am no longer concerned about fitting in. I am a professional. I know how to cash a paycheck like everyone else.

I got to *Phantom* and it was pretty cramped backstage. The choreography backstage was more involved than it was on stage. People would say to me, "You can't stand there. That is where I stand. Don't put your hat there. That's where I put my hat. You can't make your costume change over here." It was mind-boggling. The traffic patterns were cemented into a ritual of behavior backstage that could not be interrupted. People got so territorial about their "track." However, if I had to pin how the word "track" came into being, I would pin it on *Les Misérables*.

Paul Harman. *Les Misérables* (Foreman) [O], *Chess* (Arbiter) [O], *Triumph of Love* (Dimas u/s) [O], *Candide* (2nd Bulgarian Soldier) [O], *What's Wrong with This Picture?* (Mort u/s) [O], *It's So Nice to Be Civilized* [O], *Joseph and the Amazing Technicolor® Dreamcoat* (Simeon), *Ragtime* (Doctor), *Cats* (Asparagus), *Evita** (Peron u/s), *Zorba** (Niko)

When I started doing *Les Misérables*, I was new to the "track" system that they used. I didn't have a role. I had a track. What you do in the show is a track. It took me from "I'm here because I'm special" to "I'm here because I'm Track 21." It was demeaning.

Debbie Gravitte. *Jerome Robbins' Broadway* [O][T], *They're Playing our Song* (Sonia Walsk) [O], *Blues in the Night* (Woman #2) [O], *Ain't Broadway Grand* (Gypsy Rose Lee) [O], *Zorba* (The Woman) [O], *Perfectly Frank* [O], *Les Misérables* (Fantine), *Chicago* (Mama Morton)

Every day it's the same exact thing; you can't express yourself differently. You can't even put your eyebrow up on a different note. You just feel trapped. It would be like working in an office and copying the same page for three hours straight. The directors direct a show and then the stage managers keep it up. A stage manager wants everything to go as it's been going. They want you to do what the last person did and be a cookie cutter. They don't want you to change things.

David Josefsberg. *Les Misérables* (Marius u/s), *Grease!* (Doody)

In *Les Misérables*, the stage manager taught new actors their role and basically just walked them though it. It would kill your spirit for a few days. You were given a sheet that had the name of the girl you were replacing. On the sheet was a grid, which went through each scene.

"Cross from stage right to stage left."

"Enter here."

It became very technical. In the show, what you were doing was making the same crosses.

Rena Strober. *Les Misérables* (Cosette u/s)

When I was the understudy to Marius in *Les Misérables,* it was a dream come true to play the role on Broadway. I flew my mom and dad out because I had a little bit of money. I told everyone.

I would sing, "A heart full of love." Stop.

"A heart full of song." Right hand up.

"I'm doing everything all wrong." Left hand up. No, stop.

"Everything all wrong." Hand down on "wrong."

Any impulse you had as an artist, fuck you. Shut up. Go home. Learn it the way it's done. You were literally like a robot.

On the one hand, we laughed at it. "Ha, ha. This is McMiz. Aren't we clever. We're in McMiz!" But on the other hand, it really was. It was McMiz. It is McPhantom. You box it up and send it out. They could plug in any 18-year-old boy with long hair who could come close to hitting a G, and everyone would say, "Ah, isn't that cute? I saw a Broadway show. I'm cultured now." It was embarrassing. More often than not, you would hear a G-flat.

Daniel C. Cooney. *Les Misérables* (Marius u/s), *The Civil War** (Swing), *Evita** (Che), *Fiddler on the Roof** (Perchik)

Performers in *The Lion King* were treated like shit. During my time in *The Lion King*, I ended up with a herniated disc and sciatica, tennis elbow, three bruised ribs, a sprained pectoral muscle, a bruised hipbone, and a damaged SI joint. I'm in good shape, but you put a board on your head with a bunch of grass, an animal, or a puppet attached, and it ain't gonna happen. Between the costumes and being overworked, we were getting killed.

One night, we ran out of Simba's because of injuries and vacations. They had to grab a guy out of *Aida* who had done *The Lion King* the year before. They rehearsed him that afternoon and he went on.

As a result, people half-assed it on stage. One, because we were exhausted, and two, we were uninspired. This is where Broadway is most disappointing. The pay is great, and everything is top-notch in terms of production quality. It's all very exciting, and it's a packed house every night—but it's about the least creative thing I have ever done as an actor.

I was playing Ed. He's a hyena that doesn't speak. All he does is laugh. I wasn't going to turn him into Hamlet. They literally said to me, "Stop. Say it like this. Do it like this. No, stop what you are doing. Don't change anything!"

It takes a certain kind of person to come in and forgo your own integrity as an artist and become a company "yes-man." Corporations and the arts, yes-men and artists, they don't mix. You can't ask actors to come in and not be creative. It sounds a bit maudlin, but it's not the reason I became an actor. Being a corporate yes-man was not the reason that I lived in a roach-infested apartment and had enough money to choose between a can of tuna fish or a pack of cigarettes each week.

Jeff Gurner. *The Lion King* (Ed the Hyena)

Acting on Empty

During *Martin Guerre*, the cast was presented with the opportunity to be creative. The show had never before been done in the United States. It was directed by the director of the National Theater of Ireland. We were given the chance to be a part of something raw and real.

However, oddly enough, most of the cast actually preferred to be told exactly what to do. Rather than be creative, they would have preferred to be given a track and told, "Stand here, right hand up, take two steps there." We were given the chance to act, and it just became a fight. The cast would rather have been slaves than be free.

When a director challenges a cast and says, "You are a sixteenth-century peasant who is surviving in a drought amidst huge religious conflicts," an actor should say, "Awesome, I actually have something to feel and learn." But in our show, many of the actors didn't know how to handle it. If you have been conditioned to perform in shows like *Joseph and the Amazing Technicolor® Dreamcoat*, you're not used to acting, thinking, and feeling. That provided a lot of the conflict.

In musical theater, performers are often conditioned to be parrots or mimics. In this era of long-running musicals, we are praised for our ability to impersonate the actor we are replacing. Copy exactly what the other actor did on stage. They don't want creativity in this business. They want what was done before.

So, when the director in *Martin Guerre* asked the cast to actually be creative on stage, it was like putting a child behind the wheel of a car. The child might be a great back-seat driver, but that's about it.

Sean Jeremy Palmer. *Carousel** (Mr. Snow), *Martin Guerre** (Guillaume u/s)

Today, people in musicals are astonishingly ignorant of the history and literature of theater. They just know the dance steps and the songs.

They don't know the tradition out of which they came, the storytelling tradition.

Initially, it came to me as a surprise that actors were considered dumb. I always find it vaguely offensive when I am in the presence of a director who considers actors cattle. I guess a lot of actors are. Most musicals are filled with people who have no interest in reading at all, and no interest in current events. No interest in anything, really, but the fun life they are leading and the hard work they are doing—the dancing and the show itself. Show business is their whole life. I am quite surprised to find that people in musical theater generally have no interest in the history of their show or the background of the composer.

Steve Pudenz. *Hello, Dolly!* (Rudolph) [O], *Joseph and the Amazing Technicolor® Dreamcoat** (Jacob), *The Sound of Music**

I had only read half of Victor Hugo's novel *Les Misérables* when I had to start rehearsal for the show in 1986, but I managed to read it four or five times in my subsequent work with the musical. I kept the book in my dressing room. It was my bible, and I would dip into it whenever I could for inspiration and to keep the character alive. I heard a funny story about an actor who had a copy of the *Les Misérables* novel backstage, and someone said, "Oh, they've written a book about the musical?" That was an example of how far removed people were from the origins of the show.

Colm Wilkinson. *Les Misérables* (Jean Valjean) [O][t]

Just Part of the Scenery

David Hersey is a brilliant lighting designer who was responsible for the musicals *Cats*, *Les Misérables*, and *Evita*. All of those shows and more. All of his shows pin-spot the leads, and everybody else is in the background. In a David Hersey musical, if you are in the background on stage, you can be up there discussing anything you want. To the audience, it looks like you are concentrating on what is going on.

If you are doing a role, you are really working. You can't really bull-shit. When you are in the ensemble, it is a different animal. If you are not integral to the story and you are in the background, you don't feel like you are part of what is going on. When you were in the chorus of *Les Misérables*, you didn't really have to give a shit about what was going on, unless you were supposed to be quiet at a certain spot or something. You did whatever you could just to stay alive. That meant you were in a constant state of fooling around with the other actors on stage who weren't integral to the scene. You were not steeped in method. Even if you didn't give a shit, as long as you stayed active, it looked like you gave a shit.

Cats. Photo credit: Photofest

Cats ended up having to replace a lot of people in the ensemble. There was simply no activity or life on stage. Many actors didn't give a shit and didn't act like they gave a shit. It became dead.

Alex Santoriello. *Les Misérables* (Montparnasse) [O], *3 Penny Opera* (Jimmy) [O], *Chess* [O], *Jesus Christ Superstar** (Pilate), *Cats** (Asparagus)

David Hersey, who lit *Les Misérables,* is nicknamed the "Prince of Darkness" in theatrical circles. With his lighting, he paints beautiful but dark pictures, and you are inclined to bump into the furniture on stage. However, I used to sit in the stalls and watch his light cues, and they looked so wonderful that you didn't mind falling over things now and then. Theater should be the overall effect of lighting, sounds, and performances. It is not just about being seen and getting your face in the light. It is about relating to your fellow actors and making the piece work for everybody involved.

Colm Wilkinson. *Les Misérables* (Jean Valjean) [O][t]

I know the expression "there are no small parts, only small actors," but I am in this business because I like delving into a character. I like being on stage in a meaty role. If you are a nameless, faceless character sitting in the background, in the dark, you don't care. Maybe at first you do, and you try to justify things and find motivation. You can only do that for so long. Then it becomes about the paycheck. What else is there to fulfill you? Artistically, how many faces can you come up with when you are standing in the dark, covered in Rosco fog? There's only so much you can do. What does it become about? It becomes about the paycheck. I'm sorry.

Angela Lockett. *Parade* (Angela) [O], *Les Misérables* (Fantine u/s), *Martin Guerre** (Catherine), *Once on This Island**, *Ain't Misbehavin**

I played in the ensemble of *Martin Guerre*. During one performance, it was my turn to be swung out of the show and watch from the audience. I had done the show for several weeks, but had yet to really watch it. It was only then that I truly realized how insignificant I was.

During the show, while the spotlights shined brightly on the leads, everyone else was in a veil of darkness and a wash of ambient sound. Everything was sort of muddled, and you couldn't hear anything the ensemble was saying. When I was asked to watch the show, I was expecting to be thrilled and think, "Look at this show I'm in!" Watching it, I realized that no one could really even tell I was in the show.

During one scene, I wore military gear for a battle sequence. It required a tremendous amount of energy. I had to wear a fifty-pound metal costume, run around in strobe lights and amidst explosions, and use a sword, even though I couldn't quite see because I was looking through two armor slits and praying, "I hope I can make my mark."

I was a piece of scenery. That was what I was hired to be.

Sean Jeremy Palmer. *Carousel** (Mr. Snow), *Martin Guerre** (Guillaume u/s)

I have seen people "phone in" performances on Broadway. Their body is on the stage, but their mind is on their shopping list. They are not giving a full performance. They are not mentally and physically there.

If there is real integrity built into the show, and if the actors are a part of the creative process, they feel like they have something vested in the show. But when actors are just brought in and shoved around on stage and told what to do, it is harder to keep motivated.

Pamela Winslow. *Into the Woods* (Rapunzel) [O], *Beauty and the Beast* (Babette)

Malpractice

When I first was cast in *Cats*, I couldn't believe there were people who didn't care that they were on Broadway. They had this attitude of, "You can't fire me. I'm on a pink contract and I haven't missed shows."

The term "marking" means that you hit your marks and do the bare minimum to get by. Some people pull so far back to where they just don't care. They are just marking, taking it easy. It amazed me. If you are that sick, don't come in. If you hate your job that much, leave. I was surprised to see actors on Broadway pulling back and being lazy on stage, not happy to be there.

Michael Arnold. *42nd Street* (Andy Lee) [O], *The Who's Tommy* [O], *A Funny Thing Happened on the Way to the Forum* (Swing) [O], *Little Me* (Belle's Boy/Newsboy) [O], *Cats* (Mr. Mistoffelees), *Cabaret*, *Chicago*, *Martin Guerre** (Benoit), *Busker Alley**, *Durante**

Almost immediately, I was put off by many of the attitudes that I encountered on Broadway. People weren't thankful for what they were doing. I also noticed many people who were undisciplined—people who were concerned more about partying than being on time. A friend of mine left a show because he was so frustrated. He warned me.

He said, "You are going to find that there are people who are not going to work at the same level that you are going to want to."

I said, "Oh, I'm sure you aren't right. I mean, it's Broadway, for God's sake."

He couldn't have been more right. I found the goofing off unacceptable. I couldn't believe it. I was shocked.

Jeff Edgerton. *Parade* (Fiddlin' John) [O], *Grease!* (Eugene u/s)

I played the lead in the national tour of *Grease!* for two years. Over fifty actors came in and out of the show. Over fifty. Just about every two weeks, they were putting in a new person. They would hire these kids who had no idea what they were doing. I would literally say their lines for them on the opening night, and often had to do the same thing on the second night, and then on the third. I would pick up lines in the songs they were supposed to be singing. That's why I stayed on the road for two years. They kept raising my salary and telling me, "We really need you out there, because you are serving as our director."

One of the problems with modern-day corporatization is that producers are giving people jobs and Equity cards because they will perform for base pay. Half of the kids do not belong on a Broadway stage, and the other half have this "Generation X" mentality that pisses me off beyond belief.

They think, "Oh, I just got a lead in a national tour. I'll stay for three months, give my notice, go back to New York, and become a star." Two weeks go by, and they are bored.

Adrian Zmed. *Grease!* (Danny), *Blood Brothers* (Narrator), *Falsettos* (Marvin), *Chicago* (Billy Flynn), *Same Time, Next Year**

I have zero tolerance for actors who show up at the theater drunk or on drugs. There was a guy in a Broadway show with me who would show up high on cocaine. He would then proceed to mess up on stage. He was a friend of mine, but I got really angry with him. People pay a lot of money to see a Broadway show. It was just really wrong.

Lonny Price. *A Class Act* (Ed) [O][t], *Merrily We Roll Along* (Charley Kringas) [O], *"MASTER HAROLD" . . . and the boys* (Hally) [O], *Broadway* (Roy Lane) [O], *Rags* (Ben) [O], *The Survivor* (Rudy) [O], *Burn This* (Larry), *Durante** (Durante), *Apprenticeship of Duddy Kravitz**

One night, during a number in *Grease!*, an actor was talking in my ear. He said, "You are going down. You are going down." That's all I heard.

So, when it was time for me to deliver my line, I said: "I will go down. And you're in now. Grease lightning."

I was in shock. I was in front of thousands of people, saying words that made no sense. I got backstage and I unleashed on him. It was the only time I ever yelled at someone in a cast. I said, "Don't you fucking mess me up again." I wasn't secure enough to be played with. Also, I am not that irreverent that I can mess around on stage. I can have fun, but I don't try to trip people up. You hear stories of stuff like that happening.

Brooke Shields. *Cabaret* (Sally), *Grease!* (Rizzo)

Playing in the Shadows

When you were in the ensemble of *Miss Saigon*, it was about standing in the dark and holding an M-16. People felt more like scenery than part of the action. They were easily distracted and bored. That's when the screwing around started.

In the number "What a Waste," Chris, the male lead, had just learned that Kim was still alive. He came looking for her. The men in the ensemble all played a bunch of tourists. The women who played prostitutes stood on dance posts and tried to get the men to come into the club. The men roamed around while the women were stuck in one place.

There were moments in the song where all of the actors had to freeze in place. One night, one of the guys brought a water bottle on stage. He got right next to one of the girls on a dais and, during the freeze, started squirting the hell out of her. She couldn't do anything. She just stood there and got soaked.

Roger Seyer. *Les Misérables* (Jean Valjean u/s), *Miss Saigon* (Gibbons)

When I did non-union theater, they stressed professionalism backstage. When I got into professional theater, all of a sudden, there was fucking around.

I remember my last night on the road company of *Les Misérables*. I played a guard in the opening number. Hugh Panaro played Marius, and

Miss Saigon. Photo credit: Joan Marcus/Photofest

he was a prisoner in the Prologue. I had picked up one of the squirt bottles from off stage and I put it into my little ammo pouch. I would walk around and squirt the other performers. I got one guy in the ear. I attacked Hugh the worst. I made it look like he pissed in his pants.

Alex Santoriello. *Les Misérables* (Montparnasse) [O], *3 Penny Opera* (Jimmy) [O], *Chess* [O], *Jesus Christ Superstar** (Pilate), *Cats** (Asparagus)

When I was in the ensemble in *Les Misérables*, I would enter the stage as a nun at 8:41 P.M. Every night, the clock would read 8:41. However, one day, I came out on stage and it was 8:40. We had a new conductor. I started to wonder if we could ever get to 8:39.

So I bet him some beer. I wanted to see 8:39.

It took two months, but we got to 8:39. And then somebody broke that record. So we started playing this game with the conductors, who could break the record for the fastest entrance for the nun. Who could move the clock back? I think we made it to 8:37. That was the earliest.

Ana Maria Andricain. *Marie Christine* (Dakota/Emma Parker) [O], *Les Misérables* (Fantine u/s), *Beauty and the Beast* (Belle), *By Jeeves* (Stiffy Byng), *Evita** (Eva Alternate), *Annie Get Your Gun** (Annie u/s)

After nine months of *Joseph and the Amazing Technicolor® Dreamcoat,* I had a bad attitude about the show. It wasn't enough. It wasn't fulfilling. To keep things interesting and fun, the cast started playing games on stage. I tried to manage the hijinks in a way so that the audience didn't know.

We played a game called "Killer." There was a hat full of names, and you would pick a name before a performance. The actor you picked was your "target." The object of the game was to make eye contact with your target, make a gun with your hand, and shoot. Once a person got shot, they had to die some way on stage. It could be falling down, or it could be dropping your head.

One night, Janet Metz was playing the role of Narrator, and someone killed her in the middle of her big song. She did the funniest thing. As she was singing, "Strange as it seems, there's been a run of crazy dreams," on the word "dreams," she died vocally. She trilled off like she was dying. It was hysterical. It kept you on your toes and in contact with your fellow actors.

"Pass the Gumby" was another game we played on stage. You would be given a toy, and the object of the game was to pass it to another actor on stage at the worst possible time. For example, if you had a dance combination coming up that involved using your hands, you didn't want the Gumby! One night, someone had to do the whole combination with a crunched hand, hiding the toy.

Jeff Blumenkrantz. *Urban Cowboy* [O][t], *A Class Act* (Charlie/Marvin) [O], *Into the Woods* (Jack/Rapunzel's Prince u/s) [O], *How to Succeed in Business Without Really Trying!* (Bud Frump) [O], *Damn Yankees* (Smokey) [O], *3 Penny Opera* (Filch) [O], *Joseph and the Amazing Technicolor® Dreamcoat** (Brother)

I goof around a lot on stage, and I'll tell you what: from the audience's perspective, I really think I look better than those who literally just walk through the show. I try to stay active. For example, in the scene in *Les Misérables* where the men are drinking at a bar, the audience doesn't have to know if I am saying, "Oh, Paris is going to fall at our feet," or if I am saying, "Your wig looks so fucking stupid."

There were games that we played. One game was called "Freedom," where you would try to enter a scene when you were not supposed to. For example, in the "Bishop's Doorway" scene in *Les Misérables*, we would try to come into the scene when Jean Valjean was still at the Bishop's house.

Another game was "Reverse Freedom," where you would leave a scene you were supposed to be in. It was bad, but for me, there was a lot of freshness in that. We knew our limits, and we stuck to them. There are so many people on Broadway who are just bored. And they think that they are doing their job, and they think that they are telling the story, but they look horrible.

Kevin Kern. *Les Misérables* (Marius)

During *Les Misérables*, I played a game called "Stage Hockey." There were two different teams, and the object was to check as many of the opposite team's people during the show as possible. "Checking" is a hockey term when you knock someone into the boards and knock them off their feet. We had a little scoreboard downstairs. We would go around when people weren't looking and run into them. I had actors chasing me around the barricade.

> **Hunter Foster.** *Little Shop of Horrors* (Seymour) [O], *Urinetown* (Bobby Strong) [O], *Footloose* (Bickle) [O], *King David* [O], *Grease!* (Roger) [O], *Les Misérables* (Marius u/s), *Martin Guerre** (Martin u/s), *Cats** (Rum Tum Tugger)

In *Les Misérables,* there was a song in the beginning of the show called "At the End of the Day." The cast came forward and solicited the audience, explaining the hardships of being poor and their struggle to survive. Visually, the audience saw a whole bunch of people dressed in big coats and blankets moving downstage. Some people had physical affectations, some couldn't walk, and some had polio.

During the scene, we staged a contest called "Knockdown," where we would try to knock each other over the fastest. It was our little game. We would stand in the back of the stage and the scrim would come up. The chorus sang, *"At the end of the day you're another day older. And that's all you can say for the life of the poor."* I had to move on the word "poor." I knew my friend moved right after me. I tried as hard as I could to either trip him or get the hell away from him so he didn't knock me over first. I would either stick my foot out or try to bang him before he banged me.

One time, he knocked me down and, because I was wearing a huge coat, I couldn't get back up. I had to crawl the rest of the way downstage. Every night, I was scared he was going to bash my knees in the back and make me fall. It was kill or be killed. That's what we did to make it interesting. That's what we did to make ourselves feel like we were not just a part of a machine.

> **Jodie Langel.** *Les Misérables* (Cosette/Eponine), *Martin Guerre** (Bertrande Alternate), *Cats** (Grizabella), *Joseph and the Amazing Technicolor® Dreamcoat** (Narrator)

It is amazing what the audience doesn't see. In *Les Misérables,* there was a scene where Jean Valjean was given candlesticks and the ensemble was huddled in a doorway. During some performances, one actor would stand behind us and tie the backs of our skirts in knots. When we would say our goodbyes and try to exit in opposite directions, the faster we walked, the tighter the knot. We would have to exit the same way.

Another time, when we were in the barricade during the confrontation between Jean Valjean and Javert, one of the actors in the barricade was on his cell phone talking to his wife. He had his cell phone in his pocket. We passed around the phone, saying, "We are under the barricade right now!"

> **Rena Strober.** *Les Misérables* (Cosette u/s)

I used to eat M&M's on the barricade in *Les Misérables*. I would keep them in my pocket. If I happened to die before I could finish them, they would fall out as I hung upside down. One night, I dropped a whole pile of them on the floor and got into trouble. We also staged an Easter egg hunt on stage during the barricade scene. The hunt went well, but we couldn't account for one egg. We all freaked out.

Andrea McArdle. *Annie* (Annie) [O][t], *Starlight Express* (Ashley) [O], *State Fair* (Margy Frake) [O], *Les Misérables* (Fantine), *Beauty and the Beast* (Belle), *Cabaret** (Sally Bowles), *Jerry's Girls**

Watch Out, Giuliani, XXX is Back

I think audiences don't necessarily know when they are not getting the best performance. The average person is not going to know when a show is not as good as it could be. Actors can autopilot their way through and the audience won't care. They will see the costumes, lights, special effects, and the actors getting upstaged by it all. Between that and the fact that we as actors have no artistic license, I think people are uninspired and frustrated. Performances suffer. It was hard to go out on stage and dig up a performance. There are things that if the audience knew—the fucking around on stage and off—they would be blown away.

In *The Lion King*, I used to make photocopy blowups of my dressing roommate's headshot and do horrible things to it. One time, I painted him up like a drag queen. Another time, I put his head on the body of a baby and wrote filthy, foul cartoon balloons on it. Then, I would put the picture inside the mouth of my puppet. I would run out on stage at select times and flash it at the ensemble members. Six lionesses in the most dramatic scene would be standing there with their lips trembling and their shoulders shaking, trying not to break character. Finally, a stage manager said to me, "I don't know what you're doing or what is inside your puppet's mouth, but it needs to stop." I never did it again.

Here is another example. In the opening number of *The Lion King*, the hyenas were the legs of the elephant, and the audience couldn't see us. There were times when I'd drop my pants and make horrible lude gestures as the gazelles would go by. Actors mess around on stage.

Jeff Gurner. *The Lion King* (Ed the Hyena)

The cast of *The Rink* consisted of Liza Minnelli, Chita Rivera, and six guys playing more than forty different parts. That was the whole company. We got away with shit on stage that was unbelievable.

During the run of the show, the *Penthouse* scandal involving my sweet friend Vanessa Williams came out. All the men in the show were playing at least one character in drag. We did this elaborate thing where we all got into our drag costumes and took Polaroids in compromising positions à la the *Penthouse* spread. We took Polaroids and hot-glued them to every set and every prop. They were popping up all over the place. Poor Chita and Liza. Chita had to sing a song called "Blue Crystal," where she had to raise a glass and sing about it. We glued a Polaroid to the glass of two guys in drag French-kissing each other! She about died.

Jason Alexander. *Jerome Robbins' Broadway* (Emcee) [O][**T**], *Merrily We Roll Along* (Joe) [O], *The Rink* (Lino/Lenny/Punk/Uncle Fausto) [O], *Broadway Bound* (Stanley) [O], *Accomplice* [O], *The Producers** (Max Bialystock)

One night during a Broadway show, an actor ripped his pants on stage, stuck his fingers down his pants to rip them more, and then bent over to make people laugh. Another night, he came out on stage with stink bombs. Yet another night, he had a dildo hidden in his costume and he handed it to someone on stage. He did that all the time.

Jerry Tellier. *Saturday Night Fever* (Frank Junior) [O], *42nd Street* [O], *Smokey Joe's Cafe*

I was doing *Annie Get Your Gun* with Cathy Rigby. During her final performance, one of the other ladies in the show wanted to play a joke on her. So, in the wings of the theater, she attached a "strap-on" underneath her skirt. During a scene with Cathy, she lifted up her skirt and started swinging the big dildo around. She was showing off a big dick between her legs on a Broadway stage while Cathy was trying to act. Later, she also put a dildo in Cathy's pocket. Cathy reached into her pocket and pulled it out on stage.

John Antony. *Passion* (Augenti/Count Ludovic), *Titanic** (John Jacob Astor), *Sunset Boulevard** (Joe Gillis u/s), *Annie Get Your Gun** (Frank Butler)

In *Cats*, I played the role of Gus. During my big number, some of the kittens were in the background. They were supposed to be listening to my song, or sleeping. I begged them not to jump around. When they would jump around, I would see people in the audience look back at them. If the audience was watching them, I knew they were screwing around.

One day, as I started singing my song, I heard thumping sounds behind me. The audience was really close to the stage, and I could see that none of them were looking at me. I got mad. At the end of the number, when I was standing next to Deuteronomy, I asked what was going on. He said that one of the kittens was jerking off with his tail.

I said, "What?"

The actor had taken his tail, put it between his legs, held it up, and was playing with it like it was a large penis. That's what the audience was looking at.

I walked off and started yelling at him so loud that the audience could hear.

The stage manager came over and said, "Jim, you shouldn't do that. It's not your job. It's my job."

"Well," I said, "apparently you aren't doing it too well."

James Hindman. *A Grand Night for Singing* [O], *City of Angels* (Stine) [O], *1776* [O], *The Scarlet Pimpernel* (Ben), *Once Upon a Mattress* (Princess), *Dancing at Lughnasa** (Michael), *Falsettos** (Marvin), *Joseph and the Amazing Technicolor® Dreamcoat** (Simeon), *Cats** (Gus)

I grew up studying Shakespeare. Theater was taken quite seriously. You simply did not fuck around on stage.

When I got on a Broadway tour, I was shocked by the things that went on. In particular, my opening night was quite memorable. I was an understudy, and it was my first time on for the lead. We were performing the show in my hometown, and I had eighty-three friends and family members in the audience. I had never been on the stage before, nor had I ever used the microphone.

I thought everyone in the cast was going to be really supportive and calm. I was wrong. People were all over me, joking around, trying to pull me off stage when I was supposed to be on. During my solo in the opening number, people were making faces at me while I was singing. I basically couldn't connect with anyone. In order to make it through, I tried to look through people. One guy even pulled out his dick on stage and starting playing with himself to try to make me laugh. That was my opening night.

Laurie Wells. *Swing!* (Lead s/b)

Hey, My Mom's in the Audience

I was in the Broadway production of *Camelot*. One day, during the song "Fie On Goodness," out of nowhere, someone on stage decided that he was going to act like a monkey. Literally. He pushed up the skin between his upper lip and his nose and began scratching underneath his arms. He then started doing a monkey walk across the stage.

I got so mad because it was so blatant and the audience could clearly see. If his mother were in the audience, he would not have done that. Yet how did he know that my mother wasn't in the audience?

William Thomas Evans. *Camelot* (Sir Dinadan u/s) [O], *The Scarlet Pimpernel* (Hastings) [O], *Jekyll & Hyde** (Proops/Utterson u/s), *A Funny Thing Happened on the Way to the Forum** (Miles Gloriosus)

Blatant fooling around on stage gets me upset. In the "Bishop's Doorway" scene in *Les Misérables*, the doorway was flooded with ensemble members, who would often fool around and try to make each other laugh. Because of the lighting on stage, you really couldn't see the rest of the cast from the audience. But for me and the actor who played Jean Valjean, it was very hard to work.

People who saw *Les Misérables* would say, "The show was good, but . . ." They couldn't put their finger on what it was. It was because the energy wasn't there. If one person was not there, then something was just not right. I always thought that at the end of *Les Misérables*, the audience should be on their feet because they wanted to get out of their seats and join the crusade. That never happened when I was there.

Kelly Briggs. *Les Misérables* (Bishop), *Cats* (Asparagus)

No Acting Allowed

I remember the first time I played the role of Jean Valjean in *Les Misérables* when I was the understudy. There was a scene at the beginning of the show where Jean Valjean was in the Bishop's doorway, and the entire cast was standing behind him. The first time I was on, it was terrifying. I had been given this tremendously difficult and important role in a Broadway show. I was staying in my moment, and the people behind me were telling jokes about me.

"Look at his underwear!"

"Who the hell is that guy!"

They weren't supporting what I was going through, and I was really upset. There are a lot of people who feel that, unless you are jaded, you are naïve. It is sad that when you play a role the way it was intended, you become the object of ridicule by your colleagues.

Andrew Varela. *King David* [O], *Les Misérables* (Jean Valjean u/s)

When I went into the company of *Grease!*, the show had been running for eight years. I went in as a new kid with tons of energy. One of the men in the company said to me, "Calm down. Relax. What are you working so hard for? Why are you acting so much?" Many of the cast members were walking through the show. They were not open to change. They were not open to someone new coming in who would bring something fresh to the show.

Adrian Zmed. *Grease!* (Danny), *Blood Brothers* (Narrator), *Falsettos* (Marvin), *Chicago* (Billy Flynn), *Same Time, Next Year**

Many people on Broadway feel uncomfortable actually acting. This is going to sound pretentious, but when you act with skill or technique, and bring life and truth to a scene, people in certain Broadway companies will look at you and think, "What are you doing? You are an idiot!"

I was nineteen years old when I moved to the city. Without much acting training whatsoever, I rolled into the city and started auditioning. I was cast in *Les Misérables*. I thought, "So you make faces, sing high and loud, and that's how you do a Broadway show."

Then I started taking acting class, and began studying the Meisner technique. When I started applying the technique, people in the show asked, "What are you doing?"

Within a month, I was farting on the barricade during the song "Bring Him Home." I would come up with all kinds of inappropriate characters in order to entertain the actors on stage rather than engage the audience. We did this because we didn't know how to come together as a group of actors and tell a story.

Daniel C. Cooney. *Les Misérables* (Marius u/s), *The Civil War** (Swing), *Evita** (Che), *Fiddler on the Roof** (Perchik)

If you are "acting" on stage, people look at you like, "Why are you acting? We are up here walking through the show." Sometimes in *Les Misérables*, if you looked at someone on stage, they wouldn't look back or pay attention. If you "acted," you were considered silly. There was a peer pressure which arose from that. You didn't want to be the one idiot who was acting on stage when everyone else wasn't. I'm sure that I have done that too. I've looked at people like, "Cool it. I don't want to be acting right now."

David Josefsberg. *Les Misérables* (Marius u/s), *Grease!* (Doody)

I remember my first week in *Les Misérables*. It was my third day in the show. There was a scene in the show called the "Runaway Cart." An enormous cart broke loose and threatened the lives of the townspeople. The effect was amazing. At first, we all ran around the turntable. Once the turntable stopped, the cast moved in slow motion, miming running away from this cart. We were all supposed to be terrified and running for our lives.

I was twenty-two years old and it was my first Broadway show. I tried to give the scene my all. There was an actor behind me who had been in the show for a while. As I was acting, he flashed me a glare like I was the stupidest person on the planet. The look said, "What the hell are you doing? You don't actually *act* in this scene. We all goof off here." He started laughing at me. I felt really embarrassed.

I looked behind me and saw a few other cast members who clearly shared this actor's point of view. They were rolling their eyes at one another trying to make each other laugh. I couldn't believe the expressions on people's faces.

I wanted to be accepted and be a part of the group, so I began making inappropriate faces as well. There was this enormous peer pressure placed upon me not to act. I never acted in that scene again. I didn't want to be the only one.

Jodie Langel. *Les Misérables* (Cosette/Eponine), *Martin Guerre** (Bertrande Alternate), *Cats** (Grizabella), *Joseph and the Amazing Technicolor*® *Dreamcoa*t* (Narrator)

PART SEVEN

WHEN DREAMS COME TRUE

CHAPTER 18

The Base of the Tony® Is Plastic

Each year, actors gather for the Tony Awards to celebrate the best performances of the year. It is a chance for actors to gain recognition for their work in a time where, as the previous two chapters have shown, actors starring on Broadway have to fight hard just to get noticed. However, receiving a Tony nomination, or even winning the Award, does not exempt an actor from the effects of Disneyfication and the new era of Broadway. After all, the base of the Tony is not made of gold, or even stone, but plastic.

In this chapter, Tony Award winners and nominees share their thoughts about being nominated for a Tony Award and the life which follows. They reflect on the meaning of a Tony nomination and the Award itself, and the dangers involved in believing that, in today's climate, one can ever "make it" on Broadway.

The Plastic Prize

When *Cats* came around, people kept saying to me, "You're going to be nominated for a Tony. It's going to happen!" When I wasn't nominated, I wasn't crushed. I had been down that road a couple of times before. Nevertheless, I thought, "What do I have to do? What's the real problem?"

Patti LuPone called me.

"Ken, darling, how are you? Are you disappointed? Well, you should be. They should have given you one. You have a right to be disappointed."

I said, "Thank you. That's very kind."

She said, "I'm coming by and taking you to lunch."

She came to the theater, went to the stage door, and announced on the intercom, "Patti LuPone is here to see Ken!" Doors flew open all over the theater. She came up calling my name. "Ken, where are you, darling?"

She came into my dressing room. The first thing she said to me was, "Look, I'm going to say something and then we are going. The base of the Tony is plastic. Let's go have lunch."

I just stood there and looked at her. She didn't crack a smile. It took me back to reality.

Ken Page. *Cats* (Old Deuteronomy) [O], *Guys and Dolls* (Nicely-Nicely Johnson) [O], *Ain't Misbehavin'* [O], *The Wiz* (Lion), *Purlie**

Who's the Best?

I think awards are more for yourself than for anyone or anything else. For some people, it changes their life, and for others, you don't see them for years. It is not a guarantee that anything different is going to happen in your life. I have been nominated and not got, and I have been nominated and got.

I was nominated and won the Olivier Award for *She Loves Me*. Best Actress in a Musical. The most wonderful thing I remember about that night was hearing my mother say, "She got it, she got it." She was so thrilled for me. It was more for my parents. I was relieved. The year before, I had been up for *Crazy for You* and didn't win. What I realized was that it said nothing about me. It didn't mean that I was less talented or more talented, more worthy or less worthy. It meant nothing.

What you feel when you don't get an award, bearing in mind I was twenty-six, is humiliation. I felt humiliated because I thought people were looking at me, saying, "Oh, well, she couldn't be as good as they say because she didn't get the Award." You are going through all these feelings, and it is mostly about what other people are thinking. Part of you thinks that if you get the Award, you are the best actress. But it doesn't mean that at all. Everyone in the category is worthy. There are many other people who don't get nominated who are worthy. How can an award say that you are better than somebody else? No. It can't.

Ruthie Henshall. *Putting It Together* (The Younger Woman) [O], *Miss Saigon* (Ellen), *Chicago* (Velma)

I think the mistake people make about awards is that they take them way too seriously. You have to take them for what they are worth—a group of people getting together and deciding whether they want to honor you. Is it a meritocracy? It wants to be, but it's not. There are too many political things involved. A small handful of people decide who wins—the consensus of all of their tastes. Does that mean that the people who are nominated are really the most deserving? No. It is the consensus of those few people.

There is no "best" in art. Can you imagine if we had awards in other areas? Best painting of 1900? Is it a Renoir or a Degas? That's ridiculous.

Tony Award. Photo credit: Photofest

How can you possibly say that one of those paintings is better than the other? There is no "best" in art. It's not a race.

Boyd Gaines. *Contact* (Michael Wiley) [O][**T**], *She Loves Me* (Georg Nowak) [O][**T**], *The Heidi Chronicles* (Peter Patrone) [O][**T**], *Anything Goes* (Lord Evelyn Oakleigh) [O], *Company* (Robert) [O], *The Show Off* (Aubrey Piper) [O], *Cabaret* (Clifford Bradshaw)

I have experienced three Tony nominations and three losses. What I know is that I have the respect of the people with whom I work. I have the respect of my peers. That is more important than any award. That is what is going to get me jobs. Not the Tony Award. A Tony Award doesn't make anyone better than anyone else. It doesn't guarantee that someone is going to become a star. Who's the best? I just think it's crap.

Marin Mazzie. *Kiss Me, Kate* (Lilli Vanessi) [O][**t**], *Ragtime* (Mother) [O][**t**], *Passion* (Clara) [O][**t**], *Man of La Mancha* (Aldonza), *Big River* (Mary Jane Wilkes), *Into the Woods* (Rapunzel)

I don't look at a Tony Award as a pinnacle. It is not fair to artists. It's like judging painting. You either like it or you don't.

The night of the Tonys I was sitting with my girlfriend. She said, "Look, Mel Brooks is sitting across the aisle."

I asked, "What is he doing?"

She said, "He is writing his speech!"

I had more people say to me, "Oh, I am so sorry because of *The Producers*," or "you would have won." You can't be sorry. Broadway can't be geared around awards. If you think things will be different once you win a Tony or are nominated, it's not going to happen.

Patrick Wilson. *The Full Monty* (Jerry Lukowski) [O][t], *Oklahoma!* (Curley) [O][t], *The Gershwin's Fascinating Rhythm* [O], *Carousel** (Billy Bigelow), *Miss Saigon**

When my sister won the Tony Award for *Thoroughly Modern Millie*, people came up to me and said, "Congratulations on your nomination for a Tony." I wasn't nominated. I just performed during the ceremony. People assumed I was nominated.

I said to them, "Do you remember who was nominated?"

They said, "No, not really." People don't even remember who won. It happens so fast. I know so many actors who were nominated for a Tony and then couldn't get a job. It's just the way it is.

Urinetown and *Thoroughly Modern Millie* were up for the Tonys together. Everyone kept saying that *Urinetown* should beat *Millie* for the Tony. Our producers kept saying, "It's not going to happen. *Millie* will win."

I asked, "Why? Our show is better!"

Then, someone told me, "There are four unspoken criteria for Tony voters. Number one is, vote in your best interest. I'll scratch your back if you scratch mine. Number two is, vote against your enemies. Vote against shows you don't want to succeed. Number three is, vote for your friends. The last criterion is, vote for the best show."

That is why *Thoroughly Modern Millie* won for Best Musical. *Millie* was the show that was going to go on the road and make a lot of money. Our producer knew it. Everyone did. It's not fair. It's all political.

All of that said, what was remarkable was that my sister won for her talent. She wasn't a name. It gives me some hope.

Hunter Foster. *Little Shop of Horrors* (Seymour) [O], *Urinetown* (Bobby Strong) [O], *Footloose* (Bickle) [O], *King David* [O], *Grease* (Roger) [O], *Les Misérables* (Marius u/s), *Martin Guerre** (Martin u/s), *Cats** (Rum Tum Tugger)

How Does It Feel to Be a Big Star?

A dancer would never think of winning a Tony. That's like the silliest thing in the world. Dancers don't win Tonys. The whole thing was so surreal.

When the nominations came up, I thought, "Wow!" When you are nominated for a Tony, there is so much publicity. I was rooming with Jason Alexander at the time. At the Awards ceremony, I was sitting next to Madeleine Kahn. I was one of the first people out of the gates!

I cried. I laughed. I was hysterical. I walked all over Madeleine Kahn's feet. Poor thing. I had a speech in my pocket that I was going to read. By the time I got up there, I reached into my pocket and it was sopping wet. I wasn't going to sit there and peel open this piece of paper. I am a dancer. I am not an actor. Actors and singers get up there and are so articulate. If you ever see the tape, I barely got anything intelligent out of my mouth. I could barely get any names out. I didn't even thank the cast. They ushered me out, and then there was a barrage of people, pictures, and interviews. I sat next to James Earl Jones at the party.

After the Awards, I got in trouble when I was being interviewed. A journalist really irritated me.

He said, "How do you feel, now that you are a big star?"

I turned to him and said, "Well, who won it last year?" The person got mad because he didn't know. The Tony Award does not mean success. It doesn't mean you are going to work again.

Scott Wise. *Jerome Robbins' Broadway* [O][**T**], *Fosse* [O][t], *State Fair* (Pat Gilbert) [O][t], *Movin' Out* (Sergeant O'Leary) [O], *Goodbye Girl* (Billy) [O], *Damn Yankees* (Rocky) [O], *Carrie* (Scott) [O], *Guys and Dolls* (Guy) [O], *Song and Dance* (Man) [O], *A Chorus Line* (Mike), *Cats* (Plato/Macavity), *Victor Victoria* (Jazz Hot Ensemble)

Look back at the Tony Awards, at the people who were hot and won, and ask, "Where are they now?" Most of them got out of the business. If you win a Tony, it doesn't ensure that you are going to be working. If you ever feel like you are set and don't have to worry, you are setting yourself up for disappointment.

It's a validation for me to have been nominated. People ask, "Are agents calling to represent you? Have you left your agent for someone bigger?" No. No one has called me. It's over. Come next May, there will be a new hit show. *The Producers* will become history. It will fade.

Brad Oscar. *The Producers* (Franz Liebkind) [O][t], *Aspects of Love* (Swing) [O], *Jekyll & Hyde* (Archibald Proops) [O]

Where Did I Put That Thing Anyway?

Winning the Tony Award, because it comes from your peers, meant more to me than anything. However, I don't know where it is now because my cats knocked it over and I had to get it fixed.

Donna McKechnie. *A Chorus Line* (Cassie) [O][**T**], *Company* (Kathy) [O], *State Fair* (Emily Arden) [O], *On the Town* (Ivy Smith) [O], *Promises, Promises* (Vivien Della Hoya) [O], *The Education of Hyman Kaplan* (Kathy McKenna) [O], *How to Succeed in Business Without Really Trying!* (Dancer) [O], *A Funny Thing Happened on the Way to the Forum** (Philia), *Call Me Madam** (The Princess), *Sweet Charity**, *Annie Get Your Gun**

One day, when I was by myself in my dressing room, I received a box in the mail. I thought it was a box of cookies. When I finally realized it was my Tony Award, I thought, "Oh. That was anticlimactic." It just felt so lame.

Then, I mailed it to my home in California, and it broke. It totally broke. Eventually, I got it fixed.

When you pick up a Tony Award, it's like one of those trick glasses that looks like it's full of beer, but is actually empty. You think it is going to be a heavy wonderful statue, and you are wrong. When you see the shiny black thing from far away, you think, "Oh, pretty statue." But, when you get close, it's just a piece of Formica or something. The medallion is the prettiest part of the whole thing.

Now, I have the Tony on my fireplace with a little light behind it. At first, I was going to spin the medallion every day before I left the house, like on "Showtime at the Apollo," where they rub the rock. That idea died after a day or two. It's weird. You think the Tony is going to change your world. *Hairspray* changed my life, the Tony didn't.

Marissa Jaret Winokur. *Hairspray* (Tracy Turnblad) [O][**T**], *Grease!* (Jan)

They never give you the Tony right there. They take it away from you the moment you go backstage, and then they deliver it once it has been engraved. The day that the Tony Award actually arrived at the theater, Liza Minnelli was there.

I said, "Wow! Check this out. Here's the Tony."

Liza said, "It feels great, huh? Listen, hon, this Award is nothing but spit and vinegar. The most important thing is the performing. I have several of these—they fall apart in a couple of years anyway. This doesn't mean a damn thing. What's more important is the performing and what you do on stage."

So I went home and I put it right on the toilet. And I gave it a little flick, 'cause it's on a little axle, so you get to spin it around. I told people that the reason it's there is because I get to see it at least three or four times a day. It's in the bathroom. I know I will make a couple of visits there, and hey, there it is. It reminds me that I do the same thing that other people do—I just happen to have a Tony. I'm doing my business. It doesn't dignify me at all.

Wilson Heredia. *Rent* (Angel) [O][**T**]

Tony® Wanna Cracker?

There are days when this business seems downright undignified. Those are hard days. Half an hour after I unwrapped the actual Tony trophy that was sent in the mail with my engraving on it, I was at a voice-over audition making the sound of a bird. I had to say "Baaaw, super!"

That's not dignified. I just polished my Tony Award and put it on my desk.

Roger Bart. *You're a Good Man, Charlie Brown* (Snoopy) [O][**T**], *The Producers* (Carmen Ghia) [O][**t**], *Triumph of Love* (Harlequin) [O], *King David* (Jonathan) [O], *Big River* (Tom Sawyer), *The Who's Tommy* (Cousin Kevin), *The Secret Garden* (Dickon), *How to Succeed in Business Without Really Trying!* (Bud Frump)

Scott Wise had won the Tony Award for *Jerome Robbins' Broadway*, and I was so thrilled for him. He said, "Yeah, it's such a big deal to have won the Tony Award that three months later, I was at a kid's birthday party dressed up as a Teenage Mutant Ninja Turtle. Hey, look at me! Tony winner! Tony winner!"

Andrea McArdle. *Annie* (Annie) [O][**t**], *Starlight Express* (Ashley) [O], *State Fair* (Margy Frake) [O], *Les Misérables* (Fantine), *Beauty and the Beast* (Belle), *Cabaret** (Sally Bowles), *Jerry's Girls**

The Trophy on the Shelf

Winning the Tony Award is like anything else. It is an event in your life. And it lasts no longer than the event. A great meal can be the best moment in your life, and what does it turn to by that evening? It goes the way it's supposed to go. That's perfectly right.

Getting recognition is wonderful. Winning those big awards is wonderful because it's public recognition. But it really isn't any more than a giant kiss on the cheek and a pat on the back. I don't belittle it, but it isn't more than that. I have my little Tony on the shelf in the other room, and it makes me happy.

John Rubinstein. *Children of a Lesser God* (James Leeds) [O][**T**], *Pippin* (Pippin) [O], *Fools* (Leon) [O], *Getting Away with Murder* (Martin Chisholm) [O], *The Caine Mutiny Court-Martial* (Lt. Barney Greenwald) [O], *Ragtime* (Tateh), *Hurlyburly* (Eddie), *Love Letters* (Andrew), *M. Butterfly* (Rene)

How do you experience a Tony Award? You don't. It sits on your shelf. It's a line on your résumé. Quite frankly, nobody in Hollywood knows what it means. And if you perform in London and you get an Olivier Award, people in Hollywood think it's an *Oliver* Award and don't know what you are talking about.

So it's really of no use. It is certainly frosting on a piece of cake, but it shouldn't be someone's goal. I learned that real early and I was real lucky.

What you actually experience are the eight-show weeks, and on days where you don't feel like performing, performing anyway. What you actually experience is having to put on your cape and your blue dress one more time, carry your basket, and sing your song. You do it for an audience who wasn't there the last seven hundred and fifty times.

Susan Egan. *Beauty and the Beast* (Belle) [O][t], *Triumph of Love* (Princess) [O], *Cabaret* (Sally), *Thoroughly Modern Millie* (Millie), *State Fair, Bye Bye Birdie** (Kim)

A Tony Award means nothing as far as success is concerned, except, possibly, for opportunity and finance. I don't think it garners any more respect for your work. I don't think it improves your work. I don't think it validates your work. It's just someone else's opinion. Once, after I was nominated, someone said to me, "Oh, you are in the history books now!" I thought, "Well, maybe. But who cares? I mean, why do you care about that? What does that mean? It doesn't mean anything!"

Michael Berresse. *Kiss Me, Kate* (Bill Calhoun/Luciento) [O][t], *The Gershwin's Fascinating Rhythm* [O], *Chicago* (Fred Casely) [O], *Damn Yankees* (Bomber) [O], *Fiddler on the Roof* [O], *Guys and Dolls* (Crapshooter), *Joseph and the Amazing Technicolor*® *Dreamcoat** (Pharaoh), *Busker Alley**

It is very different winning the Tony Award the second time. First, with *Passion*, it felt like we opened and two days later they announced Tony nominations. We went from the whirlwind of previews, which is all about the work, to the Tony Awards, which is all about external recognition. Granted, it was recognition from your peers. It was an extended period of time in which we were under a lot of pressure.

I was so happy playing Fosca in *Passion*. I could not have been happier to receive recognition for a piece that meant so much to me. Somebody said, "Deal with it as a celebration." For the most part, I did. I couldn't help but think that two years earlier, due to my illness, I didn't know whether I would act again.

We performed live during the Tony Awards. When the curtain came up, I remember thinking, "It doesn't get any better than this. I love this role and revere the people who wrote this piece. There is artistry and purity. It makes people think and feel. I am getting to do it now in front of a television audience." I was so proud.

My character's makeup and costume consisted of a severe wig and sick makeup that exaggerated my less attractive features. My character was supposed to be wretched looking. Society viewed her as ugly. I had twelve minutes to transform and get back to my seat for my category. I was determined that I was not going to be one of those people photographed backstage still in costume. I hired a hair and makeup person. We actually rehearsed the quick change several times.

I barely made it into my seat. When they announced my name, it was like some bizarre drug was released into my system. I was moving in slow motion. I was shocked. I got up on the stage and said whatever I said. I enjoyed the party that night. The rest of the run was like a high.

My second Tony was for *The King and I*. I never felt really confident about what I was doing. There was a controversy that year because Julie Andrews, who was nominated for *Victor Victoria*, declined her nomination. She declined because no one else associated with her show was nominated. It became a political thing. Everybody wanted my comment. I wanted to be respectful and not comment. It made me uncomfortable. The whole award ceremony made me uncomfortable. I didn't feel good about my work. I questioned what I was doing.

That really begs the question, "What do awards really mean, anyway?" I was wrestling with that. I was honored for *Passion*. I enjoyed it, but I always saw it as an extension of the glory of the work. I was struck with the hypocrisy in certain ways when people asked me political questions. It seemed to be about the Awards and not about the work.

Donna Murphy. *Passion* (Fosca) [O][**T**], *The King and I* (Anna) [O][**T**], *Wonderful Town* (Ruth) [O], *The Mystery of Edwin Drood* [O], *The Human Comedy* (Bess Macauley u/s) [O], *Privates on Parade* [O], *They're Playing our Song* (Swing)

The Tony Award doesn't mean that much to me. It never did. It was exciting to be nominated. My competition was Anne Bancroft, Estelle Parsons, and Jessica Tandy. I was nominated for a Neil Simon show called *Chapter Two*.

He came into my dressing room and said, "If my name were Harold Pinter, I am sure you would win this Award. I just feel so sorry because I know you are not going to get it."

I said, "It's okay. I'm glad to be nominated."

Everyone says that. "It's great to be nominated."

But you want to win.

At our nomination lunch at Sardi's, Jessica Tandy said, "This is a horserace. We are all out here to win. The pressure to win is wrong. We should all win and be honored. Everyone should get an award."

I went to the Awards. It's just another big party. Who remembers the next year who won? It's really for the producers. It doesn't get you the next job.

Anita Gillette. *Chapter Two* (Jennie Malone) [O][t], *Guys and Dolls* (Sarah Brown) [O], *Kelly* (Angela Crane) [O], *Carnival!* (Gypsy) [O], *All American* (Susan) [O], *Mr. President* (Leslie Henderson) [O], *Jimmy* (Betty Compton) [O], *Don't Drink the Water* (Susan Hollander) [O], *Gypsy* (Thelma), *Brighton Beach Memoirs* (Blanche), *They're Playing Our Song* (Sonia Walsk), *Cabaret* (Sally)

I had no interest in being a star. It wasn't even something I thought about. I lived with my parents in Brooklyn. We had cats, and that's the way it was. I didn't want anything else. My acting and my winning a Tony Award was a sideline. I know that sounds funny. As exciting as it was, it was just a part of my life. I wasn't looking for anything else.

Daisy Eagan. *The Secret Garden* (Mary) [O][**T**], *James Joyce's The Dead* (Rita) [O], *Les Misérables* (Young Cosette)

I did not want to do *Jerome Robbins' Broadway*. I turned down the audition three times because I had been told it was a review of all of his most spectacular dances—not one of which I was capable of dancing. And all I kept hearing was that Jerome Robbins didn't know how he wanted to link the evening together.

I had done some writing for one of the producers, and he thought that I could work with Jerome Robbins to create the presentation. He kept telling me, "You'll host the night." In my mind, all I could see was Ed Sullivan. The thought of having to do that kind of uninteresting work for a year was, well, completely uninteresting.

I kept saying no, but finally I gave in. I auditioned for about three hours. At the end of the evening, I knew I was going to wind up with the part. I took the role, thinking, "This is not going to do a thing for me as an actor." But I knew Jerome Robbins was a great director and I have aspirations to direct on Broadway.

So I figured that I would sit at his heels for a year and bullshit my way through, and maybe I'd learn something from the master.

I knew the show would be a huge hit, but what really knocked me over was my becoming a highlight of the show. I was on stage with fifty or sixty of the most talented dancing performers I had ever seen. They did amazing things in the show. Actually, it was freakish what they could do. I, on the other hand, made various appearances playing about sixteen characters in the course of the evening. It was no big deal to me. I've done more shows where I played a dozen characters a night than I have where I played one. It's fun. You have to get good at changing your outward appearance and doing character work. But I've always had a knack for that kind of thing, so to me it was just a game.

That said, however, when I got nominated for the Tony, I went to the Awards almost knowing that I had the Award, because none of the other nominated musicals could really compete with us. I was up against Robbie LaFosse, who had a pure dance role in our show, and against two guys from *Starmites*, one of whom played a lizard! So how tight a contest could it be? I was the only guy with a part. I went through the night thinking, "Well, if this doesn't come to me, I guess I really suck."

I always had fantasies about what it would be like to win the Tony. Like most things, it is somewhat sweeter in the fantasy. In the musical *Pippin*—which is a seminal show for me—the story revolves around a man searching for meaning and purpose in what should be his extraordinary life. He tries many routes—politics, hedonism, and eventually war. At the end of the battle, despite being a hero and a conqueror, Pippin is disappointed, and says, "I thought there'd be more plumes."

That is what I've learned in life. You always think that there are going to be more plumes.

The night of the Tony Awards was great.

When I went home, I thought there would be a hundred messages on my machine. There were six. In rapid succession, I did *Pretty Woman* and the pilot of *Seinfeld*. Did they happen because of the Tony? I doubt it. I don't think they knew I had one.

Jason Alexander. *Jerome Robbins' Broadway* (Emcee) [O][**T**], *Merrily We Roll Along* (Joe) [O], *The Rink* (Lino/Lenny/Punk/Uncle Fausto) [O], *Broadway Bound* (Stanley) [O], *Accomplice* [O], *The Producers** (Max Bialystock)

"Hello, You Have No New Messages"

I was in the show *Starmites*. Most of us were nominated for a Tony. The weird thing about it was that the nominations came out when I was at the gym. I didn't even know they were out. When I got home, a friend who was staying with me said, "You got nominated for a Tony." He had heard it on the answering machine. I was in shock.

The next month or so, a pack of photographers followed me everywhere I went. They were always there—at the show, at a luncheon. I'd see them in packs.

At the Tonys, I sang my song and sat down with Jason Alexander, who was sitting behind me. During the commercial break, before they announced our category, I said to him, "I promise I won't trip you on the way up." We all knew he was going to win. And he did.

That night, after the party was over, I was going down the escalator, and the same pack of photographers who had followed me all that month looked right through me. They were looking to see if there were any "winners" around. It was a weird feeling to realize, "Oh, my God, the focus is totally gone." It was a reality check. It made me realize that nobody really cares. Nominations are terrific, but no one really cares.

Brian Lane Green. *Starmites* (Spacepunk) [O][t], *The Life* (Jojo), *Big River* (Huckleberry Finn), *Joseph and the Amazing Technicolor® Dreamcoat** (Joseph)

I had been performing in *Starlight Express* for about six months. I was brand new to New York and didn't know anything about the Tony Awards or what they were all about. One night, when I came home, I checked my answering machine and there were all of these messages.

"Congratulations! Oh, my God. Call me back."

"I just heard, congratulations! Call me back." Not one message said what the congratulations were for.

I finally figured out that I had been nominated for a Tony Award. It was my first time on Broadway, and I didn't even know how to skate when I was cast in the show. Furthermore, I was the only actor in the show who was nominated. It was unbelievable.

Everyone told me that I was going to be on every talk show in New

York. I waited for the phone to ring. The phone didn't ring. Not even once. The producers of the show told me that no one was interested in *Starlight Express*. Michael Maguire was also nominated in the same category for *Les Misérables*.

Two nights before the Tony Awards, I was at a McDonald's on Broadway in Midtown. A dirty, homeless, raggedy-looking woman came over to me with a nasty little book that I didn't even want to touch.

She said in an odd foreign accent, "I loved your performance in *Starlight Express*. Fabulous. Would you sign my book? Do you have a picture?"

"I don't have a picture with me," I said. "Do you have an address?"

She said, "No, it's all right. Will you sign my book, though?"

I signed it.

She then said, "But I gotta tell you, that Michael Maguire from that *Liz Miserbelees*, now that's a show! That show is good! The other show that's nominated is not so good, so it's between you and that Michael guy. Good luck!"

Then she starting rolling her cart and was on her way. It was a surreal moment.

"Wow," I thought. "I guess this is making it."

The night before the Tony Awards, I finally got a phone call telling me that I was scheduled to be on the *Regis Show* the next day. I thought, "I'm doing *Regis*, that's something!" I soon found out that the only reason I was asked to be on the show was because Colm Wilkinson had cancelled. I was still optimistic.

Then came the Tony Awards. Before the Awards, everyone wanted my picture. I had a limousine, a tuxedo, and the whole thing. The Tonys were right across the street from the Gershwin Theater, where I was performing *Starlight Express*. The limousine picked me up at the stage door, drove around the block, and dropped me off exactly where I was picked up. That's what you did. You have to arrive. When I got out of the limousine and stepped onto the carpet, there were photographers and mobs of people.

When I walked out of the theater after the Tony Awards were over, it was literally like the parting of the Red Sea. Everyone would rush over and gear up their cameras. "Here comes . . ." Slowly but surely, I heard, "Oh, he didn't win." And the cameras went away.

Just as all of the cameras went away, I heard, "Mr. Torti, right this way!" And there, standing in the street in her best party dress, was that homeless woman with an Instamatic camera. None of the paparazzi wanted my picture, but the homeless woman from McDonald's in her ratty, tatty, torn dress said, "Mr. Torti, right this way." She took my picture and left. That was my Tony experience.

Robert Torti. *Starlight Express* (Greaseball) [O][t], *Joseph and the Amazing Technicolor® Dreamcoat* (Pharaoh) [O]

I was in *Smokey Joe's Cafe*. I had no idea I could be nominated for a Tony Award. I was just a dancer who sang a few lines in the show. I knew Brenda Braxton, my dressing room–mate, was going to be nominated, so I got up early to watch the Tony nominations be announced. As expected, they announced Brenda. Then they announced another lead in our show, and a woman from *Showboat*. And then they said my name. My phone started ringing instantly. I received phone calls from people that I didn't even think liked me, saying, "Congratulations!"

The phone didn't stop ringing before the Tonys, and I was ready to hire an assistant. Every time I picked up the phone, someone would want an interview, or want me to sing for them, or something. I thought, "They've made a mistake. I'm not supposed to be getting this!"

The night of the Tonys, the girls from my show were scheduled to close the evening by singing a number from the show. We had to be at the theater early that day to rehearse. We had a matinee to do that day, so we rushed to our theater after the rehearsal. We did our show, and then we rushed home to get our hair and make-up done.

That night, the woman from *Showboat* won the Award, beating out all three of us from *Smokey Joe's Cafe*. After they gave out the Award, we had to run backstage and get ready for our number. We threw off our Tony dresses and got into our costumes. Then they cancelled our number because there wasn't enough time left.

The next day, the *Daily News* had a "Hit and Miss" section, discussing the outfits performers wore at the Tonys. It said, *"Broadway star DeLee Lively is a 'miss' in her blue dress, which was cut a little too high in the thigh."*

I tried to be optimistic. I called my mom and said, "Mom, look! It says Broadway star!" What else was I going to do? It was the perfect example of the quirkiness of my career. Something really incredible will happen, and then something comes along and kicks it in the butt.

DeLee Lively. *Smokey Joe's Cafe* [O][t], *A Chorus Line* (Val)

Going to the Tony Awards was like going to the prom I never went to. I didn't have serious boyfriends in high school, so it was like a prom. It was just so much fun.

I thought I had a chance to win for *Baby* because of the polls that people took beforehand. We were nominated for about seven Awards, and the show was suddenly sold out for that month. It was a great month. However, winning Best Score was our only hope of keeping the show open. We weren't going to win Best Musical. There was no way.

We performed "I Want it All" in the Tony Awards. When we were behind the curtain getting ready to do our number, they gave away Best Score to *La Cage Aux Folles*. We looked at each other and thought, "Well, we are out of work." Then we had to do the song. Then I lost. I was fine when I lost. Totally fine, and I had a great time at the party.

Then I went home. I lived in Chelsea and I had a cocker spaniel who had been there for hours. My answering machine light was blinking like crazy. I pressed PLAY.

The first fifteen messages were, "I know you are going to win! I am so excited for you!"

The last fifteen messages were, "I can't believe you didn't win. It's so horrible." And while I was listening, in my gown and high heels, I walked into this big thing of dog shit.

So I'm listening to all of these messages, I am stuck in this thing of dog shit, and I just cried. It was like Cinderella coming home from the ball. I was in this pile of dog shit, the show was going to close, and this fabulous night was over. I started laughing because it was so absurd.

> **Liz Callaway.** *Baby* (Lizzie) [O][t], *Miss Saigon* (Ellen) [O], *Merrily We Roll Along* (Nightclub Waitress) [O], *The Three Musketeers* (Lady Constance Bonacieux) [O], *The Look of Love* [O], *Cats* (Grizabella)

The Curse of the Tonys®

For me, the Tonys were complicated. I was glad when that night was over. I have to say that the more fulfilling moment for me was being home with a cup of coffee at 7:30 P.M., watching somebody read my name off as I was nominated. That was probably more exciting. I was home in my pajamas. No one was watching me.

It definitely made me feel like I deserved more all of a sudden. That's a dangerous thing. I felt like I deserved to have my career take off at that moment. This is the "Curse of the Tonys," as people call it. I know people who won a Tony and said that the following year was the most difficult of their lives.

I have to say it was for me too. It was the most difficult year, and I was poor.

> **Roger Bart.** *You're a Good Man, Charlie Brown* (Snoopy) [O][T], *The Producers* (Carmen Ghia) [O][t], *Triumph of Love* (Harlequin) [O], *King David* (Jonathan) [O], *Big River* (Tom Sawyer), *The Who's Tommy* (Cousin Kevin), *The Secret Garden* (Dickon), *How to Succeed in Business Without Really Trying!* (Bud Frump)

I was twenty-five years old when I was nominated for a Tony for *Jerome Robbins' Broadway.* I didn't work on Broadway for pretty much five years after that.

I went to therapy for the first time in my life. It helped. I learned that I had to be patient. For me, I have to keep working on my craft. I go to voice lessons. I go to acting class. I keep up my dancing. Otherwise, I die. That's what keeps me going. My problem is that when I get depressed, I get really lazy. I just sit in front of the television and I eat like a pig. It helps when you have a family, and I am a positive person to begin with. I can find joy in little things, which I have learned to do. It was a huge breaking point for me. I realized that I have my family. If I never work again, yes, it will be horrible, but at least I have them.

Because, I am telling you, you're suicidal to the point of, "Oh, my God, do I want to live anymore?" It is hard to change professions. Once you are into this, and you love it, there is nothing else that compares. There is nothing else I would want to do. Nothing else. So when you are out of work, what's life?

Charlotte d'Amboise. *Jerome Robbins' Broadway* (Anita/Peter Pan) [O][t], *Carrie* (Chris) [O], *Company* (Cathy) [O], *Song and Dance* [O], *Contact* (Wife), *Damn Yankees* (Lola), *Chicago* (Roxie Hart), *Cats* (Cassandra)

I have had two experiences with the Tony Awards. The first, which broke my heart, was for *Aspects of Love*. I had the very bizarre experience of being called by the press, who told me that I was on the Tony ballot. But then there was a re-vote. I think, in the whole history of the Tonys, that was the only time that had happened. They did a re-vote because somebody raised his or her hand and said, "You know, we didn't think of this person who has been around for a number of years. Maybe we should include her."

After the re-vote, I was taken off the ballot. I actually got a call that I was on the ballot and then a call that I was off. I can't tell you how devastated I was.

Some years later, when I was not expecting a nomination, I got a call that I was nominated. I never thought it possible. I remember being at Sardi's with Bernadette Peters. The event was very exciting, but then it was over.

There is a joke in this industry that after you get a Tony nomination, you won't have an audition for many months. It is true. I didn't have any auditions. My hope that it would make life easier did not materialize.

Ann Crumb. *Anna Karenina* (Anna) [O][t], *Aspects of Love* (Rose) [O], *Chess* (Svetlana u/s) [O], *Les Misérables* (Fantine u/s) [O], *Swing** (Lead), *Music of the Night** (Headliner), *Man of La Mancha** (Aldonza), *Evita** (Eva Peron)

The Tony Awards were very fun and a big high. There was all this attention that came to me the year that I was nominated. And then I didn't win. It was still okay. The next day, I went back to my life.

Years went by, and I kind of wished that the Tony nomination had done something more. The fact is, it didn't. There were many years where I would just wait for the phone to ring. I mean, I was nominated for a Tony, and then it was gone in five minutes.

Barbara Walsh. *Falsettos* (Trina) [O][t], *Blood Brothers* (Mrs. Lyons) [O], *Big* (Mrs. Baskin) [O], *Rock 'N Roll! The First 5,000 Years* [O], *Hairspray* (Velma Von Tussle), *Ragtime** (Mother), *Les Misérables** (Fantine/Cosette u/s), *Chess** (Svetlana), *Oklahoma!**, *Nine**

I have had some success and I have won some awards, but I have to audition like every one else. I don't feel like anyone owes me anything. My pattern of work is that I will be in something that is successful and then I will be largely unemployed. Then, I will work on some small things and build myself back up. If I'm lucky, I get something else that is successful. There are so many actors who are better than I am who have not had nearly as much luck. It's being in the right place at the right time. I don't take any of it terribly seriously. One hopes that the cream will rise to the top, but it doesn't always.

My first Tony Award was for *The Heidi Chronicles*. I had the expectation that it was kind of like an Oscar. I thought it would change how people think of me. I thought it would put me up a notch. I was largely unemployed for the two years that followed. I became more realistic.

Boyd Gaines. *Contact* (Michael Wiley) [O][T], *She Loves Me* (Georg Nowak) [O][T], *The Heidi Chronicles* (Peter Patrone) [O][T], *Anything Goes* (Lord Evelyn Oakleigh) [O], *Company* (Robert) [O], *The Show Off* (Aubrey Piper) [O], *Cabaret* (Clifford Bradshaw)

A Ticket to Nowhere

I am friends with Daisy Eagan. One day, I ran into her on the street after a voice-over audition.

She said to me, "Yeah, I just sent out stuff through *Back Stage* magazine."

I remember thinking, "You just won a Tony."

She said, "Donna, you've got to understand." We both just sat there, laughing.

All those credits on your résumé are nothing more than a novelty. Okay, I was Young Cosette from *Les Misérables*. That's so cute. The original Young Cosette. That's great. I realize that there are adults who also have fabulous credits and it doesn't necessarily mean anything. It really doesn't.

Donna Vivino. *Les Misérables* (Young Cosette) [O], *Saturday Night Fever* (Vocals) [O], *Hairspray**

When I was doing an Off-Broadway show, I knew people were going to think, "Oh, she is doing a little play Off-Broadway. Look at where her career is." I was scared of what the critics would say. I was terrified of how people were going to see me. I was terrified of what people would think.

"What happened to this Tony Award winner?"

"Why does she suck?"

I have a lot to overcome in terms of all of that. I have had a lot to face and let go of. I am really now just starting to be adult about it. I am really just starting to buckle down, take acting classes and voice lessons, and prepare for auditions. Until recently, I approached auditions thinking, "If I don't prepare, and I don't get the part, I can always say that I wasn't prepared." It's much easier than saying, "I worked my ass off. What the hell is wrong with me?"

Daisy Eagan. *The Secret Garden* (Mary) [O][**T**], *James Joyce's The Dead* (Rita) [O], *Les Misérables* (Young Cosette)

There was a sense that winning the Tony Award could lead to bigger and brighter things, but it doesn't always follow. I mean, you do have a Tony Award, and it does mean that for that particular year, you did pretty well. But it doesn't mean that the next year you are guaranteed a Hollywood contract.

After I left *Miss Saigon*, my agent called and said he was going to send me in for a big audition. About ten minutes later, he called back. "They don't want to see you because you are Asian." I thought, "Well, that's preposterous! That doesn't make any sense."

So then you get the reality. As fairy tale–like as my arrival might have been, you don't stay on the magic carpet ride forever. It's not always going to be a fairy tale.

You would think that having a Tony Award would immediately lead to someone offering you more things, but it doesn't always follow. I learned that. It humbles you, very, very quickly. Just because you do a Broadway show does not mean people will flock from all over, wanting to give you another Broadway show. The reality is that a Broadway show is very difficult to come by. You are very lucky if you are able to do it once in your lifetime. A lot of people pound the pavement.

Lea Salonga. *Miss Saigon* (Kim) [O][**T**], *Flower Drum Song* (Mei-Li) [O], *Les Misérables* (Eponine)

I didn't capitalize on anything after I won the Tony Award. Perhaps if I had won the Award many years ago, I would have had a starring role in my next show. No one said, "We have a brand new Broadway show and we want you to star in it."

After I won the Award, I decided to go to Hunter College and get my degree in psychology and a minor in classical studies. My professor said to me, "I see you've combined the useless with the worthless. You keep going on like this and you will be as unemployable as I am!" I finally took a job as a receptionist at a large company.

Jane Sell. *Over Here!* (Mitzi) [O][**T**], *Irene* (Jane Burke) [O], *George M!* [O], *Moon over Buffalo* (Charlotte Hay s/b) [O], *Pal Joey* (Gladys Bumps) [O], *Happy End* (Lieutenant Lillian Holiday), *I Love My Wife* (Monica)

Making It in the New Millennium

In my head, there is no "making it." I still take the train. I see people watching me on the train, thinking, "What are you doing here? You won a Tony."

I wear my sweatpants through Times Square and think, "Why are you bothering me?"

"But you play Aida!"

"Well, yeah, I do. But why are you bothering me?"

I don't think you have ever made it until you are eighty years old and you are sitting with your grandchildren and you say, "Now, I've done well. I am done, maybe."

Have I "made" it now on Broadway? No, I don't think so. I don't see it as "making it." I think that is the problem with so many kids. Some kid wrote me last night on my Web site. I read the letter and got really disturbed.

She said, "*I am really talented.*" She was twelve years old. "*I have done this and I have done that. People say I have got what it takes to be a super-star. But I am missing something. So my question to you, Heather, is which way is up? How do I get up? How do I 'make it?'*"

And I immediately thought, "You don't! Up is God." You need to think of your talent as a "gift" and a "loan." Many people think "making it" means getting to Broadway or winning a Tony. Whatever. That is the furthest thing from my mind right now. Those are simply accomplishments and part of a journey, not the end of the journey. It is always a journey.

Heather Headley. *Aida* (Aida) [O][**T**], *The Lion King* (Nala) [O], *Ragtime** (Sarah u/s)

People asked, "Have you made it?" Who knows what that means. One thing I learned years ago is that the joy is in the journey. That may sound a little transcendental, but it's absolutely true. There is no destination. There is no, "Ah, I've reached it."

Gary Beach. *The Producers* (Roger DeBris) [O][**T**], *Beauty and the Beast* (Lumiere) [O][t], *The Moony Shapiro Songbook* [O], *Doonesbury* (Duke) [O], *Something's Afoot* (Nigel) [O], *Sweet Adeline* (Dan Ward) [O], *Annie* (Rooster Hannigan), *1776* (Edward Rutledge), *Les Misérables** (Thénardier), *Of Thee I Sing**

Even though I won the Tony Award in 2003, I still haven't "made it" on Broadway. There is no "making it" on Broadway anymore. It is going to be just as hard to get my next job as it was to get *Hairspray*.

True, there are people who have "made it" and become Broadway legends—but that doesn't happen until they're dead. In this new era, there is no "making it" on Broadway. You have to do something else, like television or film.

My heart will always be on Broadway. If I could work consistently there, that's what I would choose to do. Unfortunately, even after winning a Tony Award, I don't have that choice—unless I want to be in the same show for four years straight and then kill myself.

Marissa Jaret Winokur. *Hairspray* (Tracy Turnblad) [O][T], *Grease!* (Jan)

Do I think I've made it? No. *Contact* will end in a few months. When it ends, I'll be unemployed. There isn't any "making it." There's just going on. For some, it means incredible perseverance, and for others, it means incredible luck. I don't know anyone who thinks they've "made it." Once you've made it to the top, there's really only one direction to go.

Boyd Gaines. *Contact* (Michael Wiley) [O][T], *She Loves Me* (Georg Nowak) [O][T], *The Heidi Chronicles* (Peter Patrone) [O][T], *Anything Goes* (Lord Evelyn Oakleigh) [O], *Company* (Robert) [O], *The Show Off* (Aubrey Piper) [O], *Cabaret* (Clifford Bradshaw)

CHAPTER 19

Here Today, Gone Tomorrow

No matter how many awards an actor collects, and no matter how many credits an actor acquires, pursuing a career on Broadway today can be heartbreaking. Just when many actors thinks they are about to "make it," the whole world can come crashing down on them. And, once they think they have "made it," they can find themselves waiting in a line with five hundred fellow actors, hoping to be discovered once again.

Unlike in the past, seniority and experience mean very little. Actors are asked to prove themselves over and over again. It can be exhausting, and sometimes debilitating. Rare is the occasion when a casting director will call a performer out of the blue and offer a role in a Broadway show. Even actors with numerous Broadway credits and Tony Awards must brave the audition room time and time again. Although the scene becomes familiar, the process of auditioning rarely gets easier. Sometimes, all a performer can hope for is to leave a lasting impression.

Despite having made it to Broadway, once a show closes, performers have to come to terms with the fact that they may never again perform on a Broadway stage. Despite all of the hardships endured to get to square one, in the new world of Broadway, square two is often nowhere in sight.

Sorry, We're Closed

Imagine everyone in the Broadway community as fish. We are all fish in a big ocean. The closer you float to the surface, the more important you are.

If you are cast in a Broadway show, you swim about ten feet from the top. But you are not alone. There are many other fish that are also swimming at the same level. Some are a little higher and some are a little lower. Some go down to the depths, one hundred feet below, and are never heard from again.

Imagine that metaphor. Yes, things are out of control. The tide shifts, the water ebbs, your show closes. Boom. You sink a foot or two down in the water.

Jose Llana. *Flower Drum Song* (Ta) [O], *The King and I* (Lun Tha) [O], *Street Corner Symphony* (Jessie-Lee) [O], *Rent* (Angel), *Martin Guerre** (Guillaume)

It is not an easy life. In film, you have a record of everything that lasts through the years. On Broadway, you go out and do a performance and it is lost in the air.

Ann Miller. *Sugar Babies* (Ann) [O][t], *George White's Scandals* [O], *Mame* (Mame Dennis)

I was hired to play the lead role in the Broadway-bound musical *Busker Alley*. I was going to play opposite Tommy Tune. On our eight-month pre-Broadway tour, we had rewrites every day. They would slip them under our dressing room doors during intermission. We would rehearse the changes from 1:00 P.M. until 5:00 P.M. the next day. It got to the point where we had to tape the new lyrics up on the orchestra pit because we couldn't possibly remember all of the changes. We were literally learning new material every day for eight months. We cared so much about the show.

On Broadway, they were painting the St. James Theater with a mural of the show. It featured huge images of me and Tommy Tune. Everybody was talking about me. Everyone was calling me. We were getting great reviews on the road and we were coming to New York, smelling like a rose. I was even reading about myself in *Theater Week*, *Back Stage*, and *Variety*.

Then, the week before we were scheduled to begin previews, Tommy Tune broke his foot. That was it. The show closed. We got our one-week closing notice. Literally in an instant, it was gone. When I came back to New York the next week, I went to visit the theater. There I was—a large picture of me in front of the St. James Theater, with a huge closing notice on it.

Darcie Roberts. *Dream* (Ingénue) [O], *Aida* (Amneris s/b), *Crazy for You* (Irene Ross s/b), *42nd Street** (Peggy), *Thoroughly Modern Millie** (Millie), *Copacabana** (Lola), *Busker Alley** (Libby)

In the summer after college, I was cast in a big Broadway musical. It was the musical version of *East of Eden*, and it was called *Here's Where I Belong*. It was a major production. I had a great part. It was my big break. I was in another world. We worked on the play all day and all night. It was so exciting. Also, I fell in love with my leading man.

The opening night was so wonderful that we had no inkling of what was to come. We got terrible reviews. The *New York Times* review was

especially bad. We opened and closed in one night. That was my introduction to the New York theater scene.

> **Heather MacRae.** *Falsettos* (Charlotte) [O], *Coastal Disturbances* (Faith Bigelow)
> [O], *Here's Where I Belong* (Abra) [O], *Hair* (Sheila)

One day, I got an offer to play the lead in a new workshop of *The Jazz
Singer*. At last, I was going to play Al Jolson, a role I had always wanted.
It was Broadway bound and well received. All of our money came from
one source. Everything was lined up—we had our theater in Boston, our
theater in New York, a rehearsal schedule, designers, everything. I couldn't
have been more thrilled.

On my birthday, June 4th, I opened the *New York Times* and saw a
huge picture of me in the "Arts and Leisure" section. It said, "The rumors
are true. Sam Harris is playing Al Jolson on Broadway, coming this fall."

By 5:00 that night, the show was off. All the money was gone. It was
horrifying. I couldn't understand it. The writing was wonderful. It devastated me.

Everywhere I would go, every street I would walk down, people
would say, "I'm so sorry." It killed me. I didn't go outside for two weeks.

> **Sam Harris.** *The Life* [O][t], *Grease!* (Doody) [O], *The Producers* (Carmen Ghia),
> *Joseph and the Amazing Technicolor® Dreamcoat** (Joseph)

My very first show on Broadway was *Saravà*. I made $450 a week. I have
a very vivid memory of the night the show closed. I remember standing
on the fire escape, looking at the street sign that said "52nd and
Broadway," and thinking, "When will I ever be back on Broadway?"
Eight years later, I did *Les Misérables* in the same theater. It took eight
years.

> **Randy Graff.** *City of Angels* (Oolie) [O][T], *A Class Act* (Sophie) [O][t], *Les
> Misérables* (Fantine) [O], *Moon over Buffalo* (Rosalind) [O], *High Society* (Liz
> Imbrie) [O], *Laughter on the 23rd Floor* (Carol) [O], *Saravà* (Rosalia) [O],
> *Fiddler on the Roof* (Golde) [O], *Grease!* (Rizzo u/s), *Falsettos* (Trina)

The apple really fell off the tree for me when I did *Whistle Down the
Wind*, the Andrew Lloyd Webber production that never quite made it to
New York. The show shattered my reality. I think it was the first Andrew
Lloyd Webber show to not make it to Broadway. Until then, his track
record was good.

Hal Prince was the director. He didn't want to be there, and he and
Andrew weren't getting along. While it was bad, we still never thought
the show wasn't going to happen. Although we received terrible reviews
in Washington, they told us we were still coming to Broadway. The marquee above the Martin Beck Theater on Broadway was up. Posters were
everywhere.

On the final night in Washington, Andrew Lloyd Webber and Hal Prince told us that we were closing. It was over. After that experience, it's been much harder for me to get a part.

> **Ray Walker.** *Jesus Christ Superstar* (Annas) [O], *Grease!* (Doody), *Les Misérables* (Marius), *Whistle Down the Wind** (Preacher), *Music of the Night** (Principal Soloist), *Joseph and the Amazing Technicolor® Dreamcoat** (Joseph u/s), *Falsettos** (Whizzer)

When I was in college, people told me, "If you don't make it to Broadway within five years, then you should try something new." I thought, "I'm not going to do that. I'm going to stick it out." I was cast in my first Broadway show within a year, *Uptown . . . It's Hot!*.

I didn't save any money because I was buying clothes and buying everyone and their mother tickets. I had a great apartment. I mean, there I was, my first year in New York, and I had it all. And then the rug was pulled out from underneath me.

After two weeks in the show, I walked into the theater and there was a closing notice. I had never seen a closing notice before.

I went to the stage manager and said, "I don't understand what this means."

He said, "The show is closing next week because we don't have enough money to keep the show running." I couldn't believe it. There I was, in my first Broadway show, and two weeks after it opened, a closing notice. It was devastating. No one teaches young actors about that. No one told me that shows can close in two weeks. They teach you how to audition and how to get there. Not this part.

The lead of the show called the company into his dressing room and said, "If you guys sign your checks over for this week, we will be able to stay open longer." Half the cast signed their checks over, and we closed anyway. Unbelievable.

I remember taking my stuff out of the dressing room and feeling so empty and so alone. My parents asked me, "Do you have another job lined up?" I was about to lose my apartment, I had no money, and I was jobless. I couldn't believe they would ask me that. I guess they didn't comprehend how low my self-esteem was at that moment. I felt like I was never going to work again. I felt like that was my first and last chance.

> **Gerry McIntyre.** *Once on This Island* (Armand) [O], *Joseph and the Amazing Technicolor® Dreamcoat* (Judah) [O], *Anything Goes* (Purser) [O], *Uptown...It's Hot!* (Little Richard) [O], *Chicago** (Billy Flynn), *Annie 2** (Punjab)

Onward and Upward?

A few years ago, I was playing the alternate to the lead in a brand new show called *Martin Guerre*. It was a new Cameron Mackintosh musical by the writers of *Les Misérables* and *Miss Saigon*. Everyone in New York auditioned for the show. It was the job to get. Before coming to Broadway in April, the show was scheduled for a pre-Broadway tour in Minnesota, Detroit, Washington, D.C., Seattle, and Los Angeles.

I was thrilled to be cast, and it turned out to be the artistic experience I had hoped for. We rehearsed for six weeks, and I became friendly with the creative team. For several months, we performed in front of thousands of people at the Guthrie Theater, the Kennedy Center, and the Ahmanson.

Like everyone else in the cast, I had planned my whole life around the show coming to New York. If there was ever a sure thing, this was it. The show would run for many years. My life was set.

Then it was gone. Just like that. With about two months left on the pre-Broadway tour, Cameron called the whole cast together at the Kennedy Center. He announced that the show was not coming to Broadway. Claude Michel-Schönberg's new show was not going to make it. It was simply inconceivable. Cameron told us that the tour would continue through its run in Los Angeles, and then it would all be over.

I will never forget the last few months of doing the show. The energy was different, and it showed. During the last performance, I looked around and thought, "What now? How can this be gone?" I felt like the loneliest girl in the world. The loneliness didn't go away for a while.

Over the next few months, I auditioned for all kinds of theater but I couldn't get cast in anything. I don't know if I was depressed, or angry, or if I had just lost something inside of me. The sense of inertia was eating away at me. I did some regional theater, got by, but realized my love of musical theater would have to change somehow. I ended up back in *Les Misérables* on Broadway, some eight years after I had done the show before. It was bittersweet.

There I was, on Broadway again, but it was entirely different. I wasn't the optimistic twenty-year-old who thought she was guaranteed to be the next big star on Broadway. Rather, I was thirty years old and understudying the same role I had understudied eight years earlier. I had starred in three other big shows and now I was back in the chorus.

In the show, I played a nun with Ana Maria Andricain, who had starred in several Broadway shows. We put on our habits every night, went on stage, put a cane on a chair, bowed to Jean Valjean, and walked off. No lines, just bowing. Then we had to quickly run off stage, rip off the habits, and put on our ball gowns. Eight years earlier, when I was playing Cosette, I was the one on center stage in the beautiful white wedding dress. Now I was in the back right corner, and I knew that I was lucky to be there. It was a humbling experience, and an eye-opening one.

After half a year in the show, I decided to leave and go back to school to pursue a master's degree in theater. On my last day, someone in the cast turned to me and said, "You are so lucky to be getting out." Hearing those words was hurtful because, eight years after my Broadway debut, I knew exactly what they meant.

> **Jodie Langel.** *Les Misérables* (Cosette/Eponine), *Martin Guerre** (Bertrande Alternate), *Cats** (Grizabella), *Joseph and the Amazing Technicolor® Dreamcoat** (Narrator)

This business is all about highs and lows. A year and a half ago, I was in *Martin Guerre*, the new Cameron Mackintosh musical. Many of the biggest people in New York were working on it. We thought we were going to be the toast of the town. We thought that we were going to run on Broadway forever, make an original cast recording, and be in the Tony Awards. We thought everything was going to be perfect. I thought, "That's it. I've arrived." Well, that didn't happen. We were dissed by the critics. We were abandoned. We never made it to New York.

A year later, I was doing a production of *Cinderella*. I was in the ensemble and I was understudying the role of the Prince. But in the show itself, I was a mouse who transformed into a horse.

One night, I was sitting on stage and feeling a little depressed. I thought, "Wow—a year ago, I was playing these amazing theaters with a new Cameron Mackintosh show. I was about to go to Broadway and my career was about to change forever. A year later, I am sitting here as a mouse, about to turn into a horse."

One memorable night, I was on stage and Eartha Kitt was singing. I ran offstage and ripped off my blue jumper and my blue turban, revealing a white unitard. The dresser stuck the tail into the back of my costume and put a little pony mane on my head. I ran back out onto the dark stage and grabbed the reigns with three other white unitard horses. We got into our places and froze in very unmasculine positions.

I was starting to feel a bit more depressed. We got to the part of the show where Cinderella was going to the ball and she wanted Eartha Kitt to go with her. Eartha Kitt, the fairy godmother, said that she couldn't go.

Cinderella said, "I'm not prepared for a night like this." It was a really beautiful moment in the show. Normally it would have been a beautiful moment for me too, but the way I was feeling that particular day, it wasn't.

Eartha Kitt looked at Cinderella with tears in her eyes, and said, "But everything in your life has brought you to this moment."

I slowly looked down at my white unitarded body, standing on stage left with three other unitarded bodies. I thought, "A year ago, I was on my way to Broadway in a new Cameron Mackintosh show, and now I'm a horse in a white unitard on stage left! All my life has brought me to this moment."

So, sometimes we are horses and sometimes we are princes. Once you are a prince, you'd better believe that a year later, you could be a horse.

Kip Driver. *Martin Guerre** (Swing), *Cats** (Munkustrap), *Les Misérables**

People often say to me, "Wow, congratulations! Things are going so great for your career!" I just finished starring in *Urinetown*. The show got a lot of acclaim. We won three Tony Awards, and I performed during the Tony Award ceremony. Everything was great. Then I got cast in the pre-Broadway tour of *Little Shop of Horrors*.

The thing that is so crazy about this business is that you get all these thoughts running through your head about your future. Everyone was telling me how wonderful my career was going, and I was bouncing from one Broadway show to the next. I started thinking that there will be more Tony Awards to attend. Maybe my next step is television, who knows. Your brain goes there.

I thought, "I'm doing *Little Shop of Horrors*. How can they screw that up?" Everyone was so excited. I had to wait eight months until I started rehearsals because I was cast so far in advance. There was a huge buildup.

When we opened in Florida, it was a huge disappointment. We knew the show was having problems. One Sunday night, the producer came in and said, "We are closing the show."

All those things that were in my head suddenly vanished. I realized, "Not only am I not going to be starring in a new show, but I'm not going to have a job." It's not like, "Oh, I didn't get a promotion." No. It's going from, "I'm going to make a lot of money in a Broadway show, be on *The Today Show*, and be in the Macy's Thanksgiving Day Parade," to, "How am I going to pay my mortgage?" It was night and day. To sit there and go to those extremes was horrifying. Everything on Broadway was already cast for the next season, and I could be out of a job for at least six to eight months. It was horrible.

Finally, we found out that the producers were going to retool the show. Then they started having auditions for our roles. We all started freaking out. I was sitting there in limbo for weeks, wondering if it was going to work out. I couldn't sleep. I tried to put it out of my mind and move on, but I couldn't. Part of me didn't want to go back and audition all over again, but I knew I had to come in with my tail between my legs.

It changed from everyone treating me like a star to suddenly no one caring. I got caught up in it. It fed my head for a while. It was a very humbling experience, and I realized that this business changes on a dime. What you think you have, and what you think you are, cannot be defined by what you are doing. There are countless numbers of people who starred on Broadway and are now working in banks.

Hunter Foster. *Little Shop of Horrors* (Seymour) [O], *Urinetown* (Bobby Strong) [O], *Footloose* (Bickle) [O], *King David* [O], *Grease!* (Roger) [O], *Les Misérables* (Marius u/s), *Martin Guerre** (Martin u/s), *Cats** (Rum Tum Tugger)

There is Only Square One

I had listened to the song "What I Did for Love" from *A Chorus Line* for twenty years, thinking it was just a pretty song. Now, when I hear it, after all my time in this industry, I often cry. The words are so unbelievably true. When she sings, "The gift was ours to borrow," she is right. We don't own it. We borrow this lifestyle. It is not secure enough for us to own. When she sings, "Kiss today goodbye," that is it. It's an amazing summation of this business. You can't hold on to anything. We always know that, and that's what terrifies us 98 percent of the time.

There are so many square ones—it is not like any other business. It is always square one. Maybe square one and a half, because you feel like you've got some credits. But it is never square two.

Marsh Hanson. *Les Misérables* (Marius), *Joseph and the Amazing Technicolor® Dreamcoat** (Brother)

Many people think that there is some sort of hierarchy in New York theater. You work Off-Broadway in the chorus, then you get a lead Off-Broadway, then you get a chorus job on Broadway, then a featured chorus job, then a Broadway lead, and then, finally, you become a star. Once you've done the lead, you are up for all the other lead roles in New York. Anytime they need someone like you, you are automatically considered.

Here is the reality. When I was playing a lead role in *Cats*, I couldn't even get an audition for the ensemble of *Jerome Robbins' Broadway*. I learned that you start over with each gig.

Michael Arnold. *42nd Street* (Andy Lee) [O], *The Who's Tommy* [O], *A Funny Thing Happened on the Way to the Forum* (Swing) [O], *Little Me* (Belle's Boy/ Newsboy) [O], *Cats* (Mr. Mistoffelees), *Cabaret, Chicago, Martin Guerre** (Benoit), *Busker Alley**, *Durante**

I came back to New York from the Broadway national tour of *Cats* expecting something. I deserved a job. I forgot that you start all over again. *Cats* is just four letters on your résumé. It's not like it's a free ticket to another job. I was working there for so long that I thought it was going to lead to something else. "He was in *Cats*, let's give him the benefit of the doubt." No. Not even for a moment.

Suddenly, I found myself at open calls with Victor Schlinkegart from Germany, who has never been to an audition in his life and is so very excited to be here in America. Some guy running the audition looks right at you and says, "Thank you very much for coming in today." You pack up your bag and go home. Victor gets to stay because he is two inches taller than you are. You are back to square one.

Davis Kirby. *The Boys from Syracuse* (Soldier) [O], *Thou Shalt Not* (Sugar Hips) [O], *Thoroughly Modern Millie, Cats** (Swing)

Being in the theater is powerless. I thought I would climb up a ladder, become more important, and have more money. I thought that after I had done a big Broadway lead, I would go on to bigger things. All my moves have been lateral. You never are really able to gain any ground in this business. Once it's over, you have to start over again. I've never felt like any show I've done has lead me to another.

Ray Walker. *Jesus Christ Superstar* (Annas) [O], *Grease!* (Doody), *Les Misérables* (Marius), *Whistle Down the Wind** (Preacher), *Music of the Night** (Principal Soloist), *Joseph and the Amazing Technicolor® Dreamcoat** (Joseph u/s), *Falsettos** (Whizzer)

As a Broadway performer, you are always living in fear of being out of work. Even the most wonderful stars—who have performed in the most successful shows—can't get a job now. In this business, you always have to prove yourself.

I was cast in a very special show, *Hairspray*. It's not going to happen again. If you are lucky, you get that one special show, and if you get two, well, then you are the luckiest person of all. It's not a life. It's the hardest living to make.

Marissa Jaret Winokur. *Hairspray* (Tracy Turnblad) [O][**T**], *Grease!* (Jan)

Remember Me?

I had an audition for the part of Lefou in *Beauty and the Beast*. I built a huge stunt suit with padding. I then made a fat suit around it so I looked a little portly.

During the audition, they didn't know I had a stunt suit on. I sang the song and did a dance. I did every pratfall and stunt you could imagine. The suit protected me, so I could do anything. I mean, I did things that no human should do, and I still didn't get the part.

Scott Wise. *Jerome Robbins' Broadway* [O][**T**], *Fosse* [O][**t**], *State Fair* (Pat Gilbert) [O][**t**], *Movin' Out* (Sergeant O'Leary) [O], *Goodbye Girl* (Billy) [O], *Damn Yankees* (Rocky) [O], *Carrie* (Scott) [O], *Guys and Dolls* (Guy) [O], *Song and Dance* (Man) [O], *A Chorus Line* (Mike), *Cats* (Plato/Macavity), *Victor Victoria* (Jazz Hot Ensemble)

One day, my agents left a message saying that the casting agency for *The Producers* wanted me to audition. I called them back and said, "So, they really want to see me for this?"

They said, "Yeah, there's a big open call and they might want you to move and stuff." A little alarm bell went off. I am not a dancer. That's not my forte. I'm an actor-singer. That's what I do. Nevertheless, I thought, "Well, I haven't auditioned for Vinnie Liff in a while. Let's go in. What the hell."

Susan Stroman was there with about fifty people for a movement call. I thought, "Oh, no!" Those are the most embarrassing times—doing a dance audition when you can't dance. I did it, and not very well, mind you.

Once we danced, Susan Stroman asked everybody, "What do you do? Do you have anything that's unique and special?"

When she asked me, I said, "Yes. I am an underarm mannerist."

Her eyes lit up.

I said, "Well, I'll demonstrate." I proceeded to do underarm farts.

About half of the room thought it was hilarious. The other half of the room was absolutely aghast, including Susan Stroman. Absolutely mortified!

I chuckled, put on my coat, and left.

Geoffrey Blaisdell. *Jekyll & Hyde* (Lord Glossop) [O], *Cyrano—The Musical* (Captain De Castel Jaloux) [O], *Amadeus* (Servant) [O], *Les Misérables** (Javert), *The Phantom of the Opera** (The Auctioneer)

Typecasting

In our business, we are constantly proving ourselves, over and over again. I was doing the show *All American* in the Winter Garden Theater. Irving Berlin had an office in the theater. He used to come down and watch the Wednesday matinees. He would watch me perform. I played this nymphomaniac who wore a see-through nightgown with big fat bunny slippers. I sang a song called "Nightlife." Mel Brooks wrote the show.

Weeks later, my agent called and said, "You will never believe this. I read the casting notices today, and they are casting a new Irving Berlin musical called *Mr. President*. They are looking for an Anita Gillette type to play the role of the President's daughter."

My agent called, and said, "I represent Anita Gillette."

"Fine," they said, "when can she come in and audition?"

Doesn't that say it all? I had to do two auditions for "my type."

Anita Gillette. *Chapter Two* (Jennie Malone) [O][t], *Guys and Dolls* (Sarah Brown) [O], *Kelly* (Angela Crane) [O], *Carnival!* (Gypsy) [O], *All American* (Susan) [O], *Mr. President* (Leslie Henderson) [O], *Jimmy* (Betty Compton) [O], *Don't Drink the Water* (Susan Hollander) [O], *Gypsy* (Thelma), *Brighton Beach Memoirs* (Blanche), *They're Playing Our Song* (Sonia Walsk), *Cabaret* (Sally)

So, I was out of work and feeling sorry for myself, not realizing that this was going to happen for the rest of my life every time I was out of a job. I was really anxious. I got a copy of *Back Stage* and starting looking for auditions to go to. I was looking and looking. Finally, I read, *"Wanted: A Donna McKechnie type."*

I ran to the audition. I went into the theater with great confidence. I thought, "Boy, are they going to be excited when they see me!" I walked into the room with all the other actresses. Their faces dropped. I knew what they were thinking. I felt a little cocky knowing that they were thinking, "What chance do I have now?" I tried to act as generous as possible.

I auditioned. I didn't get it. They wanted a Donna McKechnie *type*, not the real thing.

Donna McKechnie. *A Chorus Line* (Cassie) [O][**T**], *Company* (Kathy) [O], *State Fair* (Emily Arden) [O], *On the Town* (Ivy Smith) [O], *Promises, Promises* (Vivien Della Hoya) [O], *The Education of Hyman Kaplan* (Kathy McKenna) [O], *How to Succeed in Business Without Really Trying!* (Dancer) [O], *A Funny Thing Happened on the Way to the Forum** (Philia), *Call Me Madam** (The Princess), *Sweet Charity**, *Annie Get Your Gun**

Three months after I left the national tour of *Cats*, I auditioned for *The Lion King* on Broadway. I went to the first call, and got a call-back. I was really excited and felt good.

However, during the call-back, I was crammed into a tiny room, which was packed with tons and tons of girls. All of those stories I had heard about Broadway being a dog-eat-dog and sharp-elbow kind of world came painfully true. I experienced it. People gave me dirty looks and actually pushed me out of the way, just to get in the front. I was in a mass of girls who were all dying to get a job.

Then, they gave us all numbers. All of a sudden, I became a number again, and not a name. I was not even a face. Despite having been in *Cats*, both in Europe and America, I was just like all the other new girls. My experience didn't matter.

This business is so bad in that way. It is so superficial. It's all about your height, your "look," your ethnicity, and how much you weigh. It's all about the outside and not the inside. It is really sad. Most of the time, they are just looking for a type. That's the bottom line. They are just looking for someone who fits into that costume. You become a number and a body.

Christie McCall. *Cats** (Sillabub)

Broadway is becoming a modeling industry. In professional hockey, you need a certain amount of skill, experience, and fortitude. Size comes into play, but besides that, skill is important. Craft, technique, and skill don't matter on Broadway anymore. It's become a modeling industry. If they are looking for a type, they don't give a shit about real talent. They don't care if you are spontaneous, alive, and on top of the text and following your impulses. At an audition, I'll be followed by someone who is really beautiful, mediocre, and may or may not sing even half as well, and he will get the job.

Daniel C. Cooney. *Les Misérables* (Marius u/s), *The Civil War** (Swing), *Evita** (Che), *Fiddler on the Roof** (Perchik)

Wanted: Fresh Talent Only

When you are twenty-two, everyone tells you, "You are just so young. You need to go and get beaten up a little bit. Go have your heart broken a few times. You're just so young." I remember hearing that.

So you go out on the road for six years. You have your heart broken a few times. You get trampled on. You do stupid things. You drink too much. You get into compromising positions with all sorts of colorful people.

When you come back, now you are too confident. Now you are too old. It becomes difficult. Now, if they want a twenty-two year old, they will hire someone who's nineteen.

Christiane Noll. *Jekyll & Hyde* (Emma) [O], *It Ain't Nothin' but the Blues*, *Miss Saigon** (Ellen), *Grease!** (Sandy), *City of Angels** (Mallory), *Urinetown** (Hope Cladwell)

You are always proving yourself. One of the reasons that I was not brought in for *Martin Guerre* initially was that they wanted "fresh new talent." In a weird way, I felt like I was being penalized for having a résumé, for having a body of work to show for myself, for not being the cute twenty-three-year-old anymore.

When I first came on the scene in *Les Misérables* with Marius, I was fresh meat. And here we are, years later, and although I have played the Phantom, Raoul, Marius, Ravenal, and others, it's kind of like, "Oh, yeah, him. We know what he does."

So, once again, I have to prove that I am still good and that I can compete with the "fresh talent," that I haven't hit the bottom of the well quite yet. But that wears you out. And what's the reward? *Martin Guerre* closes out of town, with a lot of your heart and soul in it.

I would love to say that with all my experience, people just call me at home and ask me to star in their new show. But it doesn't work like that. I audition and have to keep proving myself and honing my craft. Hopefully, I stay on top of my game.

I have to take care of myself by going to the gym and loving myself psychologically. Otherwise, I would just throw my hands up and say, "I can't do this anymore." I've had to talk myself off of the ledge a lot of times. But, somewhere, I find it. I don't even know where that is. I just find it. I guess that is the love and the heart that I still remember from when I was thirteen and didn't know all of this.

Hugh Panaro. *Side Show* (Buddy Foster) [O], *The Red Shoes* (Julian Craster) [O], *The Phantom of the Opera* (Phantom/Raoul), *Les Misérables* (Marius), *Showboat* (Ravenal), *Martin Guerre** (Martin)

Don't I Get At Least Sixteen Bars?

During *The Mystery of Edwin Drood*, I kept hearing about certain auditions that I couldn't get seen for. I thought, "I am starring in a Broadway show. My name is on the marquee, and I can't get an audition?" I was shocked. I thought, "Do you think I am going to embarrass you? Do you think it's going to be that bad that you can't take five minutes to see me?" For whatever reason, I constantly had to challenge that. I finally came to embrace it, this crusade.

Donna Murphy. *Passion* (Fosca) [O][**T**], *The King and I* (Anna) [O][**T**], *Wonderful Town* (Ruth) [O], *The Mystery of Edwin Drood* [O], *The Human Comedy* (Bess Macauley u/s) [O], *Privates on Parade* [O], *They're Playing our Song* (Swing)

I played Cosette for over a year. After I got off the Broadway national tour of *Les Misérables*, I thought, "Things will be great now. I will get jobs easily. I now have job security."

I saw that there was an opening for Betty Schaeffer in *Sunset Boulevard*. I assumed the part was mine. I sort of mapped it out, my career, and what roles I was going to play. I was set to coast from one job to the next.

When I got back to New York, I could not even get an appointment for the *Sunset Boulevard* audition. I thought it was odd, because I had just come off this huge show, *Les Misérables*.

In order to be seen, I had to go to an open call. It was my first ever. I was so tenacious. I just thought, "It will be a great story when I get the show." I was still pretty sure that I would be cast. I set my alarm for 5:00 A.M., walked to the Equity building, stood on line, and got an appointment. Of course, I wore my *Les Misérables* show jacket.

I was the second person on line. As the line grew, I saw six other show jackets. I was shocked. This was an open call. I thought everyone except me would be a "nobody." I saw a girl in line who had starred in *Les Misérables* when I was in college. I was confused, but didn't think much of it at the time. I was still going to get the part. I got my appointment time, went home, and showered. I was so excited. I thought, "They are going to love me. I am perfect for this job!"

At the audition, I even knew a few of the people behind the table. I thought, "All I have to do is open my mouth."

After singing five bars of my song—and we are usually allowed at least sixteen—the guy behind the table stood up. Looking directly at me, he made a big axe through the air. "Jodie, thanks, that's all we need."

I just stood there. Nobody had ever stopped me from singing in such a dismissive way. And he didn't only stop me, but he axed me. I will never forget that image and the feeling I had walking out of that audition.

Jodie Langel. *Les Misérables* (Cosette/Eponine), *Martin Guerre** (Bertrande Alternate), *Cats** (Grizabella), *Joseph and the Amazing Technicolor® Dreamcoat** (Narrator)

My twin granddaughters were coming in for vacation. They already had their plane tickets purchased when my agent called. He had an audition for *Wiseguys*, the new show by Stephen Sondheim. Nathan Lane and Victor Garber were already involved in the project.

I told my granddaughters about the audition. They said, "We will stay in New York and won't go on vacation. We will come with you to the audition." I coached with Stephen Sondheim and Paul Gemignani. They wanted me to come in and sing for the director.

I went to the audition, and my grandkids sat outside. After singing, the director said, "Thank you very much." He completely dismissed me. As I walked out of the room, my two granddaughters looked at me with anticipation, and asked, "How did it go?"

I burst into tears and told them, "If you ever decide to go into this business, I will stop you immediately!" It was a very hard day.

Anita Gillette. *Chapter Two* (Jennie Malone) [O][t], *Guys and Dolls* (Sarah Brown) [O], *Kelly* (Angela Crane) [O], *Carnival!* (Gypsy) [O], *All American* (Susan) [O], *Mr. President* (Leslie Henderson) [O], *Jimmy* (Betty Compton) [O], *Don't Drink the Water* (Susan Hollander) [O], *Gypsy* (Thelma), *Brighton Beach Memoirs* (Blanche), *They're Playing Our Song* (Sonia Walsk), *Cabaret* (Sally)

Tenure Denied

Most of my friends from Broadway are my age or older. A lot of them are dancers. Now, they are in this horrible place of: (a) There are very few shows where they want mature dancers because most dancers tend to be young, (b) their bodies are breaking down, (c) they are getting paid less and less, and (d) the amount of time they have put in over the years doesn't matter. Nobody is saying, "Hey, he's been great in fourteen Broadway shows over twenty years, so let's give him more money!"

Instead, they say, "Let's give him scale, and if we can get less than scale, let's get that."

My friends don't feel like their careers have grown to a place where they are appreciated. Now they are being cast aside. They are all trying to make transitions, but to what? What do dancers and actors do when they are not invited to the ball? They can teach or choreograph, if they are lucky. Most actors my age have gotten to the point where that youthful "the next role is going to be the one" mentality is gone. They don't believe in it anymore. There's no next role that's going to be "the one." There's no new *Death of a Salesman* coming to Broadway, and if there is, Richard Dreyfuss will star in it. It won't be them. The fact that so few people in my industry know who Cherry Jones is is testament to how little you can dream about what being on Broadway can lead to.

My friends are caught in that. What other business is there where seniority doesn't have benefits? Box office appeal means a lot. Seniority means nothing. The glitter is gone.

Jason Alexander. *Jerome Robbins' Broadway* (Emcee) [O][**T**], *Merrily We Roll Along* (Joe) [O], *The Rink* (Lino/Lenny/Punk/Uncle Fausto) [O], *Broadway Bound* (Stanley) [O], *Accomplice* [O], *The Producers** (Max Bialystock)

I thought by the time I reached my age I would be a huge star. I thought I'd be a big recording artist. I thought I'd be doing concerts all across the world.

Well, I'm not.

It really pushes my buttons that I have done a certain body of work and I've paid my dues and people still don't respect me. Mostly casting people.

I have been in the business a long time. If I had been in any other business and had been there for thirty-three years, my knowledge, expertise, and professionalism would, 90 percent of the time, ensure that I had work. That's not the case in show business. I've been in the business since 1967. All my knowledge, my professionalism, and my honed talent is simply not a guarantee that I will have a job. That's the toughest thing about the business. The business has very much changed, and not for the better, I'm sad to say.

There are some casting directors who think actors will do anything. I'm not one of those actors. If I don't want to do it and if it's not interesting to me, I'd rather not be working.

Ultimately, I think you have to make the choice. Do you stay and pursue the dream? There are a lot of people who, after a while, can't.

Heather MacRae. *Falsettos* (Charlotte) [O], *Coastal Disturbances* (Faith Bigelow) [O], *Here's Where I Belong* (Abra) [O], *Hair* (Sheila)

Over the last eighteen months, I have had about a dozen auditions for production contracts. I haven't gotten one of them. I was so hard up that I auditioned to be a pit singer on the national tour of *Saturday Night Fever*. I didn't get it. Forget about pride—I've got to eat. I used to say I would never go on the road unless I was cast as a lead in a Broadway national tour. Suddenly, after nothing, nothing, nothing, you start to consider whatever you can get. I can't get arrested.

Alex Santoriello. *Les Misérables* (Montparnasse) [O], *3 Penny Opera* (Jimmy) [O], *Chess* [O], *Jesus Christ Superstar** (Pilate), *Cats** (Asparagus)

The national tour of *Sunset Boulevard* was amazing. It was a massive show and I had the male lead. When I got the role, I thought, "I'm set. This is going to run for four years. Andrew Lloyd Webber is producing it, and he has all the money in the world. I'm working with these great directors, Trevor Nunn and Peter Lawrence. What could go wrong?"

Suddenly, Andrew Lloyd Webber's empire started to fall apart. *Whistle Down the Wind* got terrible reviews. It closed. Then the Broadway company of *Sunset Boulevard* closed. Then my show closed. It didn't even last for a year. I thought, "Wow, this business is fragile."

I quickly went from thinking my road was paved with gold to realizing that I was back looking for a gig. I had no clue what I was going to do. The essence of the business is that every show closes. As great as the ride may be, you have to get back on the audition and unemployment lines. You never stop proving yourself.

I was starring in *The Scarlet Pimpernel* on Broadway. My picture was everywhere. It was one of the biggest roles in Broadway history. That doesn't necessarily weigh so much.

I went into an audition the other day with people who were fresh off the bus. I'm not treated any better. It's a business of the moment. That moment has passed and we are on to the next one.

Ron Bohmer. *Fiddler on the Roof* (Fyedka) [O], *The Scarlet Pimpernel* (Percy), *Les Misérables* (Enjolras), *Aspects of Love** (Alex), *Sunset Boulevard** (Joe Gillis), *The Phantom of the Opera** (Phantom)

After fifteen years in the business, I am going back to working a day job. It is the first time I have needed to do this in a long time. I have to make my own opportunities. My next-door neighbor is an investment partner with a man who is a day trader. Initially, I began working for him just to have some extra money. Soon, it became living money. The phone isn't ringing and no money is coming in, so I have no choice.

Nowadays, they say if you are twelve and you can talk, you can have a career on Broadway. If you are a celebrity, then you can go to Broadway. However, there's a big gap between a twelve-year-old and a celebrity. I fall somewhere in between.

I feel stupid for letting it get to this point. Until recently, I didn't realize that Broadway is a fantasy. The phone is not going to ring out of the blue with job offers, no matter what I've done.

Rather, they're going to call and say I have an audition, and if I'm lucky, I will bypass a few callbacks. They will bring me in, however, just to put some pressure on a celebrity with whom they are negotiating a contract. In the end, the celebrity will get the part, and they will say, "Thanks for coming." It's just the way it is.

Robert Torti. *Starlight Express* (Greaseball) [O][t], *Joseph and the Amazing Technicolor® Dreamcoat* (Pharaoh) [O]

A Time for Retribution

When I auditioned for *Big River*, as I was singing my song, the man who was running the audition picked up a newspaper and started reading. It was the rudest thing. I looked over at the piano player and he just shrugged. I kept on singing, but I started shooting him the bird every now and then. It was one of those rare moments when there was some kind of retribution—some kind of payback. I was singing the country song "Steal with Style" from *The Robber Bridegroom*, and just giving him the bird.

> **Bryan Batt.** *Seussical* (The Cat in the Hat s/b) [O], *Saturday Night Fever* (Monty) [O], *Sunset Boulevard* (Joe Gillis u/s) [O], *Cats* (Munkustrap), *Beauty and the Beast* (Lumiere), *Starlight Express* (Rocky One), *The Scarlet Pimpernel* (Percy s/b), *Joseph and the Amazing Technicolor® Dreamcoat* (Reuben)

CHAPTER 20

The Time in Between

The reality of a life on Broadway in this new era can be difficult to digest. One moment, you could be starring in a new Broadway show. The next, you could be dressing up as a Best Buy price tag, handing out subway passes in Central Park. You might find yourself wandering through a New Jersey strip mall disguised as Raggedy Anne or Andy, passing out balloons. There are no guarantees. Regardless of your success, money will likely be tight and your apartment cramped. You will be forced to wonder whether all of the sacrifices have been worth it.

For many, once dreams of "making it" come true, this is the harsh reality of a career on Broadway, where everything comes full circle.

Time for Therapy

The theater business is devastating. It is like one of those old beautiful porcelain vases. If you look closely, they are just filled with tiny little cracks. Tiny cracks that you know have happened over a long period of time. They never happen all at once. If all those cracks happened at once, the vase would be destroyed. But the fact that it is filled with so many tiny cracks almost makes it more beautiful. That's what this business feels like. If all the disappointments had hit me at the same time, I wouldn't have been able to take it.

Davis Kirby. *The Boys from Syracuse* (Soldier) [O], *Thou Shalt Not* (Sugar Hips) [O], *Thoroughly Modern Millie*, *Cats** (Swing)

This business is rotten. It's second only to prostitution and boxing. It's just coldhearted. There is no security. You are asking for rejection every day of your life and you are in a business that is

Rent. Photo credit: Joan Marcus/Photofest

going to give it to you. You have to be so firm in your convictions and your feelings of what you really want. Your relationship with yourself has to be so intimate. It's between you and you.

Donna McKechnie. *A Chorus Line* (Cassie) [O][**T**], *Company* (Kathy) [O], *State Fair* (Emily Arden) [O], *On the Town* (Ivy Smith) [O], *Promises, Promises* (Vivien Della Hoya) [O], *The Education of Hyman Kaplan* (Kathy McKenna) [O], *How to Succeed in Business Without Really Trying!* (Dancer) [O], *A Funny Thing Happened on the Way to the Forum** (Philia), *Call Me Madam** (The Princess), *Sweet Charity**, *Annie Get Your Gun**

This business is like a romantic relationship. A relationship starts with passion and a swirling love. You are blind to its faults. You also become blind to the unfairness and the iniquities in the relationship. When the love matures, what you are left with is reality. Then you must decide what you want to do. Some of the most amazing romantic relationships in your life have to end. That's how it has to be with musical theater.

Frank Baiocchi. *Miss Saigon* (Chris u/s), *South Pacific** (Cable u/s)

I spent a lot of the year 2000 in therapy. I had to. I was killing myself. Mentally, I was just destroying myself. I was going into this deep, dark place. My evenings would consist of drinking far too much wine, hoping that I could fall asleep, and hoping to shut off my mind. I would drink in abundance. I mean in abundance—from 10:00 P.M. until 5:00 A.M.

And I'd pass out. That's what I wanted to do. I just didn't want to deal with myself. I didn't want to deal with the outside world. I didn't even want to deal with the day.

My feeling back then was, "What's there to get up for?" There's nothing to do. No one is calling me. Yeah, I have my wife. Yeah, yeah. Actually, she is the one solace in my life who has kept me stable during the times of not working.

She's the one who kicked my ass and said, "Go into therapy. You need to fix this shit. This is not you. This is not the person I met. You are far too down on yourself right now. Far too depressed." And I got out of it.

I had to remember, "Wow. I chose this life. I chose this, and this is what comes with it."

The silence that sets in is scary. When the phone doesn't ring anymore, all you are left with is you and those little demons that hang over your shoulder, saying, "You suck."

"You were just in the right place at the right time."

"You're not that talented."

"You can't do this."

You start to read into things a lot more than you should. You forget the way the industry works. Ninety percent of the time you don't get hired, period.

Wilson Heredia. *Rent* (Angel) [O][**T**]

It's terrible that our identity has to go hand in hand with what we are doing.

People never ask actors, "How are you doing?"

Rather, they ask, "*What* are you doing?"

Even our friends do this. Those are always the first words out of their mouths. We are led to believe that if we are not working, then we are not good people and should not have self-esteem. We've lost it.

Kip Driver. *Martin Guerre* * (Swing), *Cats* * (Munkustrap), *Les Misérables* *

When I got back from being on the road with *Les Misérables*, I had a hard time. I was going out on auditions eight times a week, week upon week. I wasn't getting anything. It's easier to go out on one audition a week and not get it, than to go out twice a day for four days a week and not get anything. It was really hard. I remember locking myself in the bathroom. I have this image of me with my back to the door in the bathroom, sobbing, "What's wrong with me? Why doesn't anybody want me?"

Alice Ripley. *Side Show* (Violet Hilton) [O][t], *The Rocky Horror Show* (Janet Weiss) [O], *Sunset Boulevard* (Betty Schaefer) [O], *King David* (Bathsheba) [O], *James Joyce's The Dead* (Mrs. Molly Ivors) [O], *The Who's Tommy* [O], *Les Misérables* (Fantine), *Little Shop of Horrors* * (Audrey)

I went into an audition, and they told me that if I lost twenty pounds in a month, I had the job. That night, I sat there and thought, "Can I lose twenty pounds? Maybe, if I eat a handful of Cheerios a day."

I've had many experiences like that. That's sort of been the cross that I've dealt with since coming into the business. I will never be thin enough for most people. I will never be their ideal, or their classic vision. For years, I would starve myself and go to the gym every single day.

Three years ago, I got to the point where I said, "I can't do this anymore. I will leave the business. This is not working for me and it's just damaging." Each day, the majority of my thoughts focused on what I could and could not eat. I want my brain to be filled up with other things than that. I want my life to be about more than that.

Emily Skinner. *Side Show* (Daisy Hilton) [O][t], *The Full Monty* (Vicki Nichols) [O], *James Joyce's The Dead* (Mary Jane Morkan) [O], *Jekyll & Hyde* (Emma u/s) [O], *Dinner at Eight* (Kitty Packard) [O]

Actors Anonymous

I just came from doing a role where people were cheering. Standing ovations every night, eight times a week. It was overwhelming. It was like a great drug. But the show closed, as they always do. So obviously, there was withdrawal.

Living a life on Broadway can screw with people's heads. I've seen people deal with it through alcohol, drug addiction, and sex addiction. People look for something else to fill the void. Performing is the kind of high that you can't get from any other substance. You are lost looking for it.

Ron Bohmer. *Fiddler on the Roof* (Fyedka) [O], *The Scarlet Pimpernel* (Percy), *Les Misérables* (Enjolras), *Aspects of Love** (Alex), *Sunset Boulevard** (Joe Gillis), *The Phantom of the Opera** (Phantom)

Performing is addictive. It is like heroin or something. You can get so attached to being seen, being exalted, and being under the spotlight. It becomes your identity. It becomes about getting the next fix. It is really unhealthy.

It has taken seven years of yoga for me to understand that performing is not where happiness lies. Yes, it is wonderful to be in a Broadway show. The power of music, theater, and art all coming together is a miracle. But it is not where true happiness lies. It is always going to end, and then you go on.

Pamela Winslow. *Into the Woods* (Rapunzel) [O], *Beauty and the Beast* (Babette)

This business comes with "golden handcuffs," in the sense that we make good money when we work, so the success can lock you in.

It's the same theory as why kids on the street get into dealing drugs. They think, "Are we going to go work at the McDonald's and make minimum wage when we can sell drugs and make over a thousand bucks a week?" It's horrible, and you can't get out of it.

The same is true of this business. If you have nothing else to fall back on, and you are lucky enough to get a taste, which is really shaking hands with the devil, you are locked in.

You think, "I can do it again. I can throw the dice again. It's gonna come up seven." But a lot of times it doesn't. A lot of times, people go years without work and they go bankrupt. Their lives fall apart.

Patrick Cassidy. *Leader of the Pack* (Jeff Barry) [O], *The Pirates of Penzance* (Frederic), *Annie Get Your Gun* (Frank Butler), *Aida* (Radames), *Joseph and the Amazing Technicolor® Dreamcoat** (Joseph)

I began my career working on the West End in London, and then I played the lead on the national tour of *Carousel*. I was making a lot of money. I didn't realize that it could end. I had a car and a beautiful apartment on the Upper West Side. I had tons of credit cards with $5,000 limits. I was happy. When I left *Carousel*, I just waited for the next job. Surely it would come.

I lived off my unemployment, and then I lived off my savings. With my free time, I enrolled in French class, went to the theater, and ate at nice restaurants. I was still waiting for the job.

Eventually, my unemployment ran out and my credit cards were maxed. I started freaking out. I realized that to maintain my lifestyle, I had to make some serious cash. I believed that the only way I could make that kind of money was on a production contract. I went through a process of falling down, which included a stint of drug addiction. It was a very dark period of my life.

I remember when I auditioned for *The Lion King* and they told me, "You aren't sexy enough." It made me think, "Okay, I'm not sexy. I can't act. I can't sing." I began a relationship with someone who would treat me poorly. I felt that was what I deserved. I was on a downward spiral.

Sean Jeremy Palmer. *Carousel** (Mr. Snow), *Martin Guerre** (Guillaume u/s)

Paying the Rent

With every form I fill out, they ask, "What's your income? What's your monthly income? What's your annual income?" That's tough, because I don't know. As a professional actor, you are always committing yourself in a void. You are living from job to job, stitching a life together. It is wearing to never know your earning capacity. It just makes you weary.

This is my thirty-seventh year of working professionally. I am terribly lucky and grateful to be able to say that. But I wish it wasn't still like it was when I was starting out—hoping for that next audition, hoping to get the part, beat out the competition, be offered enough money so I can pay the mortgage. It is just like it was when I was eighteen. It gets tiring, but not tiresome. I find myself panting sometimes.

John Rubinstein. *Children of a Lesser God* (James Leeds) [O][**T**], *Pippin* (Pippin) [O], *Fools* (Leon) [O], *Getting Away with Murder* (Martin Chisholm) [O], *The Caine Mutiny Court-Martial* (Lt. Barney Greenwald) [O], *Ragtime* (Tateh), *Hurlyburly* (Eddie), *Love Letters* (Andrew), *M. Butterfly* (Rene)

Once, I was out of a job and I was really scared because I couldn't pay the rent. I didn't know what to do. I was cleaning the apartment, crying, and feeling sorry for myself, and then I turned on the television. The game show *Jeopardy* was on. Then, as I was polishing the table, I heard my name. I looked up, and I was the answer to a question. It was so ironic. I stopped crying in order to listen to what the question was. It just made me laugh. I thought, "Here I am, giving myself such a hard time." It was like a joke. I thought, "This is what your life will be, as long as you are in the business." That's what it is.

Donna McKechnie. *A Chorus Line* (Cassie) [O][**T**], *Company* (Kathy) [O], *State Fair* (Emily Arden) [O], *On the Town* (Ivy Smith) [O], *Promises, Promises* (Vivien Della Hoya) [O], *The Education of Hyman Kaplan* (Kathy McKenna) [O], *How to Succeed in Business Without Really Trying!* (Dancer) [O], *A Funny Thing Happened on the Way to the Forum** (Philia), *Call Me Madam** (The Princess), *Sweet Charity**, *Annie Get Your Gun**

My first apartment was in the basement of a brownstone in Queens. Prior to Broadway, I would take any job I could get my hands on. Money was very hard to come by. Every penny was accounted for.

Once I got to Broadway, I decided I didn't want to live in Queens anymore. I didn't want to deal with the mice and that kind of environment.

I moved to Central Park West. It was a great location, but it was smaller than my apartment in Queens and three times the price.

I thought, "It's okay, I'm making great money now!" The dollar sign takes over inside your head, but the reality doesn't kick in until it's too late.

I was in *Smokey Joe's Cafe* at the time. I was so naïve. I never picked up a *Variety* magazine and looked at how poor the numbers were for the show. Then the producers came in and told us we were going to have cutbacks. I thought, "How can a Broadway show have cutbacks?"

Small things started coming out of the budget. I started to panic. I was paying for an apartment that was three times the cost of my old apartment. I never thought that the show could close. If the show closed, I wouldn't be able to afford my apartment. I would get evicted. I knew I couldn't go back to being a karaoke host. I couldn't make enough money. I panicked.

I called my agents and told them, "Get me auditions!" Soon, I realized I was alone and I had to find a job. I had to go out and do cabaret shows, mingle with people—anything I could do in the hope that my friends could connect me to someone who might give me a job. There I was, starring on Broadway, and my agents couldn't do a thing.

When I was hired for *Saturday Night Fever*, I took a huge pay cut. I was a lead in *Smokey Joe's Cafe,* and in *Saturday Night Fever* I was a secondary character. I started to change my lifestyle. It was almost as if I went backwards in time to where I was living in the three-hundred-dollar-a-month apartment with my friend. I thought, "If I had stayed in that dumpy apartment and not moved to the city where I thought I should be, and saved, I might have done something for myself." I was spending just as much money as I was making, because I had gotten myself in a hole and had to dig myself out.

Jerry Tellier. *Saturday Night Fever* (Frank Junior) [O], *42nd Street* [O], *Smokey Joe's Cafe*

It has been six years since the last time I was on Broadway. It's been six years of a lot of hard work and a lot of being out of town, which didn't make me happy. When I took a job out of town doing *The Wizard of Oz*, I even ended up coming home with less money than I started out with. I couldn't sublet my apartment, and the money I was making in Philadelphia was not enough to support me and my empty apartment.

When I did *Joseph and the Amazing Technicolor® Dreamcoat*, I signed a lease for a $1600-a-month apartment. I thought, "I am on Broadway. I am making a lot of money." I could justifiably afford such a place at the time. What I didn't know was that the next Broadway show wasn't waiting around the corner. Not only was it not "right there," but I didn't work for six months after *Joseph*. Since then, with the exception of four months of *Les Misérables*, I have yet to be back on Broadway.

After *Joseph*, I didn't want to move out of my apartment, but I was faced with no option. So I moved into an apartment on East 70th Street. I didn't even unpack my stuff. I lived with boxes all around me. That was my way of saying, "I'm not really staying." It was hard to have a roommate again and, literally, to be counting pennies. I joined a gym and got in the best shape of my life, partly because I couldn't afford to do anything else. I was really careful about what I was buying and what I was doing.

Kelli Rabke. *Joseph and the Amazing Technicolor® Dreamcoat* (Narrator) [O], *Les Misérables* (Eponine)

This fall, my unemployment ran out and I was faced with, "Oh, gee, what should I do?" Someone offered me a job in a sales position in a rather large financial trading corporation. It was hellish. After three months, I went to my boss and said, "This is not going to work out." He begged me to stay.

I'm in the process of selling my house right now. I live in New Jersey, and I can't afford it anymore. My daughter and I are packing up and moving back to apartment life.

Nancy Opel. *Urinetown* (Penelope Pennywise) [O][t], *Evita* (Eva u/s) [O], *Triumph of Love* (Corine) [O], *Sunday in the Park with George* (Frieda) [O], *Teddy & Alice* (Eleanor Roosevelt) [O], *Ring Round the Moon* (Capulat u/s) [O], *Getting Away with Murder* (Dossie Lustig u/s) [O], *Anything Goes* (Hope Harcourt)

Back to the Day Job

I have two younger sisters who are gifted singers. My being a professional ruined it for them. They witnessed the business through what happened to me. They learned that this business is not a linear progression. Originally they thought, "I have a sister on Broadway. Life is going to be easy for her." Then they saw I had chunks of time when I wasn't working. I was borrowing money from my folks. I was working as a waitress.

Donna Murphy. *Passion* (Fosca) [O][T], *The King and I* (Anna) [O][T], *Wonderful Town* (Ruth) [O], *The Mystery of Edwin Drood* [O], *The Human Comedy* (Bess Macauley u/s) [O], *Privates on Parade* [O], *They're Playing our Song* (Swing)

My friend Maureen McNamara was the star of the Broadway show *Ain't Broadway Grand*. The show closed on a Sunday, and on Monday she was working in a restaurant again. Within twenty-four hours of the show closing, she was waiting tables.

Allen Fitzpatrick. *Sweet Smell of Success* (Senator) [O], *42nd Street* (Mac) [O], *The Scarlet Pimpernel* (Farleigh) [O], *Gentlemen Prefer Blondes* (Gus Esmond) [O], *Les Misérables* (Thénardier), *Sunset Boulevard** (Max)

After *Merrily We Roll Along* closed, I went back to being a singing waitress. That was depressing. That was hard. I waited tables on and off for three years. It was depressing—not because it was embarrassing to wait tables again, but because I had the feeling that I might never work on Broadway again.

Liz Callaway. *Baby* (Lizzie) [O][t], *Miss Saigon* (Ellen) [O], *Merrily We Roll Along* (Nightclub Waitress) [O], *The Three Musketeers* (Lady Constance Bonacieux) [O], *The Look of Love* [O], *Cats* (Grizabella)

At Least I'm Not Waiting Tables

I have struggled between shows, but I wouldn't take a job waiting tables, even if I could make $1,000 a week. I couldn't take the humiliation of being seen in that situation. So, I would pick up little odd jobs where I was out of the view of my peers. I wanted to stay out of the view of the people who might hire me—unless they were going to hire me as a fucking handyman. That is struggling. I've learned to live without material goods. It sucks. I just pay my rent and have enough to eat. That's it.

After *Chess* closed, I went to work for UPS in Newark Airport, doing weight and balance on their 727s, their DC-8s, and their 747s. That's what I did. Other people would load the big crates that go on the planes and weigh them. Then they would bring me all the weights. I would decide what containers went on which planes and where to put them so that the plane wouldn't tip out on its tail. You load it from the front and you slide it to the back.

Alex Santoriello. *Les Misérables* (Montparnasse) [O], *3 Penny Opera* (Jimmy) [O], *Chess* [O], *Jesus Christ Superstar** (Pilate), *Cats** (Asparagus)

I was in *Les Misérables* for two and a half years, and then I was cast in *The Rhythm Club*. I left *Les Misérables* to do the pre-Broadway tour. *The Rhythm Club* didn't come into New York. They also cancelled the pre-Broadway run in Chicago. Suddenly, my wife and I had no place to live. We had rented out our place for the three months that we were supposed to be in Chicago before coming to Broadway. We had to stay at a friend's house. The cats had to stay at another house because the guy we were temporarily staying with was allergic.

We had no money, so I started working as a caterer's assistant. I had to get up at five in the morning and I had to rent a truck on my own credit card. I worked the craziest hours. It was just horrible work. And then I was a bellboy at the Hudson Hotel. We would get in these ruts where we almost couldn't make the rent.

Kevin Kern. *Les Misérables* (Marius)

When *Ragtime* closed, I was out of a job. I had just bought a house in New Jersey. The next year hit and there was nothing. I couldn't get arrested, and my unemployment ran out.

Through a friend I had made in *Miss Saigon*, I got a job on the "night gang" at the Metropolitan Opera. I would show up at the Metropolitan Opera at about 11 P.M. and change the sets for the next day. I would tear down the set of the opera that had just finished and load it on a series of elevators. Then I would bring the next set up into the waiting position.

I worked all night until eight in the morning. It was the hardest, most back-breaking work that I've done in the last twenty-five years. It was unbelievable. I didn't even wear a watch because I didn't want to know how long I'd been there.

I couldn't audition because I was so exhausted. I would go home, go to sleep, wake up, grab something to eat, feel like crap, and go to the opera. I was the only actor in the group, and I didn't tell anyone.

    Craig Bennet. *Miss Saigon* (Marine/Reeves), *Les Misérables** (Thénardier u/s), *Mamma Mia!** (Bill), *Ragtime** (Willie Conklin)

Even after having done some major shows, there have been years when I had to wash dishes in order to make money. There was a small hotel on the East Side that turned into a singing cabaret at night. They needed someone to wash dishes. I said, "I'll do it."

I would go and wash dishes, run out to the cabaret, sing a song, come back and wash dishes. The only problem was that I was living way uptown. It was wintertime. There were nights when I would have to walk across Central Park in the dead of night, with snow up to my knees, just to get home.

    Sal Mistretta. *Sunset Boulevard* (Sheldrake) [O], *Welcome to the Club* (Bruce Aiken u/s) [O], *On the Twentieth Century* (Otto Von Bismark) [O], *Evita* (Magaldi u/s) [O], *Something's Afoot* (Geoffrey s/b) [O], *Cabaret* (Herr Schultz s/b), *Cats** (Asparagus), *Sweeney Todd** (Pirelli), *Wonderful Town** (Speedy Valenti)

Last year, I did *The Scarlet Pimpernel* on Broadway. It was my first Broadway show. It took me five years to get. I thought it would take a few months. I made nice money while I was in the show. It was really comfortable. It was a really nice time in my life. My family would come in every other month to see the show. I loved going to work. It lasted for eight months.

Aside from that, I've never had a big show where I've made a lot of money. I've always sort of had an extra job, either helping a friend at the office or catering on weekends.

It's still difficult. Sometimes I feel like I haven't accomplished anything because I don't have much to show for myself financially. At this point in my life, I still live month-to-month. I manage to pay my bills, but it's never easy. I never have money to spare. I've always had to work very hard. Every day, I ask myself, "Are you happy doing this? Because this might be how it's going to be for a while. Is that okay with you?"

Sometimes I feel like I'm a failure when I have to work answering phones and doing data entry. It's really difficult.

    Danny Gurwin. *The Scarlet Pimpernel* (Hal), *The Full Monty* (Malcolm MacGregor), *Urinetown* (Mr. McQueen)

Before getting cast in my first Broadway show, to fill the gaps, I would work at a temp agency. I got a temp job consulting with the New York Public Library. I was the personal assistant to one of the fundraisers. It was a nine in the morning until nine in the evening job. I did it for a few months—then I got cast in the Broadway company of *Riverdance*.

On the day I was cast, I made a deal with myself that I would never put on a tie again. I stuck with *Riverdance* for a year and did some other great shows after that. Things were really heating up for me, and I thought I would soon get my big break. All of a sudden, auditions evaporated. One moment, I was doing so well with my career. Then I turned around, and there was nothing.

I went on unemployment for a while. After two months, I was just about ready to break that promise I had made to myself and put that tie back on again. Lo and behold, I got an offer to do a tour.

Then, I was faced with a serious problem. If I went on tour, I would have to leave my wife. I had been working steadily in New York for two years. So, should I take the tie job and make considerably more money than the tour job, or do I go on the road and put a strain on my marriage?

Needless to say, I went on the road for four months.

When I came back, I had to get a bartending job to pay the rent. I couldn't get any night shifts, so I had to work the lunch shift. I showed up at ten in the morning and hauled ice from the basement into the bar all morning. It was such a surreal moment. This is the life that I chose, and sometimes it's hard to swallow.

James Sassar. *Riverdance* [O]

Has It All Come Down to This?

A couple of years ago, I was starring in the national tour of *Cats* as Rum Tum Tugger. Nevertheless, a couple of months ago, I had to get a job at a New Jersey strip mall to pay the rent. I had to dress up as Raggedy Andy and go store-to-store and hand out balloons. The only consolation was that I had Raggedy Anne with me.

When I got offered the job, they didn't tell me that I needed to bring my own white knee-high socks for the costume. Once I arrived at the strip mall, I had to rush to Express, a clothing store, and buy socks—but they didn't have the right kind. They only had the socks that came up to my ankles.

So there I was, wearing a red yarn wig, with my bare, pasty white skin showing between my ankles and my knees, walking around a mall in New Jersey and passing out balloons in Williams-Sonoma. I used to be a star of a Broadway national tour, singing to thousands, and there I was in a New Jersey mall with my pasty white legs and a red yarn wig.

Kevin Loreque. *Cats** (Rum Tum Tugger), *Hot Shoe Shuffle**

I had just returned to New York after starring in the Broadway national tour of *Cabaret*. I was once again looking for work.

A friend of mine said, "I manage a group that performs at private parties. Could I get you to do one? We are planning to do a Harry Potter party. I'd like you to play Snape." Of course, that is the evil character.

Some lady had bought a movie theater out for her son's birthday. They gave me a Bea Arthur wig, which was a horror, and a costume. I mixed potions for two hours and bantered with the kids.

It was funny. I had done children's theater before I got to Broadway, and there I was, doing it again.

Sal Mistretta. *Sunset Boulevard* (Sheldrake) [O], *Welcome to the Club* (Bruce Aiken u/s) [O], *On the Twentieth Century* (Otto Von Bismark) [O], *Evita* (Magaldi u/s) [O], *Something's Afoot* (Geoffrey s/b) [O], *Cabaret* (Herr Schultz s/b), *Cats** (Asparagus), *Sweeney Todd** (Pirelli), *Wonderful Town** (Speedy Valenti)

After the pre-Broadway tour of *Martin Guerre* closed in Los Angeles, I came back to New York and couldn't even get an audition. There was nothing. One day, I received a phone call from a friend who asked if I wanted to sing at a kid's birthday party in New Jersey. They wanted me to sing the song "Memory" from *Cats*. They were going to pay me five hundred bucks for the night. I hadn't worked in months and I needed the money. I figured, "How bad can it be?"

I was picked up in a van in the theater district, just blocks away from where my Broadway career first began with *Les Misérables*. When I got in the van, there were several other actors with whom I had worked on Broadway who were also performing in the show.

As we approached the venue, the woman who organized the event handed me a "cat outfit" which I had to wear during my performance. It looked like something you would buy in a ninety-nine cent store. She painted whiskers on my face with what looked like a children's paint set, and handed me a set of cat ears attached to a plastic headband. I looked like I was four years old and getting ready to go trick-or-treating. All I needed was a plastic pumpkin bucket.

The other cast members, all of whom had also starred in Broadway shows, looked equally ridiculous. The guy who was asked to sing a song from *Beauty and the Beast* had to wear a cheap, oversized, furry Beast head that looked like a piñata.

Just as I started walking out to sing "Memory," the woman ran up to me and said, "Where's your tail? You have to have a tail. All cats have tails." She found a safety pin and attached a long, raggedy, orange stuffed tail to my behind.

When I started to sing "Memory," all I could think about was when I was on stage with the Broadway national tour singing the song for the very first time. It was so magical. Now, a few years later, my career had taken me to a birthday party in New Jersey, and I was wearing a kiddy

Halloween costume with a bright orange tail which extended halfway across the stage. Luckily, I chose to laugh about it.

Jodie Langel. *Les Misérables* (Cosette/Eponine), *Martin Guerre** (Bertrande Alternate), *Cats** (Grizabella), *Joseph and the Amazing Technicolor® Dreamcoat** (Narrator)

In between show business gigs, I had a job where I gave out free samples of cigarettes to people on street corners. I would get up very early in the morning and meet the other sellers somewhere down in the garment district. We were all unemployed actors. They gave me a straw hat and some Salem Lights. Because we gave out the cigarettes for free, it created a stampede. In an act of self-defense, I would throw them at people, just to get away.

Randy Graff. *City of Angels* (Oolie) [O][**T**], *A Class Act* (Sophie) [O][**t**], *Les Misérables* (Fantine) [O], *Moon over Buffalo* (Rosalind) [O], *High Society* (Liz Imbrie) [O], *Laughter on the 23rd Floor* (Carol) [O], *Saravà* (Rosalia) [O], *Fiddler on the Roof* (Golde) [O], *Grease!* (Rizzo u/s), *Falsettos* (Trina)

One of my jobs was to dress up as a Best Buy price tag for the Sting concert in Central Park. Best Buy was sponsoring the event. Mind you, we had to audition for this. We had to basically play theater games with all the other price tags. While it was ninety-five degrees outside, we had to stand in Central Park, dot the walkway, and pass out gift certificates and subway tokens.

I was all dressed up and waving, and yet everyone was being a dick to me.

"How much do they pay you to wear that suit, buddy?"

Some people would even attack me once they realized I was passing out free things. I finally had to throw all the tokens in the street and hide behind a tree.

It was two weeks before I started rehearsals for my Broadway show, so I thought, "This is a joke. I am going to be in a Broadway show." The funny thing was, one of the other price tags had been in *Cats*. There she was, at the height of her career, on Broadway. And then, a week later, she was dressed up in a Best Buy box handing out gifts.

Lee Zarrett. *Jane Eyre* (Young John Reed) [O]

Didn't I Do a Show with You on Broadway?

My wife was doing the road show of *Chicago* with Charlotte d'Amboise. I was out of work, so I grabbed a flight, saw the show, and partied with the cast. The next day, I had to fly back to New York to do a catering job and audition for the upcoming Broadway show *The Civil War*.

When I arrived at the catering job, I discovered it was a party for the staged reading of a new musical by Terrence Mann. Charlotte d'Amboise, Terrence's wife, was in attendance. I had just partied with her the night before.

As I walked around the room with my tray, passing out vegetable dumplings, I noticed other actors with whom I had performed on Broadway.

The "Who's Who" of musical theater was at this party. I thought, "Holy shit, I must know about fifty people at this thing." Even the casting director of *The Civil War* was there. The next day I had to audition for him. I was so humiliated.

"Would you like ice in your soda?"

"Would you like an hors d'oeuvre?" It was horrible. I never catered again.

John Antony. *Passion* (Augenti/Count Ludovic), *Titanic** (John Jacob Astor), *Sunset Boulevard** (Joe Gillis u/s), *Annie Get Your Gun** (Frank Butler)

I worked at Candleshtick, a candle shop on the Upper West Side. Just about everyone who worked there was an actor. I worked there for a long time.

My day consisted of dealing with crazy people. I had to deal with a lot of drunken people from New Jersey who wanted to buy candles. People would come in, smell the candles for forty-five minutes, and scream: "Hey, Joey! The cucumber candle. It smells just like cucumber!"

It was a very weird thing to turn around after starring in Broadway shows and have to deal with the public in that capacity. It was not fun.

I saw people in the business all the time pass by the store. I would disappear when I would see them. I would run into the basement or run out the door. Sometimes, I would hide behind the counter.

Robert DuSold. *Les Misérables* (Javert), *Jekyll & Hyde* (Archbishop of Basingstoke), *Kiss of the Spider Woman* (Marcos), *Cats** (Deuteronomy), *The Phantom of the Opera** (André), *Chicago** (Little Mary Sunshine s/b), *Showboat** (Pete)

At the End of the Day

Today, I choreograph in the drama program at Hamilton High School in California. Some of my students are really talented. One of my students, Megan Campbell, was cast as the understudy to the lead in Broadway's *Thoroughly Modern Millie*.

Recently, I was in New York to see a show at the Public Theater. I got a phone call at 6:55 P.M. The actress who played Millie in *Thoroughly Modern Millie* was out for the night, and Megan was going to star as Millie for the first time. She was nineteen years old. I had to see her perform. I hopped in a cab and made my way to the theater.

I paid $100 for my ticket so I could be in the third row. I cried my eyes out from beginning to end. She was amazing. She didn't miss a step. She didn't miss a lyric. She was just thrilling.

When she took the last bow, she burst into tears. She had just turned nineteen. I was heaving. I thought to myself, "That's what it's all about. That's why I am here, to give back. I changed someone's life by theater. That's how I can justify the madness, the not knowing if tomorrow I will be living out of a storage unit."

It's funny. Right now I have no home. I have nothing. I live out of a storage unit. No joke. Today, coming to this interview, I showered at a friend's house and took his shirt because I have no clothes. My mail comes to me through a friend. It's always late. I always have late fees. They turn off my phone service every three months. I am forty-one years old, and I am still living the life of a gypsy. I am a working actor.

Gerry McIntyre. *Once on This Island* (Armand) [O], *Joseph and the Amazing Technicolor° Dreamcoat* (Judah) [O], *Anything Goes* (Purser) [O], *Uptown . . . It's Hot!* (Little Richard) [O], *Chicago** (Billy Flynn), *Annie 2** (Punjab)

Conclusion

Amidst all the stories shared and feelings expressed in this book, there is one thing that the authors and contributors all have in common: a love for musical theater, and a love for Broadway. It would be wrong to say that this book is anything but a product of that love. When we first began writing, our intention was simply to share with the public entertaining stories that, for the most part, had been circulated only in theater bars. However, what started out as a lighthearted and humorous book quickly turned into something quite different: a cathartic yet unsettling tale about the life of the Broadway actor in this new era of theater.

It is a life that few actors are prepared for. Most assumed that, if their dreams ever came true and they found themselves standing in the spotlight on a Broadway stage, life would be close to perfect. Neither in their dreams nor in their training did they receive any substantive hints about how the rest of their life could play out, either on stage or off.

Nowadays, despite the fact that lasting careers are seldom built in musical theater, each year thousands of students spend their education, and thousands of dollars, preparing for a career on Broadway. Moreover, hundreds of Broadway performers, after their first taste of "stardom," attempt to sustain themselves in New York, hoping the road ahead will be smoother than the road already traveled. As this book has shown, the road usually just gets rougher.

It is not our intention to discourage young hopefuls from pursuing their dreams of musical theater. Rather, to the young star: We only hope that this book provides you with an opportunity to reflect upon the life that just might await once you make it to Broadway. Musical theater can ignite strong emotions. It can make you feel that there is nothing worth doing in life but sing on a

Broadway stage. However, the reality of trying to sustain a career on Broadway is often brutal, and the life unforgiving.

In this book, you have heard from the stars you have grown up with and revered, the very stars you have listened to on cast albums late into the night. If you thought their lives were perfect, you were wrong. The hard work and the struggle begin as soon as you arrive in New York City. And, once you finally make it on Broadway, life doesn't get any easier. There are many personal sacrifices to be made, and many professional obstacles to overcome. Despite all of your success, you will likely never get beyond square one. There are no guarantees. So, proceed with caution, and if you decide to commit to a life on Broadway, remember never to lose touch with your initial love and passion for theater.

To the Broadway actor: We hope this book serves as a catalyst for positive change and growth within the Broadway community. For a wide variety of reasons, the contributors to this book have chosen to talk freely about their lives and experiences on Broadway. Through reflecting on what fellow actors have shared, we hope that you will approach Broadway with a renewed sense of purpose. To a large degree, change can only come from within. It is up to you, the working actor, to help shape Broadway into what you wish it to become.

Additionally, as this book has shown, pursuing a career on Broadway can be very isolating. It is our hope that upon reading the stories in this book and realizing that so many of your own life experiences, sentiments, and dreams are shared by others, your journey down the Great White Way won't be quite as lonely. Remember that the life of a Broadway performer is more about the journey than the destination, and make sure to enjoy yourself and your company along the way.

Lastly, to the theatergoer: We hope this book will not only put you on notice of how Broadway has changed, but more importantly, we hope this book will provide you with a glimpse into the lives of Broadway performers, and in doing so, help restore some intimacy to Broadway—an intimacy which is critical for theater to be effective and meaningful, and more than just "entertainment."

As the contributors to this book have explained, much of the intimacy which once existed on Broadway has recently been lost. First, as a result of the new economics of Broadway, a successful musical will often linger in the same theater for years, as will many of its performers. Newcomers to a long-running musical rarely have any contact with the creative team, but are simply told to fill in the gap left behind. The passion of the performance dissipates and the intimacy wanes, while ticket prices continue to rise.

Second, with ticket prices reaching $100 per seat, there is an expectation by the audience, if not a demand, for spectacle. While the musicals of the early and mid–twentieth century were built on the performers, the new musicals of Disney and company are constructed around technology and special effects. Further, it has become the imaginary characters such as Simba and Belle that draw the crowds, not the talented actors who play them. Theatergoers walk out of *The Lion King* and *Beauty and the Beast* without a clue who played the title role—and it isn't really important. It is enough that they can finally tell their friends that they saw the musical, and maybe pick up a souvenir along the way.

The art and intimacy of Broadway, and the performers themselves, have been compromised. As a result, many performers feel marginalized and estranged, and there is an increasing amount of goofing off on stage. And while the audience may not always see it, they certainly feel it, whether they know it or not. How else could people leave *Miss Saigon* remembering only the helicopter? How else could *Les Misérables* simply become an enjoyable experience, instead of an inspiring one? The spectacle has taken over, and something important has been lost. We hope that, through reading the personal stories and reflections in this book, new relationships can be formed between and among those on stage and those in the audience, and that some of the lost intimacy on Broadway can be restored.

Theater is ultimately about personal relationships. Robert Brustein, former dean of the Yale School of Drama, put it aptly when he said, "Theatergoing is a communal act, moviegoing a solitary one." So, to a large extent, the fate of Broadway is in the hands of the audience. Through better understanding the lifestyles of today's Broadway performers, their dreams and disappointments, their secrets and their struggles, you will help ensure that Broadway will flourish once again.

Chapter Guide

Part One: The Early Years

Chapter 1: Singing on the Coffee Table
Sarah Uriarte Berry, Matt Bogart, Steven Buntrock, Jeff Edgerton, Jarrod Emick, Deborah Gibson, Heather Headley, Ruthie Henshall, James Hindman, Donna McKechnie, Donna Murphy, Ken Page, Lea Salonga, Robert Torti, and Jessica Snow Wilson.

Chapter 2: First Impressions
Jason Alexander, Steven Buntrock, Liz Callaway, Kip Driver, Jeff Gardner, Marsh Hanson, Wilson Heredia, Tom Hewitt, Marin Mazzie, Gerry McIntyre, Hugh Panaro, DeLee Lively, Ray Walker, and Jessica Snow Wilson.

Chapter 3: Don't You Dare Call My Child a Thespian!
Roger Bart, Dave Clemmons, Jeff Edgerton, Mark Moreau, Joe Paparella, Alice Ripley, Sophia Salguero, and Deborah Yates.

Part Two: Getting Settled

Chapter 4: Welcome to Gotham City
Sarah Uriarte Berry, Liz Callaway, Daniel C. Cooney, Boyd Gaines, Ruthie Henshall, Rebecca Luker, Terrence Mann, Mark Moreau, Hugh Panaro, Paige Price, Doug Storm, Ray Walker, and Patrick Wilson.

Chapter 5: New Home and New Friends
Michael Berry, Ann Hampton Callaway, Jeff Gurner, Heather Headley, Sean McDermott, Marin Mazzie, Ken Page, Anthony Rapp, Alice Ripley, Doug Storm, Clarke Thorell, and Pamela Winslow.

Chapter 6: Survival Jobs
Ana Maria Andricain, Bryan Batt, Geoffrey Blaisdell, Robert DuSold, Dave Clemmons, Jeff Gurner, Kevin Loreque, Terrence Mann, Kelli Rabke, Daphne Rubin-Vega, and Ray Walker.

Chapter 7: Singing for Supper
Steven Buntrock, Ann Hampton Callaway, Tom Hewitt, Davis Kirby, Jodie Langel, Idina Menzel, Rena Strober, Barbara Walsh, Marissa Jaret Winokur, and Lee Zarrett.

Part Three: Transition to Stardom

Chapter 8: The Audition Room
Ana Maria Andricain, Gary Beach, Erin Dilly, Cory English, Marsh Hanson, Brian d'Arcy James, Jane Lanier, Jose Llana, Terrence Mann, Sean McDermott, Joe Paparella, Steve Pudenz, Kelli Rabke, John Rubenstein, Robert Torti, Jim Walton, Pamela Winslow, and Scott Wise.

Part Four: The Thrill of Live Theater

Chapter 9: Take Two
Charlotte d'Amboise, Gary Beach, Sarah Uriarte Berry, Geoffrey Blaisdell, Dave Clemmons, Ann Crumb, Robert Evan, Gina Ferrall, Randy Graff, Danny Gurwin, James Hadley, Ruthie Henshall, Brian d'Arcy James, Jodie Langel, Daniel C. Levine, Rebecca Luker, Terrence Mann, Andrea McArdle, Sean McDermott, Nancy Opel, Anthony Rapp, John Rubinstein, Brooke Shields, Emily Skinner, Lea Thompson, Colm Wilkinson, Patrick Wilson, and Scott Wise.

Chapter 10: Please Remain Seated
Michael Arnold, Anastasia Barzee, Bryan Batt, Sarah Uriarte Berry, Geoffrey Blaisdell, Dave Clemmons, Robert DuSold, Sam Harris, Wilson Heredia, Betsy Joslyn, Michael Lanning, DeLee Lively, Andrea McArdle, Idina Menzel, Ann Miller, Doug Storm, Ray Walker, and Jim Walton.

Part Five: The Secret Life

Chapter 11: The Broadway Lifestyle
Jason Alexander, Michael Arnold, Antonio Banderas, Sarah Uriarte Berry, Kerry Butler, Joseph Cassidy, Susan Egan, Cory English, Deborah Gibson, Anita Gillette, Randy Graff, Hunter Foster, David Josefsberg, Jodie Langel, Michael Lanning, Ann Miller, Jessica Molaskey, Donna Murphy, Lonny Price, Faith Prince, Ray Roderick, Craig Rubano, Brooke Shields, Emily Skinner, Doug Storm, Robert Torti, and Marissa Jaret Winokur.

Chapter 12: Sex in the Workplace
Joan Almedilla, Michael Arnold, Frank Baiocchi, Craig Bennet, Michael Berresse, Sarah Uriarte Berry, Jeff Blumenkrantz, Dave Clemmons, Lea DeLaria, Erin Dilly, Hunter Foster, Paul Harman, Jodie Langel, Michael Lanning, Sean Jeremy Palmer, Erin Leigh Peck, Craig Rubano, James Sassar, Jerry Tellier, Lucy Vance, Andrew Varela, Marissa Jaret Winokur, and John Leslie Wolfe.

Chapter 13: Forget the Picket Fence

Anastasia Barzee, Michael Berry, Liz Callaway, Robert Evan, Jeff Gardner, Tom Hewitt, David Josefsberg, DeLee Lively, Angela Lockett, Heather MacRae, Christie McCall, J. Mark McVey, Christiane Noll, Nancy Opel, Paige Price, Steve Pudenz, John Rubenstein, Craig Schulman, and Amanda Watkins.

Chapter 14: Road Trip

Ana Maria Andricain, John Antony, Dave Clemmons, Robert DuSold, William Thomas Evans, Jeff Gurner, Marsh Hanson, David Josefsberg, Betsy Joslyn, Marc Kudisch, Jodie Langel, Kevin Loreque, Christiane Noll, Rena Strober, Jessica Snow Wilson, and Adrian Zmed.

Chapter 15: What Am I Doing Here?

Frank Baiocchi, Jonathan Dokuchitz, Jeff Gurner, Daniel C. Levine, Christie McCall, Mark Moreau, Brad Oscar, Alex Santoriello, Jerry Tellier, and Jim Walton.

Part Six: A New Era

Chapter 16: The Disneyfication of Broadway

Jason Alexander, Charlotte d'Amboise, Antonio Banderas, Gary Beach, Craig Bennet, Sarah Uriarte Berry, Jeff Blumenkrantz, Ron Bohmer, Nick Corley, Harvey Evans, Hunter Foster, Alison Fraser, Anita Gillette, Debbie Gravitte, Philip Hernández, Betsy Joslyn, Michael Lanning, Sondra Lee, Heather MacRae, Terrence Mann, Andrea McArdle, Donna McKechnie, J. Mark McVey, Ann Miller, Chita Rivera, Ray Roderick, Craig Rubano, Jane Sell, Ray Walker, Colm Wilkinson, Scott Wise, Marissa Jaret Winokur, Karen Ziemba, and Adrian Zmed.

Chapter 17: Broadway, Inc.

Jason Alexander, Ana Maria Andricain, John Antony, Michael Arnold, Anastasia Barzee, Craig Bennet, Jeff Blumenkrantz, Kelly Briggs, Daniel C. Cooney, Jeff Edgerton, William Thomas Evans, Hunter Foster, Randy Graff, Debbie Gravitte, Jeff Gurner, Paul Harman, James Hindman, David Josefsberg, Kevin Kern, Jodie Langel, Angela Lockett, Andrea McArdle, Jessica Molaskey, Sean Jeremy Palmer, Lonny Price, Steve Pudenz, Lee Roy Reams, Alex Santoriello, Roger Seyer, Brooke Shields, Rena Strober, Jerry Tellier, Andrew Varela, Laurie Wells, Colm Wilkinson, Marissa Jaret Winokur, Pamela Winslow, and Adrian Zmed.

Part Seven: When Dreams Come True

Chapter 18: The Base of the Tony® Is Plastic

Jason Alexander, Charlotte d'Amboise, Roger Bart, Gary Beach, Michael Berresse, Liz Callaway, Ann Crumb, Daisy Eagan, Susan Egan, Hunter Foster, Boyd Gaines, Anita Gillette, Brian Lane Green, Ruthie Henshall, Heather Headley, Wilson Heredia, DeLee Lively, Marin Mazzie, Andrea McArdle, Donna McKechnie,

Donna Murphy, Brad Oscar, Ken Page, John Rubinstein, Lea Salonga, Jane Sell, Robert Torti, Donna Vivino, Barbara Walsh, Patrick Wilson, Marissa Jaret Winokur, and Scott Wise.

Chapter 19: Here Today, Gone Tomorrow

Jason Alexander, Michael Arnold, Bryan Batt, Geoffrey Blaisdell, Ron Bohmer, Daniel C. Cooney, Kip Driver, Hunter Foster, Anita Gillette, Randy Graff, Marsh Hanson, Sam Harris, Davis Kirby, Jodie Langel, Jose Llana, Heather MacRae, Christie McCall, Gerry McIntyre, Donna McKechnie, Ann Miller, Donna Murphy, Christiane Noll, Hugh Panaro, Darcie Roberts, Alex Santoriello, Robert Torti, Ray Walker, Marissa Jaret Winokur, and Scott Wise.

Chapter 20: The Time in Between

John Antony, Craig Bennet, Frank Baiocchi, Ron Bohmer, Liz Callaway, Patrick Cassidy, Kip Driver, Robert DuSold, Allen Fitzpatrick, Randy Graff, Danny Gurwin, Wilson Heredia, Kevin Kern, Davis Kirby, Jodie Langel, Kevin Loreque, Gerry McIntyre, Donna McKechnie, Sal Mistretta, Donna Murphy, Nancy Opel, Sean Jeremy Palmer, Kelli Rabke, Alice Ripley, John Rubinstein, Alex Santoriello, James Sassar, Emily Skinner, Jerry Tellier, Pamela Winslow, and Lee Zarrett.

The Contributors and their Credits

[O] = Original Broadway Company
Normal type = Broadway Company
* = Broadway National Tour
[T] = Tony Award® Winner
[t] = Tony Award® Nominee
u/s = Understudy
s/b = Standby

Jason Alexander: *Jerome Robbins' Broadway* (Emcee) [O][T], *Merrily We Roll Along* (Joe) [O], *The Rink* (Lino/Lenny/Punk/Uncle Fausto) [O], *Broadway Bound* (Stanley) [O], *Accomplice* [O], *The Producers** (Max Bialystock)

Joan Almedilla: *Miss Saigon* (Kim), *Les Misérables** (Fantine), *Jesus Christ Superstar** (Soul Girl)

Ana Maria Andricain: *Marie Christine* (Dakota/Emma Parker) [O], *Les Misérables* (Fantine u/s), *Beauty and the Beast* (Belle), *By Jeeves* (Stiffy Byng), *Evita** (Eva Alternate), *Annie Get Your Gun** (Annie u/s)

John Antony: *Passion* (Augenti/Count Ludovic), *Titanic** (John Jacob Astor), *Sunset Boulevard** (Joe Gillis u/s), *Annie Get Your Gun** (Frank Butler)

Michael Arnold: *42nd Street* (Andy Lee) [O], *The Who's Tommy* [O], *A Funny Thing Happened on the Way to the Forum* (Swing) [O], *Little Me* (Belle's Boy/Newsboy) [O], *Cats* (Mr. Mistoffelees), *Cabaret*, *Chicago*, *Martin Guerre** (Benoit), *Busker Alley**, *Durante**

Frank Baiocchi: *Miss Saigon* (Chris u/s), *South Pacific** (Cable u/s)

Antonio Banderas: *Nine* (Guido Contini) [O][t]

Roger Bart: *You're a Good Man Charlie Brown* (Snoopy) [T], *The Producers* (Carmen Ghia) [O][t], *Triumph of Love* (Harlequin) [O], *King David* (Jonathan) [O], *Big River* (Tom Sawyer), *The Who's Tommy* (Cousin Kevin), *The Secret Garden* (Dickon), *How to Succeed in Business Without Really Trying!* (Bud Frump)

Anastasia Barzee: *Henry IV* (Lady Mortimer) [O], *Urinetown* (Hope Cladwell), *Miss Saigon* (Ellen), *Jekyll & Hyde* (Emma)

Bryan Batt: *Seussical* (The Cat in the Hat s/b) [O], *Saturday Night Fever* (Monty) [O], *Sunset Boulevard* (Joe Gillis u/s) [O], *Cats* (Munkustrap), *Beauty and the Beast* (Lumiere), *Starlight Express* (Rocky One), *The Scarlet Pimpernel* (Percy s/b), *Joseph and the Amazing Technicolor® Dreamcoat* (Reuben)

Gary Beach: *The Producers* (Roger DeBris) [O][T], *Beauty and the Beast* (Lumiere) [O][t], *The Moony Shapiro Songbook* [O], *Doonesbury* (Duke) [O], *Something's Afoot* (Nigel) [O], *Sweet Adeline* (Dan Ward) [O], *Annie* (Rooster Hannigan), *1776* (Edward Rutledge u/s), *Les Misérables** (Thénardier), *Of Thee I Sing**

Craig Bennet: *Miss Saigon* (Marine/Reeves), *Les Misérables** (Thénardier u/s), *Mamma Mia!** (Bill), *Ragtime** (Willie Conklin)

Michael Berresse: *Kiss Me, Kate* (Bill Calhoun/Luciento) [O][t], *The Gershwin's Fascinating Rhythm*, *Chicago* (Fred Casely) [O], *Damn Yankees* (Bomber) [O], *Fiddler on the Roof* [O], *Guys and Dolls* (Crapshooter), *Joseph and the Amazing Technicolor® Dreamcoat** (Pharaoh), *Busker Alley**

Michael Berry: *Les Misérables* (Enjolras u/s), *Sunset Boulevard** (Artie)

Sarah Uriarte Berry: *Taboo* (Nicola) [O], *Les Misérables* (Eponine), *Beauty and the Beast* (Belle), *Sunset Boulevard** (Betty Schaeffer), *Carousel** (Julie Jordan)

Geoffrey Blaisdell: *Jekyll & Hyde* (Lord Glossop) [O], *Cyrano—The Musical* (Captain De Castel Jaloux) [O], *Amadeus* (Servant) [O], *Les Misérables** (Javert), *The Phantom of the Opera** (The Auctioneer)

Jeff Blumenkrantz: *Urban Cowboy* [O][t], *A Class Act* [O] (Charlie/Marvin), *Into the Woods* (Jack/Rapunzel's Prince u/s) [O], *How to Succeed in Business Without Really Trying!* (Bud Frump) [O], *Damn Yankees* (Smokey) [O], *3 Penny Opera* (Filch) [O], *Joseph and the Amazing Technicolor® Dreamcoat** (Brother)

Matt Bogart: *The Civil War* (Sam Taylor) [O], *Aida* (Radames), *Miss Saigon* (Chris), *Smokey Joe's Cafe* (White Guy)

Ron Bohmer: *Fiddler on the Roof* (Fyedka) [O], *The Scarlet Pimpernel* (Percy), *Les Misérables* (Enjolras), *Aspects of Love** (Alex), *Sunset Boulevard** (Joe Gillis), *The Phantom of the Opera** (Phantom)

Kelly Briggs: *Les Misérables* (Bishop), *Cats* (Asparagus)

Steven Buntrock: *Jane Eyre* (Mr. Eshton) [O], *Oklahoma!* (Joe/Curley) [O], *Titanic* (Frederick Barrett), *Les Misérables* (Enjolras), *Martin Guerre** (Arnaud), *Joseph and the Amazing Technicolor® Dreamcoat** (Reuben)

Kerry Butler: *Little Shop of Horrors* (Audrey) [O], *Hairspray* (Penny Pingleton) [O], *Blood Brothers* (Donna Marie u/s) [O], *Beauty and the Beast* (Belle), *Les Misérables* (Eponine)

Liz Callaway: *Baby* (Lizzie) [O][t], *Miss Saigon* (Ellen) [O], *Merrily We Roll Along* (Nightclub Waitress) [O], *The Three Musketeers* (Lady Constance Bonacieux) [O], *The Look of Love* [O], *Cats* (Grizabella)

Ann Hampton Callaway: *Swing!* [O][t]

Joseph Cassidy: *1776* (Leather Apron) [O], *Showboat* (Ravenal u/s) [O], *Les Misérables* (Courfeyrac)

Patrick Cassidy: *Leader of the Pack* (Jeff Barry) [O], *The Pirates of Penzance* (Frederic), *Annie Get Your Gun* (Frank Butler), *Aida* (Radames), *Joseph and the Amazing Technicolor® Dreamcoat** (Joseph)

Dave Clemmons: *The Scarlet Pimpernel* (Ben) [O], *The Civil War* (Sergeant Virgil Frank/Auctioneer's Assistant) [O], *Les Misérables* (Jean Valjean), *Whistle Down the Wind**, *Jekyll & Hyde** (Bishop)

Daniel C. Cooney: *Les Misérables* (Marius u/s), *The Civil War** (Swing), *Evita** (Che), *Fiddler on the Roof** (Perchik)

Nick Corley: *She Loves Me* (Keller) [O]

Ann Crumb: *Anna Karenina* (Anna) [O][t], *Aspects of Love* (Rose) [O], *Chess* (Svetlana u/s) [O], *Les Misérables* (Fantine u/s) [O], *Swing!** (Lead), *Music of the Night** (Headliner), *Man of La Mancha** (Aldonza), *Evita** (Eva Peron)

Charlotte d'Amboise: *Jerome Robbins' Broadway* (Anita/Peter Pan) [O][t], *Carrie* (Chris) [O], *Company* (Cathy) [O], *Song and Dance* [O], *Contact* (Wife), *Damn Yankees* (Lola), *Chicago* (Roxie Hart), *Cats* (Cassandra)

Lea DeLaria: *The Rocky Horror Show* (Eddie/Dr. Scott) [O], *On the Town* (Hildy) [O], *Chicago** (Mama Morton)

Erin Dilly: *Follies* (Young Phyllis) [O], *The Boys from Syracuse* (Luciana) [O], *Into the Woods* (Cinderella), *Martin Guerre** (Bertrande), *Beauty and the Beast** (Belle), *South Pacific** (Nellie)

Kip Driver: *Martin Guerre** (Swing), *Cats** (Munkustrap), *Les Misérables**

Jonathan Dokuchitz: *The Who's Tommy* (Captain Walker) [O], *Into the Woods* (Rapunzel's Prince) [O], *The Boys from Syracuse* (Antipholus of Syracuse) [O], *Company* (Peter) [O], *Dream* [O], *The Look of Love* [O]

Robert DuSold: *Les Misérables* (Javert), *Jekyll & Hyde* (Archbishop of Basingstoke), *Kiss of the Spider Woman* (Marcos), *Cats** (Deuteronomy), *The Phantom of the Opera** (André), *Chicago** (Little Mary Sunshine s/b), *Showboat** (Pete)

Daisy Eagan: *The Secret Garden* (Mary) [O][T], *James Joyce's The Dead* (Rita) [O], *Les Misérables* (Young Cosette)

Jeff Edgerton: *Parade* (Fiddlin' John) [O], *Grease!* (Eugene u/s)

Susan Egan: *Beauty and the Beast* (Belle) [O][t], *Triumph of Love* (Princess) [O], *Cabaret* (Sally), *State Fair*, *Thoroughly Modern Millie* (Millie), *Bye Bye Birdie** (Kim)

Jarrod Emick: *Damn Yankees* (Joe Hardy) [O][T], *The Boy from Oz* (Greg Connell) [O], *The Rocky Horror Show* (Brad) [O], *Miss Saigon* (Chris), *Les Misérables** (Enjolras u/s)

Cory English: *A Funny Thing Happened on the Way to the Forum* (Protean) [O], *Guys and Dolls* (Brandy Bottle Bates) [O], *Hello, Dolly!* (Barnaby Tucker) [O], *Damn Yankees* (Bubba) [O], *Gypsy* (St. Paul)

Robert Evan: *Jekyll and Hyde* (Dr. Jekyll) [O], *Dance of the Vampires*, (Count von Krolock s/b) [O], *Les Misérables* (Jean Valjean)

William Thomas Evans: *Camelot* (Mordred u/s) [O], *The Scarlet Pimpernel* (Hastings) [O], *Jekyll & Hyde** (Proops/Utterson u/s), *A Funny Thing Happened on the Way to the Forum** (Miles Gloriosus)

Harvey Evans: *Oklahoma!* (Andrew Carnes u/s) [O], *Barnum* (Phineas Taylor Barnum u/s) [O], *Our Town* (George Gibbs) [O], *Follies* (Young Buddy) [O], *The Boy Friend* (Bobby Van Husen) [O], *George M!* (Sam Harris) [O], *Anyone Can Whistle* (John) [O], *Redhead* (Dancer) [O], *New Girl in Town* (Dancer) [O], *Sunset Boulevard* [O], *Sextet* [O], *West Side Story* (Gee-Tar), *Gypsy* (Farm Boy), *The Scarlet Pimpernel* (Ozzy), *Hello, Dolly!* (Barnaby Tucker), *Damn Yankees**, *Nash at Nine**, *La Cage Aux Folles**

Gina Ferrall: *Big River* (Widow Douglas) [O], *Jane Eyre* (Mrs. Reed) [O], *The Sound of Music* (Sister Berthe) [O], *Les Misérables* (Madame Thénardier)

Allen Fitzpatrick: *Sweet Smell of Success* (Senator) [O], *42nd Street* (Mac) [O], *The*

Scarlet Pimpernel (Farleigh) [O], *Gentlemen Prefer Blondes* (Gus Esmond) [O], *Les Misérables* (Thénardier), *Sunset Boulevard** (Max)

Hunter Foster: *Little Shop of Horrors* (Seymour) [O], *Urinetown* (Bobby Strong) [O], *Footloose* (Bickle) [O], *King David* [O], *Grease!* (Roger) [O], *Les Misérables* (Marius u/s), *Martin Guerre** (Martin u/s), *Cats** (Rum Tum Tugger)

Alison Fraser: *The Secret Garden* (Martha) [O][t], *Romance/Romance* (Josefine) [O][t], *Tartuffe* (Dorine) [O], *The Mystery of Edwin Drood* (Helena) [O]

Boyd Gaines: *Contact* (Michael Wiley) [O][T], *She Loves Me* (Georg Nowak) [O][T], *The Heidi Chronicles* (Peter Patrone) [O][T], *Anything Goes* (Lord Evelyn Oakleigh) [O], *Company* (Robert) [O], *The Show Off* (Aubrey Piper) [O], *Cabaret* (Clifford Bradshaw)

Jeff Gardner: *The Wild Party* (Burrs u/s) [O], *The Scarlet Pimpernel* (Mercier) [O], *Cyrano—The Musical* (Sylvian) [O], *The Queen and the Rebels* (Traveler) [O], *Jerome Robbins' Broadway* (The Setter u/s), *Les Misérables** (Foreman)

Deborah Gibson: *Cabaret* (Sally Bowles), *Les Misérables* (Eponine), *Beauty and the Beast* (Belle), *Grease!* (Sandy), *Joseph and the Amazing Technicolor® Dreamcoat** (Narrator)

Anita Gillette: *Chapter Two* (Jennie Malone) [O][t], *Guys and Dolls* (Sarah Brown) [O], *Kelly* (Angela Crane) [O], *Carnival!* (Gypsy) [O], *All American* (Susan) [O], *Mr. President* (Leslie Henderson) [O], *Jimmy* (Betty Compton) [O], *Don't Drink the Water* (Susan Hollander) [O], *Gypsy* (Thelma), *Brighton Beach Memoirs* (Blanche), *They're Playing Our Song* (Sonia Walsk), *Cabaret* (Sally)

Randy Graff: *City of Angels* (Oolie) [O][T], *A Class Act* (Sophie) [O][t], *Les Misérables* (Fantine) [O], *Moon over Buffalo* (Rosalind) [O], *High Society* (Liz Imbrie) [O], *Laughter on the 23rd Floor* (Carol) [O], *Saravà* (Rosalia) [O], *Fiddler on the Roof* (Golde) [O], *Grease!* (Rizzo u/s), *Falsettos* (Trina)

Debbie Gravitte: *Jerome Robbins' Broadway* [O][T], *They're Playing Our Song* (Sonia Walsk) [O], *Blues in the Night* (Woman #2) [O], *Ain't Broadway Grand* (Gypsy Rose Lee) [O], *Zorba* (The Woman) [O], *Perfectly Frank* [O], *Les Misérables* (Fantine), *Chicago* (Mama Morton)

Brian Lane Green: *Starmites* (Spacepunk) [O][t], *The Life* (Jojo), *Big River* (Huckleberry Finn), *Joseph and the Amazing Technicolor® Dreamcoat** (Joseph)

Jeff Gurner: *The Lion King* (Ed the Hyena)

Danny Gurwin: *The Scarlet Pimpernel* (Hal), *The Full Monty* (Malcolm MacGregor), *Urinetown* (Mr. McQueen)

James Hadley: *Thou Shalt Not* (Swing) [O], *Bells Are Ringing* (Swing) [O], *The Red Shoes* (Swing) [O], *Cats* (Coricopat), *Chicago* (Swing), *The Producers**

Marsh Hanson: *Les Misérables* (Marius), *Joseph and the Amazing Technicolor® Dreamcoat** (Brother)

Sam Harris: *The Life* (Jojo) [O][t], *Grease!* (Doody) [O], *The Producers* (Carmen Ghia), *Joseph and the Amazing Technicolor® Dreamcoat** (Joseph)

Paul Harman: *Les Misérables* (Foreman) [O], *Chess* (Arbiter) [O], *Triumph of Love* (Dimas u/s) [O], *Candide* (2nd Bulgarian Soldier) [O], *What's Wrong with This*

Picture? (Mort u/s) [O], *It's So Nice to Be Civilized* [O], *Joseph and the Amazing Technicolor® Dreamcoat* (Simeon), *Ragtime* (Doctor), *Cats* (Asparagus), *Evita** (Peron u/s), *Zorba** (Niko)

Heather Headley: *Aida* (Aida) [O][**T**], *The Lion King* [O] (Nala), *Ragtime** (Sarah u/s)

Ruthie Henshall: *Putting It Together* (The Younger Woman) [O], *Miss Saigon* (Ellen), *Chicago* (Velma)

Wilson Heredia: *Rent* (Angel) [O][**T**]

Philip Hernández: *The Capeman* (Reverend Gonzalez) [O], *Kiss of the Spider Woman* (Esteban) [O], *Les Misérables* (Jean Valjean/ Javert), *Copacabana** (Rico)

Tom Hewitt: *The Rocky Horror Show,* (Dr. Frank N. Furter) [O][**t**], *The Boys from Syracuse* (Antipholus of, Ephesus) [O], *Art* (Serge u/s) [O], *The Lion King* (Scar), *School for Scandal* (Charles Surface), *Sisters Rosensweig* (Geoffrey), *Urinetown** (Officer Lockstock)

James Hindman: *A Grand Night for Singing* [O], *City of Angels* [O], *1776* [O], *The Scarlet Pimpernel* (Ben), *Once Upon a Mattress* (Princess), *Dancing at Lughnasa** (Michael), *Falsettos** (Marvin), *Joseph and the Amazing Technicolor® Dreamcoat** (Simeon), *Cats** (Asparagus)

Brian d'Arcy James: *Sweet Smell of Success* (Sidney) [O][**t**], *Titanic* (Frederick Barrett) [O], *Carousel* (Captain) [O], *Blood Brothers*

David Josefsberg: *Grease!* (Doody), *Les Misérables* (Marius u/s)

Betsy Joslyn: *High Society* (Patsy) [O], *Sweeney Todd* (Johanna) [O], *The Goodbye Girl* (Paula s/b) [O], *A Doll's Life* (Nora) [O], *A Few Good Men* (Lt. Galloway s/b) [O], *Into the Woods* (The Witch), *Sunday in the Park with George* (Dot), *Les Misérables* (Madame Thénardier), *Beauty and the Beast** (Mrs. Potts), *City of Angels** (Oolie/Donna), *Camelot** (Guenevere), *Of Thee I Sing**, *Let 'em Eat Cake**

Kevin Kern: *Les Misérables* (Marius)

Davis Kirby: *The Boys from Syracuse* (Soldier) [O], *Thou Shalt Not* (Sugar Hips) [O], *Thoroughly Modern Millie, Cats** (Swing)

Marc Kudisch: *Thoroughly Modern Millie* (Trevor Graydon) [O][**t**], *Bells are Ringing* (Jeff Moss) [O], *The Wild Party* [O] (Jackie), *Joseph and the Amazing Technicolor® Dreamcoat* (Reuben) [O], *High Society* (George Kittredge) [O], *Assassins* (Proprietor) [O], *The Scarlet Pimpernel* (Chauvelin), *Beauty and the Beast* (Gaston), *Bye Bye Birdie** (Conrad)

Jane Lanier: *Jerome Robbins' Broadway* [O][**t**], *Anything Goes* (Virtue) [O], *Sweet Charity* (Frenchy) [O], *Fosse* [O]

Jodie Langel: *Les Misérables* (Cosette/Eponine), *Martin Guerre** (Bertrande Alternate), *Cats** (Grizabella), *Joseph and the Amazing Technicolor® Dreamcoat** (Narrator)

Michael Lanning: *The Civil War* (Captain Emmett Lochran) [O]

Sondra Lee: *Peter Pan* (Tiger Lily) [O], *High Button Shoes* (Playmate of the Boy at the Picnic) [O], *Hotel Paradiso* (Victoire) [O], *Hello, Dolly!* (Minnie Fay) [O], *Sunday in New York* (Woman) [O]

Daniel C. Levine: *Jesus Christ Superstar* (Disciple) [O], *The Rocky Horror Show, Chicago** (Mary Sunshine), *Les Misérables** (Marius u/s), *Mamma Mia!**

DeLee Lively: *Smokey Joe's Cafe* [O][t], *A Chorus Line* (Val)

Jose Llana: *Flower Drum Song* (Ta) [O], *The King and I* (Lun-Tha) [O], *Street Corner Symphony* (Jessie-Lee) [O], *Rent* (Angel), *Martin Guerre** (Guillaume)

Angela Lockett: *Parade* (Angela) [O], *Les Misérables* (Fantine u/s), *Martin Guerre** (Catherine), *Once on This Island**, *Ain't Misbehavin'**

Kevin Loreque: *Cats** (Rum Tum Tugger), *Hot Shoe Shuffle**

Rebecca Luker: *The Music Man* (Marian) [O][t], *Showboat* (Magnolia) [O][t], *The Sound of Music* (Maria) [O], *The Secret Garden* (Lily) [O], *The Phantom of the Opera* (Princess/Christine) [O], *Nine* (Claudia)

Heather MacRae: *Falsettos* (Charlotte) [O], *Coastal Disturbances* (Faith Bigelow) [O], *Here's Where I Belong* (Abra) [O], *Hair* (Sheila)

Terrence Mann: *Les Misérables* (Javert) [O][t], *Beauty and the Beast* (Beast) [O][t], *Cats* (Rum Tum Tugger) [O], *The Scarlet Pimpernel* (Chauvelin) [O], *Barnum* (Chester Lyman) [O], *Rags* (Saul) [O], *Getting Away with Murder* (Gregory Reed) [O], *Jerome Robbins' Broadway* (Emcee), *The Rocky Horror Show*, (Dr. Frank N. Furter)

Sal Mistretta: *Sunset Boulevard* (Sheldrake) [O], *Welcome to the Club* (Bruce Aiken u/s) [O], *On the Twentieth Century* (Otto Von Bismark) [O], *Evita* (Magaldi u/s) [O], *Something's Afoot* (Geoffrey s/b) [O], *Cabaret* (Herr Schultz s/b), *Cats** (Asparagus), *Sweeney Todd** (Pirelli), *Wonderful Town** (Speedy Valenti)

Marin Mazzie: *Kiss Me, Kate* (Lilli Vanessi) [O][t], *Ragtime* (Mother) [O][t], *Passion* (Clara) [O][t], *Man of La Mancha* (Aldonza), *Big River* (Mary Jane Wilkes), *Into the Woods* (Rapunzel)

Andrea McArdle: *Annie* (Annie) [O][t], *Starlight Express* (Ashley) [O], *State Fair* (Margy Frake) [O], *Les Misérables* (Fantine), *Beauty and the Beast* (Belle), *Cabaret** (Sally Bowles), *Jerry's Girls**

Christie McCall: *Cats** (Sillabub)

Sean McDermott: *Starlight Express* (Prince of Wales) [O], *Miss Saigon* (Chris u/s) [O], *Falsettos* (Whizzer), *Grease!* (Danny Zuko)

Gerry McIntyre: *Once on This Island* (Armand) [O], *Joseph and the Amazing Technicolor® Dreamcoat* (Judah) [O], *Anything Goes* (Purser) [O], *Uptown . . . It's Hot!* (Little Richard) [O], *Chicago** (Billy Flynn), *Annie 2** (Punjab)

Donna McKechnie: *A Chorus Line* (Cassie) [O][T], *Company* (Kathy) [O], *State Fair* (Emily Arden) [O], *On the Town* (Ivy Smith) [O], *Promises, Promises* (Vivien Della Hoya) [O], *The Education of Hyman Kaplan* (Kathy, McKenna) [O], *How to Succeed in Business Without Really Trying!* (Dancer) [O], *A Funny Thing Happened on the Way to the Forum** (Philia), *Call Me Madam** (The Princess), *Sweet Charity**, *Annie Get Your Gun**

J. Mark McVey: *The Best Little Whorehouse Goes Public* (Sam Dallas s/b) [O], *Les Misérables* (Jean Valjean), *The Who's Tommy* (Captain Walker), *Carousel**

Idina Menzel: *Rent* (Maureen Johnson) [O][t], *Wicked* (Elphaba) [O], *Aida* (Amneris)

Ann Miller: *Sugar Babies* (Ann) [O][t], *George White's Scandals* [O], *Mame* (Mame Dennis)

Jessica Molaskey: *Dream* (Performer) [O], *Parade* (Mrs. Phagan) [O], *Crazy For You*

(Irene Roth u/s) [O], *Oklahoma!* [O], *Chess* [O], *The Who's Tommy* (Mrs. Walker), *Les Misérables* (Madame Thénardier u/s), *Cats* (Jellylorum u/s), *Falsettos**, *City of Angels**, *Joseph and the Amazing Technicolor® Dreamcoat**

Mark Moreau: *Cats* (Swing), *The Music Man* (Traveling Salesman), *The Will Rogers Follies*, *Grease!*

Donna Murphy: *Passion* (Fosca) [O][T], *The King and* I (Anna) [O][T], *Wonderful Town* (Ruth) [O], *The Mystery of Edwin Drood* [O], *The Human Comedy* (Bess Macauley u/s) [O], *Privates on Parade* [O], *They're Playing Our Song* (Swing)

Christiane Noll: *Jekyll & Hyde* (Emma) [O], *It Ain't Nothin' but the Blues*, *Miss Saigon** (Ellen), *Grease!** (Sandy), *City of Angels** (Mallory), *Urinetown** (Hope Cladwell)

Nancy Opel: *Urinetown* (Penelope Pennywise) [O][t], *Evita* (Eva u/s) [O], *Triumph of Love* (Corine) [O], *Sunday in the Park with George* (Frieda) [O], *Teddy & Alice* (Eleanor Roosevelt) [O], *Ring Round the Moon* (Capulat u/s) [O], *Getting Away with Murder* (Dossie Lustig u/s) [O], *Anything Goes* (Hope Harcourt)

Brad Oscar: *The Producers* (Franz Liebkind) [O][t], *Aspects of Love* (Swing) [O], *Jekyll & Hyde* (Archibald Proops) [O]

Ken Page: *Cats* (Old Deuteronomy) [O], *Guys and Dolls* (Nicely-Nicely Johnson) [O], *Ain't Misbehavin'* [O], *The Wiz* (Lion), *Purlie**

Sean Jeremy Palmer: *Carousel** (Mr. Snow), *Martin Guerre** (Guillaume u/s)

Hugh Panaro: *Side Show* (Buddy Foster) [O], *The Red Shoes* (Julian Craster) [O], *The Phantom of the Opera* (Phantom/Raoul), *Les Misérables* (Marius), *Showboat* (Ravenal), *Martin Guerre** (Martin),

Joe Paparella: *Jesus Christ Superstar* (Swing), *Les Misérables* (Thénardier u/s), *Martin Guerre** (Martin u/s), *Mamma Mia!** (Eddie), *Joseph and the Amazing Technicolor® Dreamcoat** (Swing), *Ragtime**, *Big**

Erin Leigh Peck: *Dance of the Vampires* (Zsa-Zsa) [O], *Grease!* (Swing), *Brighton Beach Memoirs**

Faith Prince: *Guys and Dolls* (Miss Adelaide) [O][T], *Bells Are Ringing* (Elle Peterson) [O][t], *Jerome Robbins' Broadway* (Ma/Tessie) [O], *Noises Off* (Belinda Blair) [O], *Nick and Nora* (Lorraine Bixby) [O], *What's Wrong with This Picture?* (Shirley) [O], *Little Me* (Belle) [O], *The King and I* (Anna), *James Joyce's The Dead* (Gretta Conroy)

Lonny Price: *A Class Act* (Ed) [O][t], *Merrily We Roll Along* (Charley Kringas) [O], *"MASTER HAROLD" . . . and the boys* (Hally) [O], *Broadway* (Roy Lane) [O], *Rags* (Ben) [O], *The Survivor* (Rudy) [O], *Burn This* (Larry), *Durante** (Durante), *Apprenticeship of Duddy Kravitz**

Paige Price: *Saturday Night Fever* (Stephanie) [O], *Beauty and the Beast* (Silly Girl) [O], *Smokey Joe's Cafe*

Steve Pudenz: *Hello, Dolly!* (Rudolph) [O], *Joseph and the Amazing Technicolor® Dreamcoat** (Jacob), *The Sound of Music**

Kelli Rabke: *Joseph and the Amazing Technicolor® Dreamcoat* (Narrator) [O], *Les Misérables* (Eponine)

Anthony Rapp: *Rent* (Mark Cohen) [O], *You're a Good Man, Charlie Brown* (Charlie

Brown) [O], *Precious Sons* (Freddy) [O], *Six Degrees of Separation* (Ben) [O], *The King and I** (Louis)

Lee Roy Reams: *42nd Street* (Billy Lawlor) [O][t], *Lorelei* (Henry Spofford) [O], *Applause* (Duane Fox) [O], *Sweet Charity* (Young Spanish Man) [O], *Hello, Dolly!* (Cornelius Hackl) [O], *An Evening with Jerry Herman* [O], *Beauty and the Beast* (Lumiere), *La Cages Aux Folles* (Albin), *The Producers** (Roger De Bris)

Alice Ripley: *Side Show* (Violet Hilton) [O][t], *The Rocky Horror Show* (Janet Weiss) [O], *Sunset Boulevard* (Betty Schaefer) [O], *King David* (Bathsheba) [O], *James Joyce's The Dead* (Mrs. Molly Ivors) [O], *The Who's Tommy* [O], *Les Misérables* (Fantine), *Little Shop of Horrors** (Audrey)

Chita Rivera: *Kiss of the Spider Woman* (Spider Woman) [O][T], *The Rink* (Anna) [O][T], *Nine* (Liliane La Fleur) [O][t], *Jerry's Girls* [O][t], *Merlin* (The Queen) [O][t], *Bring Back Birdie* (Rose) [O][t], *Chicago* (Velma) [O][t], *Bye Bye Birdie* (Rose) [O][t], *Bajour* (Anyanka) [O], *West Side Story* (Anita) [O], *Shinbone Alley* (Mehitabel s/b) [O], *Mr. Wonderful* (Rita Romano) [O], *Seventh Heaven* (Fifi) [O], *Born Yesterday** (Billie Dawn), *3 Penny Opera** (Jenny), *Zorba** (The Leader), *The Rose Tattoo**, *Call Me Madam**, *Sweet Charity**, *Can-Can**, *Kiss Me, Kate**

Darcie Roberts: *Dream* (Ingénue) [O], *Aida* (Amneris s/b), *Crazy For You* (Irene Ross s/b), *42nd Street** (Peggy), *Thoroughly Modern Millie** (Millie), *Copacabana** (Lola), *Busker Alley** (Libby)

Ray Roderick: *Grind* (Knockabout) [O], *A Funny Thing Happened on the Way to the Forum* (Protean) [O], *Crazy For You* (Billy) [O], *Wind in the Willows* [O], *Cats* (Carbucketty), *Barnum** (Tom Thumb)

Craig Rubano: *The Scarlet Pimpernel* (Armand St. Just s/b) [O], *Les Misérables* (Marius)

John Rubinstein: *Children of a Lesser God* (James Leeds) [O][T], *Pippin* (Pippin) [O], *Fools* (Leon) [O], *Getting Away with Murder* (Martin Chisholm) [O], *The Caine Mutiny Court-Martial* (Lt. Barney Greenwald) [O], *Ragtime* (Tateh), *Hurlyburly* (Eddie), *Love Letters* (Andrew), *M. Butterfly* (Rene)

Sophia Salguero: *The Green Bird* (Singing Apple) [O], *The Capeman* (Bernadette) [O], *Juan Darien* (Green Dwarf) [O], *Martin Guerre**, *Carousel**

Lea Salonga: *Miss Saigon* (Kim) [O][T], *Flower Drum Song* (Mei-Li) [O], *Les Misérables* (Eponine)

Alex Santoriello: *Les Misérables* (Montparnasse) [O], *3 Penny Opera* (Jimmy) [O], *Chess* [O], *Jesus Christ Superstar** (Pilate), *Cats** (Asparagus)

James Sassar: *Riverdance* [O]

Jane Sell: *Over Here!* (Mitzi) [O][T], *Irene* (Jane Burke) [O], *George M!* [O], *Moon over Buffalo* (Charlotte Hay s/b) [O], *Pal Joey* (Gladys Bumps) [O], *Happy End* (Lieutenant Lillian Holiday), *I Love My Wife* (Monica)

Craig Schulman: *Les Misérables* (Jean Valjean), *Jekyll & Hyde* (Dr. Jekyll), *The Phantom of the Opera** (Phantom)

Roger Seyer: *Les Misérables* (Jean Valjean u/s), *Miss Saigon* (Gibbons)

Brooke Shields: *Cabaret* (Sally), *Grease!* (Rizzo)

Emily Skinner: *Side Show* (Daisy Hilton) [O][t], *The Full Monty* (Vicki Nichols) [O],

James Joyce's The Dead (Mary Jane, Morkan) [O], *Jekyll & Hyde* (Emma u/s) [O], *Dinner at Eight* (Kitty Packard) [O]

Doug Storm: *Dance of the Vampires* [O], *The Scarlet Pimpernel* (Leggett), *Les Misérables* (Feuilly)

Rena Strober: *Les Misérables* (Cosette u/s)

Jerry Tellier: *Saturday Night Fever* (Frank Junior) [O], *42nd Street* [O], *Smokey Joe's Cafe*

Lea Thompson: *Cabaret* (Sally Bowles)

Clarke Thorell: *Hairspray* (Corny Collins) [O], *Titanic* (Jim Farrell) [O], *The Who's Tommy*

Robert Torti: *Starlight Express* (Greaseball) [O][t], *Joseph and the Amazing Technicolor® Dreamcoat* (Pharaoh) [O]

Lucy Vance: *Miss Saigon* (Ellen u/s), *Les Misérables* (Eponine/Cosette u/s)

Andrew Varela: *King David* [O], *Les Misérables* (Jean Valjean u/s)

Daphne Rubin-Vega: *Rent* (Mimi) [O][t], *The Rocky Horror Show* (Magenta) [O], *Anna in the Tropics* [O]

Donna Vivino: *Les Misérables* (Young Cosette) [O], *Saturday Night Fever* (Vocals) [O], *Hairspray**

Ray Walker: *Jesus Christ Superstar* (Annas) [O], *Grease!* (Doody), *Les Misérables* (Marius), *Whistle Down the Wind** (Preacher), *Music of the Night** (Principal Soloist), *Joseph and the Amazing Technicolor® Dreamcoat** (Joseph u/s), *Falsettos** (Whizzer)

Barbara Walsh: *Falsettos* (Trina) [O][t], *Blood Brothers* (Mrs. Lyons) [O], *Big* (Mrs. Baskin) [O], *Rock 'N Roll! The First 5,000 Years* [O], *Hairspray* (Velma Von Tussle), *Ragtime** (Mother), *Les Misérables** (Fantine/Cosette u/s), *Chess** (Svetlana), *Oklahoma!**, *Nine**

Jim Walton: *The Music Man* (Harold Hill s/b) [O], *Merrily We Roll Along* (Franklin Shepard) [O], *Sweeney Todd* (Anthony Hope) [O], *Perfectly Frank* [O], *Stardust* [O], *42nd Street* (Billy Lawlor)

Amanda Watkins: *Cabaret* (Sally u/s), *Cats* (Demeter), *Urinetown*, *Beauty and the Beast* (Silly Girl), *Grease!* (Marty)

Laurie Wells: *Swing!** (Lead s/b)

Colm Wilkinson: *Les Misérables* (Jean Valjean) [O][t]

Jessica Snow Wilson: *Little Shop of Horrors* (Audrey u/s) [O], *Les Misérables* (Eponine), *A Funny Thing Happened on the Way to the Forum* (Philia)

Patrick Wilson: *The Full Monty* (Jerry Lukowski) [O][t], *Oklahoma!* (Curley) [O][t], *The Gershwin's Fascinating Rhythm* [O], *Carousel** (Billy Bigelow), *Miss Saigon**

Marissa Jaret Winokur: *Hairspray* (Tracy Turnblad) [O][T], *Grease!* (Jan)

Pamela Winslow: *Into the Woods* (Rapunzel) [O], *Beauty and the Beast* (Babette)

Scott Wise: *Jerome Robbins' Broadway* [O][T], *Fosse* [O][t], *State Fair* (Pat Gilbert) [O][t], *Movin' Out* (Sergeant O'Leary) [O], *Goodbye Girl* (Billy) [O], *Damn Yankees* (Rocky) [O], *Carrie* (Scott) [O], *Guys and Dolls* (Guy) [O], *Song and Dance* (Man) [O], *A Chorus Line* (Mike), *Cats* (Plato/Macavity), *Victor Victoria* (Jazz Hot Ensemble)

John Leslie Wolfe: *Parade* (Tom Watson) [O], *Passion* (Fosca's Father) [O], *Evita* [O], *Saravà* [O], *Martin Guerre** (Pierre Guerre), *Cabaret** (Ernst Ludwig).

Deborah Yates: *Contact* (Girl in the Yellow Dress) [O][t], *Dream* (Swing) [O]

Lee Zarrett: *Jane Eyre* (Young John Reed) [O]

Karen Ziemba: *Contact* (Wife) [O][T], *Steel Pier* (Rita Racine) [O][t], *Never Gonna Dance* (Mabel) [O], *Teddy & Alice* (Alice u/s) [O], *Crazy For You* (Polly Baker), *42nd Street* (Peggy Sawyer), *Chicago* (Roxie Hart), *A Chorus Line* (Bebe)

Adrian Zmed: *Grease!* (Danny), *Blood Brothers* (Narrator), *Falsettos* (Marvin), *Chicago* (Billy Flynn), *Same Time, Next Year**

Acknowledgments

First and foremost, the authors wish to thank each and every contributor. Your voices and stories made this book possible. Thank you for your trust, your courage, your time and effort, and above all, your honesty. After three years of working on this project, we have listened to and read your stories and reflections a countless number of times. Each time, we are simply overwhelmed at the incredible experiences you have all had and your willingness to share your lives with us. Your stories will forever be embedded in our minds. Now the world will get a glimpse.

We are forever indebted to Jason Alexander for not only introducing the book, but for helping refine its message. Special thanks to Kevin Goering, Philippe Bennett, Robert Hanlon, and everyone else at Coudert Brothers LLP who supported this project. Thanks to Peter Sharp for your counsel.

The authors would also like to individually thank the following people for their help in making this book possible: Michael Borowski, Craig Carnelia, Dave Clemmons, Paul Davis, Kip Driver, Jeffrey Dunn, Robert DuSold, Deborah Gibson, Paul Hart, Wilson Heredia, Joy at PMK/HBH, Daniel Lebor, Wendy Lebowitz, Daniel C. Levine, Kevin Loreque, Terrence Mann, Robyn Martin at Gendler & Kelly, the cast of *Martin Guerre*, Roy Miller, Austin Mitchell, the cast of *The Rocky Horror Show* for my many backstage visits, John Rubinstein, Dan Paier, Sean Jeremy Palmer, Tara Sands, Karen Saunders, Mark Shacket, Brooke Shields, Doug Storm, Lea Thompson, Ray Walker, Jim Walton, Amanda Watkins, Michael Weiner, and all of our family and friends who stood by us with love. And, of course, this book would never have been written if Alison Wissot hadn't introduced the coauthors to each other many years ago.

Thank you to Colm Wilkinson for putting up with all of our international phone calls, and congratulations on your CD, *Some of My Best Friends Are Songs*, which can be found at *www.colmwilkinson.com*.

We offer special gratitude to Tad, Nicole, Jessica, Birte, and everyone else at Allworth Press. You understood the importance of this book from the first time you read it, and we are thrilled to be a part of the Allworth family. Thank you for believing in the power of this book and making everything possible.

About the Authors

DAVID WIENIR is an entertainment lawyer in New York City and an associate with the international law firm Coudert Brothers LLP. He earned a J.D. from the University of California, Berkeley (Boalt Hall School of Law), an M.Sc. (Econ) from the London School of Economics, and a B.A. (cum laude and departmental honors) while studying as an Oxford-Cambridge Scholar at Columbia College, Columbia University. Additionally, he earned a certificate from the faculty of law at the Vrije University in Amsterdam, and was a visiting scholar at the University of Oxford (Harris-Manchester College) and an Eesti Fellow at the University of Tartu in the former Soviet Republic of Estonia.

Making It on Broadway is David's third book. He is the coeditor of The Diversity Hoax: Law Students Report from Berkeley (New York: Foundation for Academic Standards and Tradition, 1999, afterword by Dennis Prager) and is the coauthor of Last Time: Labour's Lessons from the Sixties (London: Bellew Press, 1997) with Austin Mitchell, Member of British Parliament.

Prior to moving to New York City, David was the host of the talk radio show Estonia Today on Estonia National Radio in the former Soviet Union, a researcher both within the British House of Commons and for The Survivors of the Shoah Visual History Foundation, and a professional whitewater river rafting guide in California and Oregon. He is a founder and former musical director of the Oxford Alternotives, Oxford University's first rock a cappella close harmony group.

JODIE LANGEL began her Broadway career starring as Cosette in Les Misérables on Broadway while still pursuing her B.F.A. from New York University's Tisch School of the Arts, and has subsequently played the role of Eponine. Jodie starred as the Narrator in the national tour of Joseph and the Amazing Technicolor® Dreamcoat, and is the youngest person ever to play the role of Grizabella in an Equity production of Cats. She toured with the pre-Broadway company of Martin Guerre as the alternate to Bertrande and starred in the Off-Broadway musical I Sing.

Jodie has performed as a lead soloist with the Colorado Springs Symphony Orchestra and has participated in the acclaimed Lyric and Lyricists series at the 92nd

Street YMCA. Regionally, she has played many roles, including Eva Peron in *Evita* with the North Carolina Theater. In 2001, Jodie had the honor of singing the National Anthem at the reopening of the American Stock Exchange alongside Governor Pataki and New York City firefighters and policemen. Currently, Jodie is pursuing her M.F.A. in theater at the University of California, Los Angeles, where she is a recipient of the Streisand-Sony Fellowship. Jodie also teaches undergraduate acting and theater at U.C.L.A., and has taught master classes at universities, high schools, and acting programs across the country.

Those interested in having the authors and various contributors address the issues raised in *Making It on Broadway* and appear for group discussions, lectures, musical performances, master classes, educational workshops, or a combination thereof, should contact them at *www.makingitonbroadway.com* or *www.allworth.com*.

If you enjoyed this book, please post a review to your favorite online bookstore today.

Index

Books from Allworth Press

Allworth Press is an imprint of Allworth Communications, Inc. Selected titles are listed below.

Improv for Actors
by *Dan Diggles* (paperback, 6 × 9, 256 pages, $19.95)

The Perfect Stage Crew: The Compleat Technical Guide for High School, College, and Community Theater
by *John Kaluta* (paperback, 6 × 9, 256 pages, $19.95)

Business and Legal Forms for Theater
by *Charles Grippo* (paperback with CD-ROM, 8½ × 11, 192 pages, $29.95)

Movement for Actors
edited by *Nicole Potter* (paperback, 6 × 9, 288 pages, $19.95)

Acting for Film
by *Cathy Haase* (paperback, 6 × 9, 224 pages, $19.95)

Creating Your Own Monologue
by *Glenn Alterman* (paperback, 6 × 9, 192 pages, $14.95)

Promoting Your Acting Career
by *Glenn Alterman* (paperback, 6 × 9, 224 pages, $18.95)

An Actor's Guide—Making It in New York City
by *Glenn Alterman* (paperback, 6 × 9, 288 pages, $19.95)

Career Solutions for Creative People
by *Dr. Rhonda Ormont* (paperback, 6 × 9, 320 pages, $19.95)

Building the Successful Theater Company
by *Lisa Mulcahy* (paperback, 6 × 9, 240 pages, $19.95)

The Health and Safety Guide for Film, TV and Theater
by *Monona Rossol* (paperback, 6 × 9, 256 pages, $19.95)

Creative Careers in Hollywood
by *Laurie Scheer* (paperback, 6 × 9, 240 pages, $19.95)